Curriculum Planning for Young Children

Curriculum Planning for Young Children

Janet F. Brown, Editor
Director of Publications, NAEYC

National Association for the Education of Young Children
Washington, D.C.

Cover photograph: Marietta Lynch
Cover design: Melanie Rose White

Copyright © 1982. All rights reserved.
Second printing November 1983. Third printing August
1985. Fourth printing February 1989.
National Association for the Education of Young Children
1834 Connecticut Avenue, N.W.
Washington, DC 20009-5786

Pages 171-176 copyright © 1978. All rights reserved.
Constance Kamii and Lucinda Lee-Katz. Reprinted by permission.

Library of Congress Catalog Card Number: 82-61723
ISBN Catalog Number: #0-912674-83-0
NAEYC #113

Printed in the United States of America.

For Erica

Contents

Introduction

How do young children learn?

What are appropriate activities and materials for young children?

Which teaching techniques are most effective?

If these are familiar questions, whether you are new to the profession or are still building upon your knowledge and experiences, the ideas in this book may help lead you to some answers. You will find *why* as well as *how* to implement an early childhood curriculum—thus furthering your professional growth and increasing your effectiveness as a teacher.

As early childhood educators we are committed to providing the best for young children, and to making the most of our time with each child in our care. This enormous task is not easy, and to do it well requires a great deal of both energy and knowledge. Children's interests, and the world, are always changing, so that our best plans must sometimes be altered or even scrapped to take advantage of an equally valuable learning experience that couldn't be anticipated. How can we make the most of our planned and unexpected activities with children?

Teachers who make wise curriculum decisions usually can explain why their decisions are the best at that moment for their particular group. A recipe book of lesson plans can't take into account what you as the teacher know about the children in your class—and is an insult to you as a professional. Before you choose what to do tomorrow morning,

you will consider the needs of the children in your group, keeping in mind what other teachers have found effective and what you know you can expect from children.

If you find yourself skimming or jumping over sections of professional materials that deal with research and theory, you are probably shortchanging both yourself and the children you teach because you won't be familiar with what others are learning in our fast-growing field. At the same time, busy teachers can't be expected to read all the research and theory that is constantly adding to our knowledge about children.

Curriculum Planning for Young Children was designed to help you keep up with current research and theory—but it was also designed to help you see how what we know about children can be applied in your classroom. The ideas included here reflect the best of early childhood educational practice. We trust that your perspective will be broadened, and that the lives of children everywhere will be fuller once you have read this book.

* * * * * *

Each article in *Curriculum Planning for Young Children* was originally printed in *Young Children*, the professional refereed journal published by the National Association for the Education of Young Children. This book was developed in response to reader requests, and follows in the tradition of excellence established by three earlier volumes:

- *Ideas That Work with Young Children*, Katherine Read Baker, Editor
- *Providing the Best for Young Children*, Jan McCarthy and Charles May, Editors
- *Ideas That Work with Young Children, Volume 2*, Leah Adams and Betty Garlick, Editors

If *Curriculum Planning for Young Children* is valuable to you in your work with young children and you are not already a member of NAEYC, we invite you to join more than 36,000 others committed to providing quality services to young children and their families.

Janet F. Brown
November 1982

1

Building a basic curriculum

Many of you may be inclined to skip this section in your eagerness to get to the more specific components of a good early childhood curriculum which follow. To do so would cause you to miss some invigorating ideas about how we as professionals can learn from each other, and what we as teachers can learn from children. Elkind and Honig set the stage for the remainder of the book, offering insights about how early childhood teaching practice has evolved, and how we can apply what we know about children to our work each day. How can you work more closely with your colleagues and children to improve the quality of life for future citizens?

David Elkind

Child Development and Early Childhood Education: Where Do We Stand Today?

In the best of all possible worlds, at least for me, early childhood practice would be the embodiment of the latest findings and conceptions of developmental psychology. Developmental psychology, in turn, would be the science of education in that it would take its problems and form its concepts on the basis of life in classrooms. How nice it would be, for example, to say to parents and administrators that there is strong evidence to support the view that early entrance into formal schooling is less efficacious than later entrance. If this statement were made on the basis of large numbers of children studied over long periods of time and with accepted measures, such a statement would carry much weight. As it is, we lack a strong data base to argue that one educational practice is more beneficial than another.

The benefits of a reciprocal relation between early childhood education and child development research are not one-sided. There are a host of interesting, conceptually fruitful, and eminently researchable problems that arise in classroom practice. For example, studying how children actually go about learning to read or mastering mathematics is more likely to aid our understanding of the learning process than experimentally rigorous studies of children's memory for nonsense syllables. This is true because the nature of the task we set for children necessarily limits the kinds and levels of abilities brought to bear upon it. The more holistic the task we study, the more holistic a picture we will get of the range and nature of human abilities.

We are, however, very far from the ideal depicted above. The reasons are historical, dynamic, social, and economic all intertwined. That convoluted history cannot be recorded here. The outcome is well known. Child development research, methods, concepts, and theories have been developed independently of educational practice. Early childhood educational practice has grown almost, but not entirely, by oral tradition, with good practitioners passing on to their students their insights about young children and how best to educate them. When researchers and practitioners interact, they lack a common language and a common outlook on what is important and upon what is real.

For a while, much too short a while, the work of Piaget changed all that. Without meaning to, because he wanted first and foremost to address philosophers, Piaget spoke both to practitioners as well as to researchers. He spoke to practitioners be-

Keynote address given at the annual conference of the National Association for the Education of Young Children, San Francisco, November 22, 1980.

David Elkind, Ph.D., is Professor and Chairman, Eliot-Pearson Department of Child Study, Tufts University.

cause the children he described were the children seen in classrooms. Moreover Piaget was concerned with relevant content about children's ideas of space, time, and number that were the basis of the school curriculum. Likewise he demonstrated the evolution of relevant processes like seriation and classification that undergird many of children's learning activities.

Piaget also spoke to researchers. He demonstrated that significant contents and processes could be investigated, albeit by less rigorous methods and experimentation. Perhaps more than anyone else, Piaget lessened American psychology's fixation upon experimentation as the *only* or at least the only valuable, scientific method. He showed, as did Freud before him, that in the early stages of a science, classification and the establishment of norms are the most appropriate and important tasks.

Because of their shared interest in Piaget, like an earlier shared interest in Montessori, child development and early childhood workers began to move closer together. In Piaget there was a bridge of discourse that could be crossed in either direction. And, quite aside from the intellectual bridge, there was an affective one as well. There was a feeling that Piaget's work provided a very rich ore that could be mined by both the applied and the research disciplines. It is truly miraculous how the work of one man or woman can break down long-standing disciplinary boundaries.

But, and it is an all important *but*, those interactions need to be worked at in order to be sustained. Unfortunately, this has not happened. Each discipline has reverted to type. Child development researchers have gone back to experimentation, and teachers have lost some of their enthusiasm for research and theory. Some of the gains were of course retained, but from a giant step forward toward integration we have taken a number of elflike steps backward to our previous encap-sulated positions.

This, or so it seems to me, is where we stand today in regard to the relations between child development and early childhood education. The exciting days of Head Start, day care, integration, and the like, when many of us worked together, are past and may well be buried for the near future. The question now is *how can we salvage and restore the best of what was inherent in the interactions of child development and early childhood education?* One very important thing is to continue to interact professionally at conferences. Unfortunately, early childhood educators appear to be more open in this regard than the child development people. I would guess that more child development people attend NAEYC conferences than early childhood educators attend Society for Research in Child Development meetings.

Indeed, now that I head a department concerned with early childhood education, I have fallen from the already low level of prestige that I held within that organization. I was appointed to take charge of the child care services at the SRCD convention. Whatever my colleagues feel, and I am sure that there are many smiles at how low I have fallen, I considered it perhaps the most important task of the conference. To provide adequate child care services at a conference of child development specialists was a very important task. Nancy Rambusch, the director of our children's school, and I intended to make it a showpiece and used it to demonstrate what good early childhood education is all about. It was a chance to build a bridge that should not be missed.

Now I would like to demonstrate with concrete examples the potential mutual benefits to be derived from child development and early childhood people working together. With respect to child development I would like to address the issue of socialization. And with respect to education I would like to present some of the recent work on mediated learning experience.

Socialization research

One of the primary aims of early childhood education is to broaden the child's social understanding. Such understanding includes, among other things, cooperative play and work, sharing, taking turns, and courtesy. We know that there are major changes in the child's social understanding and behavior from ages two to eight, and many early childhood education practices, such as show and tell, are meant to encourage this social learning.

While the goals of social understanding are reasonably clear, the best way to get there may not be. Developmental psychology, for example, provides at least four different models. The social learning model suggests that children learn the appropriate social behavior from observing (modeling) others engaged in such behaviors and according to a system of rewards and punishments. This position suggests that aggression shown on television is bad because children who observe this behavior will model it in their own actions. From this standpoint the teacher's behavior and other children's behavior are all important in the child's social learning. They not only model behavior, they also reward and punish.

A somewhat different theory is offered by the developmentalists who as a group are known as social cognition theorists. What unites this group is the belief that children come to know the social world via the same cognitive operations and the same sequential stages as those observed in their coming to know the physical world. Likewise, inasmuch as the physical world children construct is a series of progressive approximations to the adult physical world, the same should be true of their construction of the social world.

In contrast to the social learning theory position, the social cognition position suggests that children do not copy the social model but more likely transform and distort what has been modeled according to their mental limitations. From this perspective, modeling is not the major factor in social learning. Rather the child's cognitive development is what ultimately determines social understanding. Accordingly, to encourage social learning, classroom practice should be aimed at fostering cognitive growth, particularly social perspective taking, that would enhance social understanding.

Still a third approach derives from traditional learning theory and might be called the behavior management approach. According to this model, social learning is primarily a matter of rewarding desired behaviors and not rewarding undesired behaviors. Neither modeling (as in the social learning position) nor cognitive ability (as in the social cognition approach) is required. All one has to do is to decide which behaviors are desirable and which undesirable and then apportion rewards and punishments (failure to reward) accordingly.

The behavior management approach has the appeal of simplicity. For teachers it provides a clearly worked out methodology that is targeted to behavior and that is not freighted with concerns about modeling or social cognitions. If teachers want children to be cooperative, they merely reward children's cooperative efforts and do not reward or attend to their aggressive efforts. The approach also provides means for objectively measuring a child's progress toward a stated goal, such as the number of cooperative behaviors demonstrated per day or week.

The last approach to social learning derives from dynamic developmental psychology, particularly from the work of Freud and Erikson. According to these writers the important ingredients in social learning are the unconscious motives that derive from the kind of caregiving the parents provide. For example, a rejecting parent might produce an insecure child who unduly seeks undue attention. Or an aggressive parent might produce a fearful and docile child. Clearly, much more than modeling is involved here because the

Elkind

child may demonstrate behaviors opposite to those displayed by the parent. Likewise, although cognition is involved, it does not explain the powerful motivational forces in play. The dynamic approach also presents problems for the behavior management approach. One would think that a rejecting parent would provide negative reinforcement for attention-getting children, yet rejected children are often attention seeking.

From an educational point of view, the psychodynamic theory suggests still another approach to encouraging social understanding. Such an approach would emphasize the quality of the interpersonal relationships. It would argue for teachers who are warm, understanding, and accepting, but who are also firm and willing to set limits. In the psychodynamic view there is not a direct modeling relation between the child and the parent or teacher, but rather a reciprocal one, a kind of action/reaction wherein the first action may be quite different from the one it provokes. The reaction of a piece of metal to an impact is a dent which is different from the impact.

We have then at least four different theories about how social learning comes about and four different implications for classroom practice. For brevity we can say that these different approaches argue that social learning comes about as a consequence of modeling, or of thinking, or of rewards and punishments, or of feelings and motives. One has the impression, in reviewing these theories, that one is seeing different sides of the same alphabet block. Clearly *children learn in many different ways and what mode of learning is employed depends very much upon what is to be learned.* Even within the domain of social learning there are many quite different sorts of knowledge that have to be acquired, and the kind of content will determine which mode of learning is most appropriately applied.

Let me put the matter somewhat differently. Psychologists concerned with social learning are repeating the mistake that was made in studies of nonsocial learning. Namely, they are ignoring the content of what is to be learned. Each position wants to arrive at a set of principles that will describe all social learning regardless of content. But that is the search for the Holy Grail. To abstract learning processes from the material to be learned is a distortion of both. That is why Piaget never discussed assimilation and accommodation when he talked about the acquisition of particular subject matter. In writing about a particular concept he described in detail the unique way in which mental operations were employed in acquiring it. The methods of learning were embedded in the content to be learned.

The same must be true for social learning. A child who is learning to say please and thank you is applying different processes than the child who is trying to con another child out of a toy. Likewise a child who is learning to share a toy may be using different learning activities than when learning to play cooperatively. What we really need first is a detailed catalog of the social units that must be acquired in early childhood. Only then can we begin to explore, in systematic ways, the processes of acquisition. To study acquisition processes before knowing what it is that is to be acquired is like building a sailboat in the desert.

I would like, before closing this section, to give you an example of the approach I have in mind. It suggests how important it is for developmentalists and practitioners to work together. This approach again deals with social learning but from the standpoint of what is learned rather from that of the learning process.

The rules, expectancies, and understandings which regulate repeated or common social interactions are called "frames" by Goffman (1974). Similar ideas are being explored by other investigators using terms such as schemas and scripts, particularly in language learning. It is my contention that the fundamental unit of social learning is the frame and that even infants acquire rudimentary frames. Whenever the infant and adult are involved in a repeated patterned activity, a frame unit is said to be involved. Feeding, changing diapers, and display to strangers are all frames in which certain expectancies and understandings are in play. When the infant is readied for food, sat in a highchair, a bib placed around her or his neck, etc., food had better be forthcoming or the child will give evidence of a broken frame, namely crying.

Frames, therefore, are at once cognitive as well as affective. They have an emotional rhythm, as it were. If this rhythm is broken, negative consequenes are likely to occur. Some frames, however, are primarily affective and they are broken if the feelings are not permitted to appear. If children are prepared for a fight and fighting is not permitted, then they are angry.

What we have been doing is looking at frames in the early childhood setting. Block play, dramatic play, circle activities, outdoor activities, nature walks, and story time are all frames. Each has a set of expectancies, rules, and understandings which allow the activity to successfully run its course. In block play children must understand that the blocks are not to be thrown or to be used as hammers but are to be put together to form some sort of structure. They must also know that the blocks are to be used in a particular place and are not to be carried elsewhere. There is also a place where the blocks are to be put after the block play is over. When more than one child is involved, rules of cooperation must also be understood.

At story time other frame rules and understandings are in effect. The children must sit quietly and listen. They must not bother other children or get upset if a teacher or teacher's aide is holding another child. They must also learn not to interrupt the story with personal anecdotes unless these are called for by the storyteller.

Each of these frames has its own emotional rhythm because everyone who participates in a frame is *invested* in it. Investment means that you have put something into it and want to get something out of it. For example, a child engaged in block play has invested in the activity. If the child's structure is knocked down, that investment is lost and the child is justifiably angry. However, if the structure is admired by others, or just by the child, the frame has paid off. Conflicts arise when children are unequally invested in a frame. The child who wants to hear the story is annoyed by the fussy child who does not. Diagnostically it is important to know whether a child's lack of involvement in a frame derives from an ignorance of it or from a failure to invest in it. There is much more to be learned about frames and we have only begun to catalog them. Even at this point frames prove to be powerful analytic tools. Even beginning students find it easy to observe frames and to dissect them.

Perhaps the most interesting thing about frames, from a theoretical point of view, is that they presuppose intellectual structures that young children are not supposed to have from a strict developmental point of view. According to Piaget, for example, children are not supposed to operate according to rules until they attain concrete operations. Yet young children clearly learn frames and behave as if they knew the rules. The problem is similar to that of language behavior. Young children use language constructions that a cognitive development point of view would say is impossible.

There is a solution that would allow us to keep cognitive development theory and frames too. Piaget has proposed that children acquire mental operations at least in part by abstracting not from things, but rather from their actions upon things. (He calls this "reflective abstraction.") A child who arranges ten pebbles in a row, then in

Elkind

a circle, then in a square, discovers that they remain ten. The child has abstracted not "tenness" but rather the actions of transformation that leave tenness invariant. The child acquires general operations of thought by reflective abstraction from her or his own actions upon things.

Although, insofar as I know Piaget did not propose this, it seems possible that children can reflectively abstract from the actions of significant adults in their lives as well as from their own behavior. Thus, children might be able to abstract frame rules from adult language and behavior long before they could construct these on the basis of their own actions. The adult, of course, engages in behaviors far in advance of what children can do. Accordingly, by abstracting from adult behavior children can give the impression of precocity, of having powers beyond those they demonstrate in other domains.

Children can thus operate according to frame rules without having constructed them on their own. I call such rules or operations abstracted from adult behavior *mediating structures*. Frames are one, but only one, type of mediating structure. The acquisition of frames is, however, one of the unsung heroes of early childhood education. The child's knowledge of classroom frames makes her or his transition to formal schooling relatively smooth and uncomplicated. Kindergarten and first grade teachers often take these frames for granted except when a child appears who does not possess them. It is only then that they appreciate how rule regulated the "normal" child is.

Frames then are basic units of social learning that need to be identified and studied in school settings. Such studies may well benefit both practitioners and child development researchers. Teachers will have a more explicit knowledge of the social skills children are learning. Developmental psychologists, in their turn, can gain a better understanding of the diversity and complexity of social learning

by studying classroom frames.

Contributions of education

There are numerous examples of educational experiments that have given rise to educational and developmental theories and concepts. Itard, Pestalozzi, Froebel, and Montessori all developed their ideas out of actual work in the classroom. It is not clear, however, how much Dewey learned from his school and how much he brought to it. Child development theory and concepts have been enriched by the contributions of educators even if this is not always fully acknowledged. The issue of critical periods raised by Montessori, for example, is now regarded as a research rather than an applied issue. Likewise mental testing introduced by Binet and Simon for educational purposes has been transformed into a research instrument to study the contributions of nature and nurture to intelligence. One could go on but the contributions of educational practice to research and theory are numerous although often forgotten.

Among the most recent applied contributions comes from the work of Feuerstein (1980). Feuerstein has been concerned with the assimilation of children from various countries into Israeli society. Many of these children come from Oriental countries. (In Israel, the Orient or the East includes countries such as Yemen and Morocco.) What Feuerstein observed was that many of the Oriental children had good native intelligence but could not use this intelligence to acquire academic knowledge. After working with these children for many years, Feuerstein came to believe that what these children lacked was what he calls "mediated learning experiences." These experiences are those in which the adult plays a part in the child's efforts at learning and adaptation. Adults, particularly parents and teachers, are at a crucial point—not providers of knowledge and skills to be learned but part of the child's adaptive activity.

Let me give some examples of what I have in mind. I will use illustrations from early childhood education although Feuerstein's work has been primarily with early adolescence. Perhaps the most important mediated learning experience young children have in school is that of attention getting and holding. Teachers engage in a number of actions such as clapping, turning lights on and off, or strumming on a guitar to capture the children's attention. By attracting and directing the children's attention, the teacher becomes a part of the child's adaptive apparatus. This is true because attention mediates much of the child's other learning or adaptations. *By having someone else attract and control their attention, children progressively learn to control their own attentional processes.*

Another example comes from the work of Tough (1976) who argues for the importance of talk. She argues that when adult talk encourages children to rehearse past experience and to anticipate future experience, children themselves acquire the capacity to bring past and future experience to bear upon present situations. Consider the difference between a child who grabs a toy because she wants it and another who says, "You have used this a lot, now it's my turn, you can use it again when I am through." The ability to use past and anticipated experience in problem-solving situations is mediated by adults who use experience in this way.

At the early adolescent level, Feuerstein has identified a number of skills that are acquired through mediated learning experiences. These are not content or skills in a curricular sense and are not something on which the child can be examined. They include mental activities such as inference, delay of judgment, and so on. But like attention, and the utilization of past and future experience for coping with present situations, they play an important mediating role in academic learning. Bright children who have had mediated learning experiences will have a good chance of succeeding at school. However, equally bright children who have not had these experiences will be disadvantaged educationally.

Clearly, the sorts of structures that Feuerstein and Tough are talking about are what I called mediating structures earlier. They too, are acquired when children abstract from adult actions. These mediating structures may be our greatest legacy to young children. Indeed, the resistance of good early childhood educators to the inculcation of curricular skills may well reside in the sound intuition that the early childhood educator's task is of a different order. Our task is to provide children with the mediating structures such as attention, patience, and use of past and future experience in problem solving that make formal academic learning possible. Perhaps if we can make parents and administrators aware of the child's need for mediating structures, the pressure for teaching academic skills in the early years may be lessened.

The recognition of mediating structures in the child's learning complements the recognition of frames as the building blocks of social learning. In a very real sense frames are one type of mediating structure which prepares the child to deal with social learning experiences. Mediating structures such as attention-focusing and holding relate to nonsocial as well as to social learning. Both developmentalists and educators are thus coming to similar understandings from somewhat different perspectives and with different concerns.

What emerges is a new conception of learning that is at once holistic and social. It suggests that the child's earliest learning experiences are mediated by adults and are complex frames or regulational activities. It is likely that children acquire frames and other mediating structures by means of reflective abstraction from parental behavior. Such mediating structures may give the appearance of precocity because the child is using structures previously acquired by adults.

In a very real sense then *the child's social learning—the acquisition of mediating structures—is primary and all the curricular learning provided by schools is secondary* in that it necessarily builds upon this mediated learning experience base. The relation between children's academic performance and their intellectual power is thus always indirect, always dependent upon the acquisition of the requisite mediating structures. It is time we gave these mediating structures their due both experimentally and practically in the classroom. It will help us conceptually and practically and will highlight the complementarity of interest between child developmentalists and early childhood educators.

References

Feuerstein, R. *Instrumental Enrichment*. Baltimore: University Park Press, 1980.

Goffman, E. *Frame Analysis*. New York: Harper & Row, 1974.

Tough, J. *Listening to Children Talking*. London: Ward Lock Educational, 1976.

Alice S. Honig

The Young Child and You—Learning Together

What can adults learn from working with children, and what can children learn from interacting with adults? The special relationship of teacher, caregiver, or parent with a young child helps the adult develop as much as it helps the child grow. Adults and children benefit from seeing the world and themselves from the other's perspective.

What adults learn

How children think

We learn about how children think from children, particularly if we look and listen with open eyes and ears. How does the child perceive and understand the world? As Piaget has shown, young children have contradictory views of how the physical world works.

Today Robbie is sure that his toy will sink if dropped in a pail of water. Tomorrow he may confidently guess that the same toy will float. Amanda may judge that you and she have the same amount of orange juice if both of your tall glasses are full. As you carefully pour your juice into several shorter, skinnier glasses, the child may decide that you have more to drink than she does.

Young children can usually handle a change in one perceptual aspect of a situation, but they may be confused as they try to judge and balance a variety of factors (such as height and width) which need to be considered simultaneously. Think of the four-year-old eating at the kitchen table. His mother rushes in too late to stop a pot of food from burning on the stove. "Why didn't you call me?" she asks in exasperation. "But Mommy, you told me not to say another word until I finished everything on my plate!" protests the child. It is hard for the young child to hold two concepts in mind simultaneously and evaluate the importance of each.

Children spend years actively exploring materials to learn about the properties of substances. For example, children gradually realize the total mass or weight of solids and liquids does not change despite changes in container shape or distribution of materials. Kamii and DeVries (1978) and Kamii and Lee-Katz (1979) have provided a variety of planned science experiences that can help young children understand levers or the properties of round versus square-sided objects.

An observant adult watching a child's behavior during many similar well-planned experiences can perceptively find out *how* a child thinks and reasons. Drisana pours a coffee pot full of water into a small cup. She watches intently as

Alice S. Honig, Ph.D., is Professor of Child Development, College for Human Development, Syracuse University, Syracuse, New York.

the water overflows and spills all over her hand. Mischief—or discovery of the relationship between container size and liquid quantity?

After Leticia has carried her load of large building blocks to the far end of the room, she may firmly announce that the blocks are much heavier in this corner than they were at the other end of the room. Young children often confuse their subjective internal feelings with the actual physical characteristics of toys or materials. Toys, just as groceries, feel heavier after they have been carried around for awhile.

Adults can begin to learn *how* a young child thinks and reasons by *watching* each child's response to physical changes, such as breaking up a ball of clay into many pieces and judging the amount of clay present when compared to an unbroken ball. Most adults grin when a small child prefers to have a large copper penny rather than a skinny tiny dime. "More" may mean "bigger" at this stage rather than "more monetary value."

Five-year-old Erik, helping his mother dust and polish furniture, carefully poured a small amount of polish out on his dusting cloth. When mother turned around, the furniture polish bottle was lying on its side, and a puddle oozed onto the sofa. That viscous substances need to be stored upright or they will flow out is a lesson in the physics of liquids.

Adults need to learn about children's concepts of number, space, quantity, time, and length; in addition to being aware of their knowledge of physical properties. Jovan easily counts by rote from 1 to 10 (1 2 3 4 5 6 7 8 9 10—maybe even " 'leven"). Yet if Jovan counts the number of bottles on his toy milk truck (which has five bottles), he may confidently start out "1, 2, 3, 4, 5" and continue on "6, 7, 8, 9, 10," counting some bottles more than once. The idea that the concept of number relates to the final count of single objects, each counted once, is difficult for young children to understand.

Have you ever watched the intense surprise on a child's face when a teacher counts snap-apart beads laid out first in a straight line and then in a circle? Even if the adult helps the child count beads in each position, the child may still refuse to believe that the circle and the straight line have the same quantity of beads. The child reasons that a straight line looks much longer, and therefore, should have more beads.

Children's sense of time also differs from adults'. After his parents have promised a holiday family visit, Kenny decisively and proudly announces, "I'm visiting my Grandpa tomorrow." Several months of waiting time, combined with the child's wishes, become "tomorrow."

Children's thoughts are often influenced by how things seem to them. Treating a young child to a Magic Show may disappoint a caregiver who expects her to be amazed. There may be nothing unreasonable to a four-year-old who delightedly watches a magician pull a rabbit out of a hat.

A strong relationship exists between a child's level of thinking and the ability to decide "moral" issues. Adults who are concerned about the moral development of small children can learn by child watching that a child's behavior, seemingly identical to that of an adult, may have a different meaning compared to the same action carried out by an adult. A teacher was driving a mother and toddler to a play group program. The young toddler reached out to touch the teacher's pocketbook lying on the car seat. The purse was invitingly stuffed with papers, keys and other mysterious shapes. As the baby slid her hand into alluring "toy," the mother exclaimed sharply, "You little thief! What are you trying to steal now?" The toddler cried as the mother snatched baby's hand away from that interesting, leathery-slithery feeling bag bulging with treasures to handle, squeeze, and play with.

Adults need to learn to look at a child's behavior from the child's viewpoint. Otherwise, a child's curious explorations may be labeled deliberately as "naughty" by an adult who thinks about the meaning of the act from an adult perspective. Children can be helped to behave in appropriately polite ways without an adult's shaming them or expecting them to reason at an advanced level.

Teachers need to make sure that children understand their expectations for a class activity. Otherwise, teachers might inappropriately label a child as "disobedient." One nursery school teacher gave out collage materials to each child: a large sheet of construction paper; an assortment of feathers, buttons, glitter, and paper scraps; plus paste and a pair of scissors. Joey picked up his pair of scissors and vigorously and cheerfully cut up the large sheet of construction paper. "Oh no, Joey," his teacher called out, "You're spoiling the collage paper." Joey looked up at her in bewildered surprise. Explanations are needed to help children understand the adult expectations for games and activities. We must be sensitive to the fact that children's initiative and creativity may be more important than our limited expectations and demonstrations.

Diane was happily coloring the inside of a paper plate. "No, Diane, color the outside," called out the teacher. Diane continued to adorn the center of her plate. "Diane, you'll need the inside to paste a picture on later," remarked a classroom aide passing by. The child tuned out the adult. "Oh, honey, you're supposed to color only the outside," reminded another teacher five minutes later. Diane looked up, thoroughly annoyed with the pestering adults. She turned her paper plate entirely over to the back side and retorted, "Outside! Why should I color the outside?" Be sure a child's understandings and values are considered before chastising.

How children feel

Children's emotional patterns, as well as their perceptions of the world, differ from adults. The young baby may be uncertain when Daddy or Mommy goes out that the parent will ever return again. Emotionally trivial events for adults may seem distressfully overwhelming to a young child who is just beginning to understand the social world as well as the physical world. Three-year-old Daryl and his mother were ready for a trip. Their plane was delayed, and hours dragged on as maintenance crews replaced some equipment. Suddenly Daryl sobbed aloud, "I'll never seen Daddy again!" He felt genuinely terrified. Exaggeration? Not to a three-year-old who believed in this terrible possibility.

Five-year-old Daren cried as his father took a large pair of pruning shears and clipped the hedges hanging out over the driveway. A parent may be amused at such "babyishness," but to a child, the bushes were alive and should not be cut and hurt. Adults need to understand the stages of emotional development of children and their relationship to intellectual understanding.

Social understandings develop as young children interact with adults and other children. We need to notice how children play together. How do they solve their arguments? Does every quarrel end in fighting or a whining retreat to an adult? Does a child seem to need or demand adult attention quite frequently? Many emotional tensions of children are evidenced in actions such as sudden toy throwing, trouble falling asleep at naptime, hair or finger chewing, teeth grinding, irritability, and frustration at mild provocations such as another child's brushing past or having to wait for a turn at the new tricycle.

Do we learn when tiredness triggers troubles? Do we recognize when a child needs to wind down peacefully as a quiet time approaches? Transition times can be particularly difficult for toddlers in day care.

It is not enough for us to become perceptive observers of signals of social or emotional distress. We also need to develop strategies for helping children cope with their problems. A variety of skills may be needed. For example, an adult may calm a tense child by rubbing her back and crooning softly. Sometimes eye contact, a firm voice, and a light touch on impulsive hands will help a child to wait before grabbing a toy. Many adults are adept at forestalling problems before they begin. Mr. Richmond noticed that Arby had a short supply of patience. When an activity was planned which required each of four children to take a turn feeling under a cloth to find a toy that matched one of those items visible on the table, Mr. Richmond made sure that Arby was not the last child in the group to get a turn.

Adults can use many good discipline techniques (Hipple 1978) to help children who have emotional difficulties. Adults who resort to "Stop being a crybaby" or "Don't be so rough with Maria" are using techniques about as efficacious as snake oil remedy for ailments! A good YOU message (Gordon 1974) can help a child become able to express feelings and needs and helps reduce anger and tensions. "It looks like you are having troubles." "You seem to be really struggling with that puzzle." "It looks like you are feeling very mad right now." YOU statements can help children become aware of their feelings instead of just acting out.

Jason pouted and glared. He had just walked over to his favorite teacher to ask her to read a story to him. She was busy tying one child's shoelace and getting ready to toilet another child. Ms. Perez looked quietly at Jason. "Jason, are you feeling angry at me?" she asked gently. "Were you coming over to have a story time—and here I am, busy helping Lisa and Jackie?" Jason's eyes widened. How could his teacher understand all that? He stood stiffly and silently. "Jason, I promise you that I will come back and read with you right after I finish helping these children." She smiled at him. Jason's shoulders relaxed. Some of the stormy look

cleared from his face. Adult promises, made perceptively and honestly, help ease emotional upsets for some children. Adult modeling of patience, consideration, tolerance, and generosity assists children in the long process of learning prosocial skills that will help them get along more easily with others.

We need to listen to and observe ourselves as we interact with young children. How many times do our voices get edgy or express our irritation? Would I want to hear my own voice tones if I were the child? Many young children have learned that if teachers or parents raise their voices three more times, then the children will really have to obey. Children learn from experience that an adult doesn't mean the prohibition until the adult voice takes on a certain edge or lowers to a special warning tone. We need to listen to ourselves as well as children to help them develop emotionally.

How can we help children learn more peaceful ways of playing and learn to share, empathize, and cooperate with each other? Caldwell (1977) has suggested that teachers need to use clear rules to help minimize crowd frictions. When children crowd up in a school corridor for a drink or when children are playing exuberantly outdoors, vigorous jostling can turn suddenly into aggression. Helping children find solutions to their interpersonal quarrels is a challenge. If both children want to carry a bucket of water to the wading pool outside at the same time, can they both find a way to resolve that conflict to the satisfaction of each? Sometimes an adult finds it hard to deal with aggravating situations between children. It seems easier to scold or disapprove or order a ready-made solution for the difficulties than to help children find their own solution.

Shure and Spivack (1978) have developed a program for parents and teachers to promote the use of problem-solving strategies in child conflict situations. They suggest four important aspects in helping young children learn to consider ways of

The creative genius of a teacher lies in the ability to find ways to interact with each child according to that child's needs, to stretch an attention span, motivate a child to persist at a task, or provide opportunities to experiment with materials actively and autonomously.

solving their own conflicts in a play situation with peers:

a. Help a child *state the problem*.

b. Help children *become aware of their own and of other's feelings*.

c. Help a child *figure out the consequences* of her or his actions. (If Jack hits Joan to make her give him the red truck, then she is well likely to hit him back and hold on tight to the toy.)

d. Help children *think of alternative solutions* which they can accept in order to solve their difficulties.

Space, materials, and timing promote development

Planning is important in child care. Have you ever watched the chaos that can occur if nine children are permitted to play at a rectangular water table? In contrast, have you noted how peacefully and with what absorbed concentration four children can participate at each side of that same water table? If enough attractive activities are set out for children when they arrive at a child care facility, they will be able to make choices and busy themselves with a variety of materials.

Rules are important, although they need to be few and clear. Keeping promises to children and restating rules firmly and quietly often increases the children's sense of comfort about the child care environment. Intellectually, rules help a child focus on relevant details. Caregivers who can be relied on to keep rules and promises reinforce a child's faith and trust in adults. Tina and Lonnie were seated at a small table with a great hunk of red playdough available for both. Assorted cookie cutters and props were also available. Little by little the playdough managed to be drawn closer and closer toward Lonnie's end of the table. Tina pulled at the mass. Lonnie ignored her glares. She sang out loudly "Mrs. Kay, Lonnie's not *sharing*!" Mrs. Kay walked over to the table and quietly restated the sharing rule to both children. She explained briefly why the hunk of playdough needed to sit in the middle of the small work table. Both children continued creating playdough shapes together.

Children need time to make choices and change from one activity to another. Adults need to think carefully about how activities are sequenced. Are there enough alternations of quiet times with more active times? Do children get an opportunity to simmer down after vigorous outdoor play before being expected to come back inside and sit quietly for circle story time? Some teachers and parents use signals, such as a special chant or song or the dimming of lights, to indicate when children need to start getting ready to change activities.

Good room arrangements can facilitate good play experiences (Honig 1979) and vice versa. In one center, teachers strongly disapproved of children inundating their clay with water and then smearing the mushy clay. Yet the clay table was temptingly positioned adjacent to the sink. The five-year-olds at the clay table waited for the teacher to turn his back before they poured even more water onto their squishy clay wads. We can improve the quality of children's learning and living experiences as we increase environmental planning for young children.

How children develop physically

Many children feel joyous and free using their limbs vigorously to run, jump, climb, roll, tumble, slither, skip, and hop. Others need adult encouragement to learn to climb on a jungle gym or to walk on a walkboard suspended a few inches up from the floor. Observation skills are necessary to evaluate each child. Program planning helps facilitate the growth of grace, agility, and facility both in dextrous small muscle activities, in sports and large muscle games, and in movement-to-music experiences (Honig 1978).

We must balance our fears for safety against the need of a child to explore, to test her limits, to try to throw a ball further, to climb higher, to add another block to that precariously balanced block tower. When we arrange for a baby to pick up cereal from a high chair tray or we set up a basketball hoop outdoors, we facilitate children's coordination and motor development. Adult warnings such as "Be careful, you will spill it all over you," often guarantee the occurrence of just such a mishap.

Motor skill building is important for handicapped children as well. A young college graduate, born without arms or legs, writes eloquently of his parents who constantly challenged him to try: "The basic thing my parents did was just to let me experiment and to encourage me to go and be Terry Haffner. I was never smothered or kept away from the action. I got snow inside my special boots and mud and dirt and stones inside my artificial arms" (Haffner 1976, p. 15).

Mears (1978) researched motor play in very young monkeys. She stressed the importance of self-reinforcing, self-motion play in presenting natural opportunities for encouraging and positively reinforcing pleasure in achievement: "Those individuals, both monkey and human, who gain self-confidence in the physical environment have made vital progress toward social role readiness (p. 378)." Learning skills in one area frequently increases confidence and competence in other areas of functioning.

How to encourage language competence

Children naturally talk when they play together. Adults can help children gain power and mastery over their ability to understand others and to communicate their own needs and ideas about the world with these techniques:

- Listen actively when children talk.
- Give children chances to talk about their experiences.
- Respond positively to children's talking.
- Use music, chant, rhymes, and rhythms to enhance children's ease and delight in words.
- Label experiences: "We are stroking the gerbil's *soft* fur." "Jimmy is brushing his teeth so *carefully*." "We are *almost* ready to bake our muffins." "The ball rolled *under* the table."
- Read lots and lovingly and ask relevant questions to find out if the child is understanding what is happening (Blank 1973).

How to be better matchmakers

We are not just Ms. or Mr. X, teaching the four- or five- or two-year-olds. We are Beth's teacher or José's teacher. How small are the steps we need to move to help a particular child learn a new skill or idea? Each of our children has special talents, special needs for support and encouragement, a special tempo, an individual response to frustration or overstimulation. The creative genius of a teacher lies in the ability to find ways to interact with each child according to that child's needs, to stretch an attention span, motivate a child to persist at a task, or provide opportunities to experiment with materials actively and autonomously.

What children learn

Children are learning about their environment and people in every situation. What do they learn when they are in a good child care center?

I know what is expected here

Children learn the routines, rules, and rhythms of their days. As they play, they learn about what activities occur regularly and which routines increase their sense of assurance. They notice how adults pace activities. Perhaps they also notice when they feel rushed or comfortable, restless and bored, or involved and energized.

A sense of order helps children develop a logical way of thinking about the world. There are places and spaces for different toys and activities. We wash before meals. When we want to join a jump rope game, we ask, "Can I play too?" We don't yank the rope away from the child holding it. A differentiated, well-arranged environment helps a young child know what activities happen in what spaces. Orderliness does not mean inflexible schedules for special trips and opportunities.

Children learn daily what they *can* do. They can slide, play with shaving cream, feed fish, play house, try new foods. They learn how to use materials. Sand is for sifting and pouring, but not for throwing. Books are for reading, not for tearing up or using as weapons.

Some rules can be made with the help of young children. For example, what are their ideas about what to do if they are mad at a friend? One child in a day care center was stopped by the secretary as she saw him walking determinedly out of the building. He explained to the surprised staff member, "I gotta get out of this place. I am feeling so mad at Tommy."

What happens to the child's expectations and understandings of adults when there are different rules for home and for center? Behaviors such as punching with fists, saying scatalogical words to others, and using napkins rather than sleeves may be sanctioned in one place but not another. Teachers can explain calmly, "We have our rules here. In your home, there may be another rule. Sometimes we have to learn different ways to be in different places." There should be rapport and congruence between home expectancies and rules and those in the child care setting. Whenever possible, build comfortable bridges so that ways familiar at home, such as the serving of ethnic foods and the use of culturally special songs, will be promoted in both environments.

I can choose

Children need to learn to be responsible for their own actions through taking the initiative. A child also needs to feel comfortable making incorrect guesses. Family-style meals allow children to take as many spoonfuls of a food as needed. Children can dish out a second portion without adult help if bowls of food are available at the table.

Adults can give children choices within the boundaries of the rules for the center. "What area do you want to play in *first* this morning?" "Would you like two carrot sticks or four?" Helping children make responsible choices does not mean that an adult abdicates a guidance role. Responsible functioning means that children will learn how to serve and help at mealtimes and how to sort and put away toys in appropriate spaces at cleanup time.

I am lovable

Children can feel free to learn and try different activities if they feel loved or cared for by adults. Bronfenbrenner remarked that every child needs "someone to be crazy about him or her (1977)." As adults show their pleasure and pride in the small daily accomplishments of young children, they build a secure trusting foundation for children to want to try to learn. Building a loving relationship is easier if the adult is readily available for cuddling, listening, and sharing when the child feels the need.

I can do it

From earliest toddlerhood, children express their need to do things for themselves and by themselves. Children often grow in self-satisfaction as they try to accomplish new developmental tasks. If a caregiver has learned to match needs with abilities, children will have more experiences with success than failure as learning progresses. "I can figure out how to fix it." "I can read that book." "I can swim."

Young children are so anxious to prove their competence that sometimes they inaccurately gauge their skill levels. Children will increase in competence as we arrange their learning activities, as we interact with them in growth-enhancing ways, and as we encourage their trying hard at slightly difficult tasks. Carew (1976) described in detail ways in which fathers and mothers encourage and validate the competence of their small children. Teachers can learn much from these observational records.

I can use language to express myself

The gift of language is a great power for young children. Language enables children to ask for what they need rather than fight or whine for it. Language also permits sociability between children and between adults and children. Preschool language communication may still be at a level where each child in a dialogue is unaware of the intent of the other, yet the conversation is eminently satisfying to each.

Children also play with language. Sometimes young children use language in picturesque ways used by adult poets. "They highered the price and they smallered the candy bar," exclaimed a child on receiving candy from an airport machine dispenser. Another toddler, whose father was taking her to the pediatrician for a checkup of an oral infection was told that the doctor would have her open her mouth wide. She asked whether the doctor was a dentist. When told no, the child thought awhile and asked, "Is he a doctor *pretending* to be a dentist?" Helping children develop their language skills entails priceless rewards for caregiving adults as well as pleasure and skill for children.

Adults can be trusted

We have all seen older children who distrust adults. There are children in high schools who would never go to a teacher and ask for special tutoring. Other children grow up learning to avoid adults and adult responsibilities in their lives. They do not see adults as caring and cared for resource people.

Children need to learn that adults can be teaching, loving, and helping people. Teachers show children this through daily actions, courtesies, and gestures that do not detract from the child's feelings of competence. Such actions by adults will help children want to grow up like the caring adults around them.

This article is adapted from a keynote speech presented at the annual conference of the Canadian Association for the Education of Young Children, Carleton University, Ottawa, Canada, September 1978.

References

Blank, M. *Teaching Learning in the Preschool. A Dialogue Approach.* Columbus, Ohio: Charles E. Merrill, 1973.

Bronfenbrenner, U. "Who Cares for America's Children?" Keynote address presented at the annual conference of the Association for Children's Services, Syracuse, New York, April 4, 1977.

Caldwell, B. M. "Aggression and Hostility in Young Children." *Young Children* 32, no. 2 (January 1977): 5-14.

Carew, J. V.; Chan, I.; and Halfer, C. *Observing Intelligence in Young Children.* Englewood Cliffs, N.J.: Prentice-Hall, 1976.

Gordon, T. *Parent Effectiveness Training.* New York: Wyden, 1974.

Haffner, T. "The Cap and Gown Feeling." *The Exceptional Parent* 6, no. 1 (1976): 13-17.

Hipple, M. L. "Classroom Discipline Problems? Fifteen Humane Solutions." *Childhood Education* 54 (1978): 183-187.

Honig, A. S. "Comparison of Child-Rearing Practices in Japan and in the People's Republic of China: A Personal View." *International Journal of Group Tensions* 8, nos. 1 and 2 (1978): 6-32.

Honig, A. S. "What You Need to Know to Select and Train Your Daycare Staff." *Child Care Quarterly* 8, no. 1 (1979): 19-35.

Kamii, C. and DeVries, R. *Physical Knowledge in Preschool Education.* Englewood Cliffs, N.J.: Prentice-Hall, 1978.

Kamii, C. and Lee-Katz, L. "Physics in Preschool Education: A Piagetian Approach." *Young Children* 34, no. 4 (May 1979): 4-9.

Mears, C. F. "Play and Development of Cosmic Confidence." *Developmental Psychology* 14, no. 4 (1978): 371-378.

Shure, M. B. and Spivack, G. *Problem-Solving Techniques in Childrearing.* San Francisco: Jossey-Bass, 1978.

2

Play *is* learning

"All they do is play all day. When will they start learning something?"

How would you respond to this question? If parents or other teachers have asked you, you know how difficult it is to answer satisfactorily. Most adults are unfamiliar with the child development research such as that which you are about to review, and which would help them understand the role of play in learning.

For those who question the value of play, Fein documents how complex different types of play can be and how they relate to children's total learning. You may want to share this article with those who are skeptical.

What have you done in your classroom to make a difference in the quality of children's play? Blocks and dramatic play are two of the most popular areas. Kinsman and Berk, and Griffing tell us about their experiences in making some slight changes in the environment that resulted in expanded play opportunities.

Playgrounds are more than just a break from being indoors—they are an exciting part of the early childhood curriculum. Ideas for a quality *and* safe playground are offered by Frost and Henniger.

research in review

Pretend Play: New Perspectives

by Greta G. Fein

Children's pretend play is a familiar phenomenon to early childhood educators. But it is only recently that its origins, forms, and implications for development have received systematic attention (see Fein 1979 for an extensive review of the research literature). A variety of terms are used, often interchangeably, to refer to this type of play. *Fantasy play, imaginative play, make-believe play,* and *pretend play* are typically used as generic terms for play that has an "as if" quality, and these terms will be used in a similar fashion in this discussion. By contrast, the terms *symbolic play* and *sociodramatic play* are used to designate particular forms of pretend play that appear at different stages of development. *Symbolic play* will be used to refer to solitary play in which the child represents one thing as if it were another with no attempt to develop or coordinate pretend activities with a partner, and *sociodramatic play* will be used for pretense that is shared or coordinated with a partner. Although this distinction can be viewed as a convenient way of classifying a complex form of behavior, there are empirical grounds for believing children shift from solitary to social pretense, and that this shift marks a developmental accomplishment of considerable importance.

Symbolic Play

At about 12 months of age, a new behavior emerges in the young child's repertoire. Prior to this time, the baby eats when hungry, sleeps when tired, and cries when distressed; objects such as bottles, cups, spoons, pillows, and blankets are used either to manipulate or to obtain nourishment and rest. Then, with apparent suddenness, the meaning of these objects subtly changes. Seemingly sated, the baby pretends to eat and, seemingly rested, the baby pretends to sleep. Although these behaviors were noted by others, Piaget (1962) was the first to offer a theoretical framework for understanding their developmental significance. According to Piaget, these behaviors mark the beginnings of representational thought, the first sign that the child is beginning to construct mental symbols and images of the real world of substances, objects, and actions.

According to Piaget and others who have subsequently extended and refined these observations, early pretend behaviors become more stable and elaborated during the second year of life (Inhelder, Lezine, Sinclair, and Stambak 1972; Nicolich 1977; Fein and Apfel 1979). By about 18 months, the child discovers that a doll can be fed or put to bed as if it were a baby. But at this age, the doll must be doll-like and the cup must be cuplike if they are to be used this way. Between 18 and 24 months, the requirement of likeness becomes relaxed. In Vygotsky's terms, dissimilar objects (a hank of wool, a piece of wood, a shell, a fist) can substitute

Greta G. Fein, Ph.D., is Professor and Director of Child Development Research, The Merrill-Palmer Institute, Detroit, Michigan.

for lifelike objects and, gradually, an immediately present object is not needed for pretending. Over the next few months, symbolic play becomes increasingly elaborate and well-formed until, by about 30 months, it can become a collaborative effort undertaken with others.

Piaget and Vygotsky agree that symbolic play reflects the child's mastery of mental symbols, elements of thought that permit the child to detach ideas about the world from the influence of objects in the immediate environment. Vygotsky (1967) views the acquisition of stimulus-free mental symbols as a gradual process in which the requirement of likeness is relaxed by degrees. Recent research supports this idea. When two-year-olds are given a realistic cup and a realistic toy horse to pretend feeding with, they have no difficulty. If a less realistic object is substituted for one of these, pretense drops slightly. If less realistic substitutes are provided for both objects, pretense decreases markedly (Fein 1975). It is as if at this age, the symbol system is too fragile to operate without firm anchors in the immediate setting. Studies of preschool children suggest that the child's liberation from the immediate situation continues to develop over the next two years (Elder and Pederson 1978; Golomb 1977). But even five-year-olds have difficulty substituting one object for another under certain circumstances (e.g., a hairbrush for food to feed a hungry baby in Golomb's study).

These and other studies suggest that symbolic play is influenced by the play materials available to the child. In young children, play is enhanced by realistic materials and realistic toy props. With age, the need for realistic materials diminishes and, according to some researchers (Pulaski 1973), less realistic toys might even enhance the imaginativeness of play in older children. Although sleek, abstract forms are appealing to adults, their play value for children seems to depend on the age of the child.

Sociodramatic Play

Sociodramatic play can be viewed as a reorganization of solitary symbolic play that takes into account the symbolic representations of a partner. In a sense, solitary pretense rests primarily on the child's ability or desire to imagine familiar, novel, or even bizarre events. Sociodramatic play requires, in addition, the ability to respond to the imagination of another person. Evidence from a classic study by Parten (1933) suggested that cooperative sociodramatic activities of this type do not appear until children are about three years of age.

Recent play episodes, taken from a current Merrill-Palmer Institute study of peer interactions in children between the ages of two and six years, seem to confirm Parten's observations. In the Merrill-Palmer study, well-acquainted children come in pairs to a playroom where their behavior is videotaped through a one-way mirror. The playroom is equipped with two sets of toys. Each child is videotaped playing with different peers in four 15-minute sessions. The data illustrate some general features of the pretend play behavior of children within this age range. First, sociodramatic episodes become more frequent and sustained with age. At two years these episodes are rare, but by five years it is not unusual for sociodramatic episodes to occupy an entire 15-minute period. Second, the content of the play changes from simple imitative motor actions (such as one

This is one of a regular series of research columns edited by Shirley G. Moore, Ph.D., Professor, Institute of Child Development, University of Minnesota, Minneapolis.

child feeding another) to enactment of full blown social roles (such as the parent).

Two verbatim episodes from the Merrill-Palmer data follow. The first involves an exchange between two unusually sophisticated two-and-a-half-year-olds, a boy named Herman (H) and a girl named Sally (S). Herman begins the action.

H: (Takes the baby bottle and the spoon) "Take your medicine, OK?"
S: "OK, put it on my spoon."
H: (Puts it on her spoon and says,) "It's not medicine, it's for your nose. Hey, you know what?"
S: "Yeah, put it in my nose."
H: "I put it in your nose OK?" (S. bends head back. H. brings spoon to her nose.)
S: "OK" (She continues to comb her hair.)
H: "Drink some of that."
S: "OK" (S. pretends to drink what H. is feeding her.)
H: *"You feed me, OK?"* (H. puts down the bottle and the spoon.)
S: *"OK"* (S. picks up the bottle and the spoon and feeds H.) "It's medicine. It's medicine. Look, it's medicine."
H: *"It's mine."* (takes the bottle from S.)
S: *"OK. Where's my bottle?"*
H: (Looks in her carriage.) *"Your bottle is down there."*
S: *"Oh thank you."*
H: *"I'll show you, OK? (Pause.) "Where's the spoon?"* (H. takes the spoon from S.)
S: "No!" (S. reaches for the spoon. H. turns around and pours from the bottle to the spoon.)
H: "This is for your nose, OK? This is for your nose."
S: "OK."
H: "You're gonna be alright."
S: "I'll be alright." (Pause.) *"Come here. Give me your medicine, I'll feed you, OK? Want me to feed you?"*
H: *"You want me to feed you?"*

S: *"No, I'll feed you."*
H: *"Unh, unh."*
S: *"Yeah."*
H: "No" (H. leaves.)
S: (Sweetly.) "It's medicine. You will be OK."
H: "Unh, unh."
S: (Sweetly and insistently.) "Come here, it's medicine. You will be OK." (S. takes a taste of it.) "It's Kool-Aid, you want some Kool-Aid?"
H: Nods yes, drinks from the spoon, and smiles.
S: (Smiling back.) "Oh, it's good."

Note that Herman and Sally are preoccupied with the concrete, sensorimotor roles of "giver" and "taker." They are able to negotiate role reversals, and Sally is even able to employ successfully the adult ruse of presenting medicine as Kool-Aid. And yet, although the play lasted for almost 10 minutes, the children never extended either by gesture, clothing, or verbal labeling the sensorimotor roles of "giver" and "taker" to the social roles of parent and child, or doctor and patient.

The second episode involves two five-year-olds, a girl named Lil (L) and a boy named Jim (J). As the action begins, Jim is playing with a fire truck and miniature people while Lil is walking back and forth with a broom.

L: *"Are you the father or the son?"*
J: *"I'm the big brother."*
L: *"OK, then I'll be the big sister."*
J: *"Cause fathers don't even play with toys."*
L: *"Well, I'm the big girl, I'm the big sister. Anyway, Mom told me to take care of the two babies, our little brother and sister and you better not touch them or I'm gonna tell Mom on you."*
J: "You're not gonna tell anybody on me."

L: "Huh! I'm gonna tell someone on you, don't you think I'm not. So brother if you want to say something keep it to your own self."

J: "You know I'm bigger than you."

L: "Huh, you're not bigger than anybody."

J: "Hey, I'm bigger than you—you're just nine. So you better watch it!"

L: "You're the biggest cause you're just twelve years old. You're even bigger than me."

J: "You're just. . . ."

L: "If you want to fight just go fight yourself."

J: "You think I'm bigger than you cause I'm twelve years old. You, you're just nine. Hey, hey, you better watch it cause I'm babysitting for you all."

L: "You mean us three?"

J: "Yeah."

L: "One, two, three."

J: "There, just. . . ."

L: "One, two, three, four, and your own self. You're a baby: your own self."

J: "Hey, I ain't no baby girl, what goes and tattles on you."

Jim and Lil begin to whisper.

L: "You better watch it cause they're waking, brother."

J: "Shut up."

L: "Well make me."

J: "Shut up before you make me wake the babies up."

L: "Then I'll really tell Mom on you."

J: "Hey you can't, you cannot tell Mom on me. I'll. . . ."

L: "Then I'll tell Dad on you. *Let me tell you; you be the dad and. . . .*"

J: *"Uh uh, I ain't playing no dad and I'm certain not no daddy."*

L: *"And I'm certain not no mommy."*

J: *"If you wanna find a daddy, if you wanna find a daddy, ask John"* (the children's teacher).

Note that action roles preoccupy Herman and Sally, whereas social roles are of central importance to Lil and Jim. Father, son, brother, mother, sister, baby, along with the obligations, responsibilities, and privileges that accompany these roles are major issues for older children in defining the boundaries of the play that is to occur. Jim is quite explicit in rejecting the father role because it would not permit him to play with the toys. But as big brother, he retains some authority even though as the play unfolds, it becomes clear that this authority must be vigilantly asserted and defended.

As Garvey and Berndt (1977) have noted, two forms of communication characterize sociodramatic episodes. Meta communications (italicized in the transcripts) are communications *about* the play. In these exchanges, the children retain their own identities, and as themselves, talk about the roles and scenes being performed. By contrast, pretend communications are exchanges held *within* the play mode. In these exchanges, the children relate to one another in the roles they have agreed to perform. For the younger children, Herman and Sally, communication boundaries are more evident in tone of voice, gestures, and supplementary props than in the words themselves. For the older children, the boundaries are sharper. Having decided to play brother and sister, Lil and Jim can pretend to fight about the things brothers and sisters often fight about, such as status and the ultimate authority. By contrast, Sally and Herman have difficulty managing conflict until Sally, in an inspired move, manages to commandeer the play role of medicine-giver.

The Contribution of Pretend Play to Social and Cognitive Development

Early childhood educators have long believed that pretend play was beneficial for young children. Until recently, however, there was little evidence to support this belief. Studies by Rosen (1974), Saltz and Johnson (1974), Saltz, Dixon, and Johnson (1977), and Golomb and Cornelius (1977) report changes in children's social and cognitive ability as a function of training in sociodramatic and fantasy play.

Rosen (1974) gave two groups of kindergarten children 40 days of instruction and practice in sociodramatic play during their free play time. This intervention produced a significant increase in sociodramatic play. In order to examine whether increases in sociodramatic play would have an impact on nonplay abilities, the children were assessed before and after intervention on several abilities thought to benefit from such play. For example, sociodramatic play might enhance children's sensitivity to the point of view of others. In one of the tasks assessing this ability, children were asked to choose from a set of objects (woman's hose, man's necktie, toy truck, doll, and adult book) the birthday gift he or she would choose if they were a father, a mother, a brother, a sister, or themselves. The children who received sociodramatic play training improved significantly in their ability to choose a gift appropriate for another person. In another task, small groups of children were asked to work together as a team in constructing an object out of blocks. Children who received sociodramatic play training showed significant improvement in facilitative group behaviors (planning, cooperating, and group reference behaviors). These results confirm the findings of other investigators indicating that sociodramatic play enhances children's social skills.

There is additional evidence to suggest that fantasy activities might enhance children's performance on IQ tests (Saltz, Dixon, and Johnson 1977) and on Piagetian tests of conservation (Golomb and Cornelius 1977). In the latter study, nonconserving four-year-olds were as-signed to special symbolic play sessions in which the adult first joined the child's pretend play and then challenged the child to explain how an object could be both itself and a make-believe something else. Experimental and control children (those who did not participate in the special play sessions) were given four tasks assessing conservation of quantity. On one task, for example, the children were shown two identical glass beakers containing the same amount of pink liquid. The contents of one beaker was then poured into a narrower and taller beaker, and the children were asked whether the amount of liquid in the two beakers was the same or different. On these tasks, children who judged that the amount of liquid was different after it had been poured were considered nonconservers. On the conservation tests, the symbolic training group produced more correct conservation judgments than did children in the control group. According to Golomb, symbolic play facilitates children's ability to maintain the identity of an object in spite of its transformation. In symbolic play the transformation is imaginary, whereas in conservation the transformation is perceptual.

Enhancing Play

If recent research is beginning to clarify the ways children benefit from play, it is also clarifying the ways adults can enhance play. In an earlier section, evidence was presented that well-chosen materials can enhance play. Play can be encouraged in other ways as well. Properly chosen materials, realistic toys for toddlers and more abstract toys for preschoolers, can facilitate pretense. Encouragement from parents and teachers can enhance the play and its benefits.

Smilansky (1968) describes in detail a method for recording on a daily basis the pretend play of individual children.

Then, for children who pretend infrequently, the teacher can suggest how a toy can be used more imaginatively or how a pretend game can be elaborated by the addition of new roles or changing scenes. Several studies using such procedures have demonstrated striking changes in the richness and complexity of sociodramatic activities (Smilansky 1968; Rosen 1974).

Conclusion

Pretend play seems to be an important activity for young children. Recent research has begun to document its contribution to children's social and cognitive development. The capacity for pretend play seems to be acquired without special toys or tutelage. Yet some children do not use this ability as much as others. Especially in the case of sociodramatic play, a combination of social and communication skills seems necessary for the play to happen. But once the basic skills are available and sociodramatic play occurs, the evidence suggests that these skills are refined and consolidated. New areas of cooperation and social sensitivity then emerge in children's nonplay activities. Play and nonplay seem to be related in such a way that accomplishments in one domain feed into the other.

As increasing numbers of young children spend increasing amounts of time in group care settings, the functions of play, and techniques for supporting it, will become increasingly important areas of study in early childhood research.

References

Elder, J. L., and Pederson, D. R. "Preschool Children's Use of Objects in Symbolic Play." *Child Development* 49 (1978): 500-504.

Fein, G. "A Transformational Analysis of Pretending." *Developmental Psychology* 11 (1975): 291-296.

Fein, G. G. "Play and the Acquisition of Symbols." In *Current Topics in Early Childhood Education*, ed. L. Katz. Norwood, N.J.: Ablex, 1979.

Fein, G. G., and Apfel, N. "Some Preliminary Observations on Knowing and Pretending." In *Symbolic Functioning in Childhood*, ed. N. Smith and M. B. Franklin. Hillsdale, N.J.: Erlbaum, 1979.

Garvey, K., and Berndt, R. "Organization of Pretend Play." *Catalogue of Selected Documents in Psychology* 7 (1977): no. 1589, American Psychological Association.

Golomb, C. "Symbolic Play: The Role of Substitutions in Pretense and Puzzle Games." *British Journal of Educational Psychology* 47 (1977): 175-186.

Golomb, C., and Cornelius, C. B. "Symbolic Play and Its Cognitive Significance." *Developmental Psychology* 13 (1977): 246-252.

Inhelder, B.; Lezine, I.; Sinclair, H.; and Stambak, M. "Les Debut de la Function Symbolique." *Archives de Psychologie* 41 (1972): 187-243.

Nicolich, L. "Beyond Sensorimotor Intelligence: Assessment of Symbolic Maturity Through Analysis of Pretend Play." *Merrill-Palmer Quarterly* 23, no. 2 (1977): 89-99.

Parten, M. B. "Social Participation in Preschool Children." *Journal of Abnormal Social Psychology* 28 (1933): 136-147.

Piaget, J. *Play, Dreams and Imitation in Childhood*. New York: Norton, 1962.

Pulaski, M. A. "Toys and Imaginative Play." In *The Child's World of Make-Believe*, ed. J. L. Singer. New York: Academic Press, 1973.

Rosen, C. E. "The Effects of Sociodramatic Play on Problem-Solving Behavior among Culturally Disadvantaged Preschool Children." *Child Development* 45 (1974): 920-927.

Saltz, E., and Johnson, J. "Training for Thematic-Fantasy Play in Culturally Disadvantaged Children: Preliminary Results." *Journal of Educational Psychology* 66 (1974): 623-630.

Saltz, E.; Dixon, D.; and Johnson, J. "Training Disadvantaged Preschoolers on Various Fantasy Activities: Effects on Cognitive Functioning and Impulse Control." *Child Development* 48 (1977): 367-380.

Smilansky, S. *The Effects of Sociodramatic Play on Disadvantaged Preschool Children*. New York: Wiley, 1968.

Vygotsky, L. S. "Play and Its Role in the Mental Development of the Child." *Soviet Psychology* 5, no. 3 (1967): 6-18.

Cheryl A. Kinsman and Laura E. Berk

Joining the Block and Housekeeping Areas
Changes in Play and Social Behavior

Are you a teacher who frequently rearranges your room? Or one who prefers to leave everything in the same place? Simply removing one wall of shelves caused some dramatic changes in children's play. How does the environment influence activities where you teach?

Although early childhood teachers plan the arrangement of classroom activity centers to promote desirable behaviors in children, little empirical knowledge is available to guide them in improving early childhood learning environments (Gordon and Jester 1973). Despite the fact that systems for analyzing the ecology of nursery schools and child care settings are available, and many observational instruments have been developed for studying the relationship of environments to children's behavior (Boyer, Simon, and Karafin 1973), most teachers rely on intuition, practical considerations, or conventional habit rather than on an objective appraisal of classroom designs.

This study is an intensive empirical look at how two traditional early childhood activity settings—the block and housekeeping areas—influence young children's play and social behaviors. We chose to investigate these two settings because they have historically been and continue to be a salient part of the environment and curriculum in most programs. In exploring the influence of nursery and kindergarten activities on how children express themselves in play,

Hartley, Frank, and Goldenson (1952) describe blocks as the most widely accepted early childhood classroom materials. Play with blocks, they speculate, helps the child to release energy, aids social integration, and combines creative expression with mastery. Housekeeping, a form of dramatic play, provides social education through role playing, imitation of adults, and opportunities to play out home relationships and life experiences.

In view of their social functions, it is not surprising that the block and housekeeping areas have also been considered to be an important part of early sex role socialization in schools and as play environments that may condone and perpetuate traditional sex roles. Even when there is no conscious effort on the part of teachers to sex type, it has been suggested

Cheryl A. Kinsman, M.S., was a vocational evaluator and counselor in a rehabilitation agency for the psychiatrically disabled, Chicago, Illinois.

Laura E. Berk, Ph.D., is Associate Professor of Psychology, Illinois State University, Normal, Illinois.

that girls, who play with dolls, may receive a very different education from boys, who play with blocks (Stacey, Bereaud, and Daniels 1974). A number of studies report that boys spend more time playing in the block area, and girls spend more time in the housekeeping area (Clark, Wyon, and Richards 1969; Coates, Lord, and Jakabovics 1975; Sears 1965; Vance and McCall 1934). In most classrooms these two settings are either clearly divided or physically separated from one another, an arrangement that serves to promote this separation of the sexes in play. Shure (1963) examined the type of play that occurred in each setting and found that when children did enter the "opposite sex" setting, they did not constructively make use of its play opportunities. Boys engaged in more irrelevant behavior in the housekeeping area (behavior that is not "appropriate" to the area, such as running or playing with cars), whereas girls exhibited more irrelevant actions in the block area.

Both Hartley et al. (1952) and Shure (1963) suggested joining the housekeeping and block areas so that materials from both settings could be used together to enrich children's play. By linking the two areas, the range of children's play experiences could be expanded by offering a greater variety of materials and providing interaction with more varied groups of peers.

The purpose of this study was: (1) to investigate how children's social and play behaviors are influenced by a divided arrangement of housekeeping and block areas in an early childhood classroom; and, (2) to find out how behavior changes when a wall of shelves separating the two settings is removed and children can move freely from one area to another. As a result of joining the two areas, we expected more mixed-sex play, more spatial overlap of activities between the two settings, and an increase in children's integration of materials from one area into the play activities of the other. We also anticipated that girls

Marietta Lynch

By linking the housekeeping and block areas, the range of children's play experiences could be expanded by offering a greater variety of materials and providing interaction with more varied groups of peers.

would spend more time in the block area and engage in more relevant behavior there, and that the same would be true for boys in the housekeeping area.

Method

The children. Seventeen children who attended a morning nursery school session and twenty children who attended an afternoon kindergarten session at a university laboratory school were observed at play in the block and housekeeping areas. In all, there were 37 children, 21 boys and 16 girls. They ranged in age from three to six years, and almost all of them came from middle class homes. Due to frequent absence from school, two children were eventually excluded from the study, making the final number of children 35. Both the nursery and kindergarten sessions were taught by the same teacher in the same classroom environment.

The setting. Figure 1 shows the layout of the classroom, including the location of the block and housekeeping areas and the divider of shelves that existed between them. For the first phase of the study, no modifications were made in the activity areas, and they are shown just as the teacher had arranged them and as they had existed for the seventeen years she had been teaching in this classroom.

The block area was carpeted and contained a variety of wooden play objects: large blocks, long narrow boards, two saw horses, a seesaw, and small trucks and cars. A large stationary car that could support several children was located on one side of the entrance to the setting. On the other side of the entrance was a slide, con-

sidered to be part of the block area equipment.

The housekeeping area contained a wide assortment of furnishings, including a refrigerator, sink, stove, china cabinet, table and chairs, high chair, bed, crib, ironing board, dolls, and dress-up clothing. A large mirror stood at one end of the area. The row of shelves separating the housekeeping area from the block area was low enough so children could climb on them and reach across.

The daily program for the nursery and kindergarten sessions offered much time for free play and ample opportunity for children to use the two environments. Puzzles, games, and art materials were readied on tables for children's use in other areas of the classroom. However, special activities were not provided by the

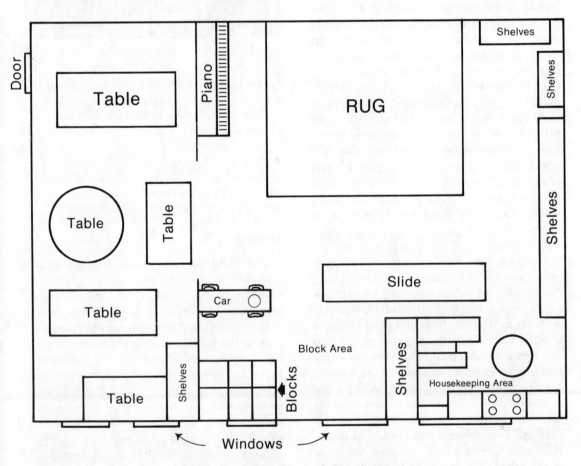

Figure 1. The layout of the classroom

Kinsman and Berk

teacher in the block and housekeeping areas. Instead, the forms and themes of activities occurring in these two areas emanated from the combination of materials and children inhabiting the settings. The teacher observed and intervened to provide help when necessary; otherwise, during free play she allowed the children much autonomy to work and play according to their own motivations.

Categories of behavior observed. The following aspects of behavior were observed as the children spontaneously entered the two play areas:

1. *Group size.* **(Categories drawn from Berk 1976.)**
   a. *Solitary*—the child played alone and independently, centering attention on his or her own activity which was pursued without reference to what other children in the area were doing. The child might have played with the same materials as other children nearby but did not try to interact with them or influence their activity.
   b. *Pair*—the child played with one other child. Playing with another child involved interaction of some kind, including conversation, borrowing or sharing toys, following or chasing, physical contact, or organized play in which children assumed different roles.
   c. *Small cluster*—the child played with a group of three to five other children.
   d. *Large cluster*—the child played with a group of six or more children.

2. *Group composition.* **If the child played in a group of two or more children, the group's sexual composition was noted.**
   a. *Same-sex*—the child played with other children of the same sex.
   b. *Mixed-sex*—the child played with a child of the opposite sex or in a group with children of both sexes.

3. *Nature of play activity.* **These categories were concerned with identifying the type of play materials a child used along with the major intent of play. (The first two categories were borrowed from Shure 1963.)**
   a. *Relevant*—the child was engaged in an activity and use of materials appropriate to an area and used only props

and equipment that belonged in the area. In the block area, building with blocks or using them as imaginary cars or furniture were examples of relevant play, as were playing with dolls or playing house in the housekeeping area.
   b. *Irrelevant*—the child was engaged in an activity or use of materials that was in no way related to the area in which he or she was present. For example, putting together a puzzle or playing tag in either area or dressing a doll in the block area was considered irrelevant.
   c. *Integrative*—materials from either the block or housekeeping area were used to support and elaborate the appropriate use of materials in the other area. For example, a child placed dolls on a "chair" built of blocks in the block area, or blocks were used as "food" in the housekeeping area.
   d. *Uninvolved*—the child was not engaged in an activity or involved with any materials in the area, but was merely standing, wandering, sitting, or talking with others.

4. *Location of play activity.* **These categories referred to the spatial arrangement of the child's activity.**
   a. *Contained*—the child's activity was spatially confined to either the block or housekeeping area.
   b. *Overlapping*—the child's activity occupied space in both the block and housekeeping areas.

5. *Affect.* **This referred to the general feeling tone or mood expressed by the child.**
   a. *Positive*—the child expressed a momentarily positive feeling. Contented, happy, friendly, affectionate, sympathetic, and enthusiastic were examples.
   b. *Negative*—the child expressed a momentarily unfavorable feeling, such as cross, irritable, angry, or antagonistic.

Observational procedure. The housekeeping and block areas were observed for a total of six weeks. For the first three weeks, the settings remained unaltered, with the shelves separating one from the other. The shelves were removed for the final three weeks of observation.

Child behaviors in the block and housekeeping areas were observed for a total of nine hours a week, five in the morning nursery school class and four in the afternoon kindergarten class. Because the first hour of each class session was a free play period, the observations were made at that time.

Four observers participated in data collection, with two of them observing primarily in the morning and two in the afternoon. The observer focused on the block and housekeeping areas alternately for five minutes at a time. Every 20 seconds the observer dictated into a tape recorder the identity of each child in the setting, the group size and composition, type of play, location of the child's activity, and the child's affective expression. The information on the tapes was later transcribed onto data sheets.

The number of 20-second intervals each child was observed to be present in the block and housekeeping areas and the frequency of occurrence of the behavior categories for each child were tabulated. Due to child absences, the greater amount of observation time in the nursery school than in the kindergarten class, and the fact that children varied in the extent to which they entered the two settings, percentage rather than frequency scores were used to analyze the data.[1]

Results and Discussion

Overall incidence of social and play behaviors. Children in this study were observed to appear for an average of 13 percent of their free play time in the block or housekeeping areas. Confirming results of previous research, blocks and housekeeping in this classroom served a predominantly social function that brought together children of the same sex. Children spent an average of 50 percent of their time in the two areas involved in play with same-sex children and 21 percent with opposite-sex children. During interactive activities, play consisted mostly of the more intimate social arrangements of small clusters and pairs with large cluster groups of six or more children occurring only 3 percent of the time. That children also spent 35 percent of their time in solitary play indicates the great flexibility of these activity areas in serving a variety of children's needs—from retreat, withdrawal, and absorption in private activity to active group participation and cooperative efforts with other children.

For a majority of the time (55 percent), children used the two activity environments and the materials in them in a setting-appropriate, relevant fashion. Irrelevant play occurred in only 16 percent of children's observations. A 20 percent incidence of uninvolved behavior indicated that children also used these areas as safe, enclosed places in which to back off and seek a respite from the busy, involved, social atmosphere of the classroom. The "separate" arrangement of the blocks and housekeeping areas appeared to discourage integration of play materials from one area to the other. Integrative activities occurred only 5 percent of the time, and activities that spatially overlapped the two areas occurred only 1 percent of the time.

Differences between the block and housekeeping areas. In contrast to previous research (Clark, Wyon, and Richards 1969; Coates, Lord, and Jakabovics 1975; Sears 1965; Vance and McCall 1934), there was no indication of a sex-typed attraction to either play area in this study. Boys did not spend more time in the block area and girls in the housekeeping area. Instead, all children preferred the block area and were observed playing there more than twice as often as they were in the housekeeping setting. Nevertheless, an examination of qualities of children's behavior indicated that children used the two settings differently and that play and social behavior in them varied according to age and sex.

---

[1] A full report of the data analysis, interobserver reliabilities, and tabular presentation of results may be obtained from the authors.

Children used the housekeeping area for more solitary pursuits (p < .01) and the block corner for more clustered social play (p < .01). This difference was especially marked for the nursery school children who were found to engage in far more large cluster play in blocks than in housekeeping (p < .004). When children entered the block setting, it was not long before they joined a group working on a project. The observers informally noted that blocks were often used to build transportation toys which, as Beehler (1974) has observed, encourages high rates of social interaction. The children rarely "traveled" alone in their cars constructed with blocks. Since children spent more time in the block area, it was likely to be more crowded than the housekeeping area and to provide much more opportunity for cooperative group play.

When social interaction occurred in the housekeeping area, girls were observed playing in small clusters more often than were boys (p < .05). Furthermore, girls' social clustered play in housekeeping consisted primarily of play with other girls, whereas boys' small cluster play in the block area more often involved play with other boys (p < .01).

As the block area was the main attraction, it also elicited a greater amount of relevant play (p < .01), and a larger quantity of irrelevant play occurred in the housekeeping setting (p < .01). This may be a function of the greater flexibility of play objects, thereby permitting a wider range of play activities with them to be considered relevant. Conversely, the objects in the housekeeping area had a more prescribed usage, and this more limited opportunity for relevant play gave way to the greater quantity of irrelevant behavior that occurred there. Irrelevant play in the housekeeping area was also typical of older children more often than younger

Integration of play materials from one area into the other increased for older children when the two settings were joined.

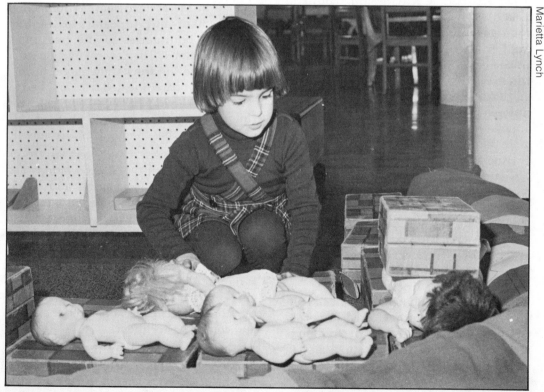

Marietta Lynch

children (p < .05). Put another way, the older children were less influenced by the materials in the housekeeping area, and they tended to use it simply as a play space where, for example, they sat at the table looking at books or engaged in fantasy play (e.g., playing radio station, King Kong, or Batman), without incorporating any of the housekeeping materials into their activity. Older children also showed less positive affect than younger children while in the housekeeping area (p < .05). This, along with the more irrelevant nature of their play, might indicate that the five- and six-year-olds were beginning to "outgrow" the play possibilities of the housekeeping environment.

As in Shure's study (1963), the sex-stereotyped nature of children's play in the two corners was evident in this study. Boys engaged in more relevant play in the block area than in the housekeeping area, whereas no difference existed for girls (p < .01). This finding suggests that the greater social pressure for boys to engage in sex-appropriate activities (Maccoby and Jacklin 1974) was already present in the spontaneous play of these very young children. Also, boys exhibited more uninvolved behavior in the housekeeping area, whereas girls were more uninvolved in the block area (p < .01), indicating that children may have been less at home in an opposite-sex setting, where they spent more time standing around, wandering, or watching others play.

Changes in children's behavior after removal of the divider. In contrast to what was expected, after the shelves were removed, girls did not spend more time in the block area and boys in the housekeeping area. However, several other aspects of their behavior were influenced by joining the two settings.

The most evident change involved children's social behavior. As predicted, solitary play and associations with children of the same sex decreased (p < .01). Play in mixed-sex groups increased in both settings (p < .01), especially in small and large cluster social arrangements (p < .01). The increase in mixed-sex play was especially dramatic in the housekeeping area (p < .01).

However, a finer examination of the results revealed that the decrease in same-sex play and increase in mixed-sex interaction was characteristic of younger children, and older children's social partners remained relatively stable over time (p < .01). Younger children's opposite-sex play was especially evident in the large cluster arrangement (p < .01), and sometimes observers saw the entire morning class playing together in the block area.

Whereas joining the two play settings produced a wider range of social experience for the nursery school children, the kindergarten children in some ways appeared undaunted by the environmental change. The observers noticed that the older children's immediate reaction to removal of the shelves was to replace them with some kind of barrier. They resisted change in the accustomed environmental arrangement and appeared to want to keep the boundaries of the two areas sharply defined. They successively used a line of large toy trucks, the large mirror, the ironing board, the doll crib, and bed to redivide the two play areas. The younger children were far less rigid in their adjustment to the changed environment.

Perhaps they were simply less aware of the traditional sex-typed expectations associated with housekeeping and block play. Or, as their teacher suggested, since many of the kindergarten children had previously spent their nursery school years in the classroom, their familiarity with and dependence on the activity arrangements had developed over two years. Therefore, removal of the divider may have been especially overwhelming and confusing for them.

Several additional findings emerged. Boys engaged in more irrelevant play after the shelves were taken out in both activity

Kinsman and Berk

settings. In contrast, girls showed an increase in appropriate use of blocks and housekeeping. They engaged in less irrelevant play than they had exhibited under the divided arrangement (p < .02). A finer analysis revealed that the decrease in irrelevant play for girls was largely due to an increase in integrative play in the block area. Girls reacted to modification of the settings optimally by expanding and enriching their play activities in the "opposite-sex" environment.

Integration of play materials from one area into the other increased for older children when the two settings were joined, although the younger nursery age children showed no increase in this type of play (p < .01). Since only the shelves were removed and the materials and equipment in the two play areas were not intermingled, perhaps the idea of integrative play necessitated the increased cognitive sophistication of the older children, whose play was not so closely tied to location of materials and the concrete usage immediately suggested by the toys.

Expression of negative affect, initially very low in occurrence, declined even more after removal of the divider. Perhaps the greater access to play materials in an enlarged, open play space reduced crowding, jostling, and competition for play materials and was responsible for this change.

Conclusion

In this study, environmental qualities and personal characteristics of children combined to shape children's social interaction and play in the block and housekeeping areas. An adequate explanation of the behavior observed must take into account both the nature of the child and the ecology of the environment the child inhabits (Barker 1968). In fact, no simple and direct effect of children's age or sex on their behavior was found in this study. Instead, the impact of these child characteristics on play and social activity was tempered by the nature of the setting the

Elaine M. Ward

Modification of the block and housekeeping areas led the teacher to consider changing old forms and practices in ways that would extend and enrich children's experiences.

child entered—whether it was blocks or housekeeping and whether these areas were discrete or joined.

The findings of this study showed no differences between boys and girls in setting preferences but great differences in how children of the two sexes utilized the two play environments and how they reacted to removal of the divider. The results confirmed the sex-typed nature of behavior supported by blocks and housekeeping. The separate environments promoted interaction among children of the same sex, separation of boys from girls, and less constructive and involved play by children who entered an "opposite-sex" area. Girls, for whom sex-related play alternatives are less rigid and prescribed, adapted more readily to the removal of the shelves than boys. Girls showed an especially impressive increase in relevant, constructive use of the block area after the settings were joined.

Like two other studies on the relation of school environment to behavior (Berk and Lewis 1977; Minuchin, Biber, Shapiro, and Zimiles 1969), this investigation suggests that sex cleavage in children's play, generally accepted as a natural outcome of development during the early school years, can be influenced by the constraints of the child's environment. The younger three- and four-year-old children interacted more often with children of the opposite sex after the shelves were removed. The fact that the older children rigidly resisted rearrangement of the environment may be related to the especially long time they had been inhabitants of the classroom and their consequent strong attachment to familiar surroundings. It is also possible that the rapidly developing awareness of sex roles in the five- and six-year-olds was strong enough to offset the environmental pressures toward mixed-sex play.

The partnership established between the classroom teacher and the researchers in this study made it possible for the teacher to take a detailed look at the behavioral achievement of her curricular goals in the block and housekeeping areas. The fact that modification of the environments particularly enhanced the social and play experiences of girls and younger children suggested that the teacher think carefully about whether or not to introduce other interventions especially designed to reach the boys and the older kindergarteners. Removal of the divider resulted in less enclosed space, and children decreased the extent to which they sought solitary refuge in blocks and housekeeping. Places where children could find time to be alone needed to be provided elsewhere in the classroom. Spatially overlapping play seldom occurred, and integrative play was enhanced only for older children. These findings suggest that with younger children the teacher model these more complex play forms directly or stimulate them by intermingling materials from the two environments.

Bronfenbrenner (1977), in a discussion of the ecology of human development, points out that in order to understand the impact of environments, we must try to change them. In this study, the teacher's knowledge of the nature, strengths, and weaknesses of the environments she creates for children was broadened by an attempt to change those environments. Modification of the block and housekeeping areas called into question the beliefs and practices that the teacher originally used to design them and led her to consider changing old forms and practices in ways that would extend and enrich children's experiences.

"Natural experiments" involving modifications of other activities (for example, art, music, or outdoor play) could be conducted. Not only the spatial arrangements and activity props, but also such program characteristics as group size and teacher's activity role could be systematically varied. More research of this kind will help teachers understand those factors in the classroom environment that influence how children utilize a program and what they learn from it.

References

Barker, R. G. *Ecological Psychology*. Stanford, Calif.: Stanford University Press, 1968.

Beehler, K. A. "Social Interactions of Preschool Children as Correlates of Play Activities." Paper presented at the annual meeting of the American Psychological Association, September 1974.

Berk, L. E. "How Well Do Classroom Practices Reflect Teacher Goals?" *Young Children* 32, no. 1 (November 1976): 64-81.

Berk, L. E., and Lewis, N. G. "Sex Role and Social Behavior in Four School Environments." *Elementary School Journal* 77 (1977): 205-217.

Boyer, E. G.; Simon, A.; and Karafin, G. R. *Measures of Maturation: An Anthology of Early Childhood Observation Instruments*. Philadelphia: Research for Better Schools, 1973.

Bronfenbrenner, U. "Lewinian Space and Psychological Substance." *Journal of Social Issues* 33 (1977): 199-212.

Clark, A. H.; Wyon, S. M.; and Richards, M. P. M. "Free Play in Nursery School Children." *Journal of Child Psychology and Psychiatry* 10 (1969): 205-216.

Coates, S.; Lord, M.; and Jakabovics, E. "Field Dependence-Independence, Social-Non-Social Play and Sex Differences in Preschool Children." *Perceptual and Motor Skills* 40 (1975): 195-202.

Gordon, I. R., and Jester, R. E. "Techniques of Observing Teaching in Early Childhood and Outcomes of Particular Procedures." In *Second Handbook of Research on Teaching,* ed. R. M. W. Travers. Chicago: Rand McNally, 1973.

Hartley, R. E.; Frank, L. K.; and Goldenson, R. M. *Understanding Children's Play.* New York: Columbia University, 1952.

Maccoby, E. E., and Jacklin, C. N. *The Psychology of Sex Differences.* Stanford, Calif.: Stanford University Press, 1974.

Minuchin, P.; Biber, B.; Shapiro, E.; and Zimiles, H. *The Psychological Impact of School Experience.* New York: Basic Books, 1969.

Sears, R. R. "Development of Gender Role." In *Sex and Behavior,* ed. F. A. Beach. New York: Wiley, 1965.

Shure, M. B. "Psychological Ecology of a Nursery School." *Child Development* 34 (1963): 979-992.

Stacey, J.; Bereaud, S.; and Daniels, J. *And Jill Came Tumbling After: Sexism in American Education.* New York: Dell, 1974.

Vance, T. F., and McCall, L. T. "Children's Preferences Among Play Materials as Determined by the Method of Paired Comparisons of Pictures." *Child Development* 5 (1934): 267-277.

Penelope Griffing

Encouraging Dramatic Play in Early Childhood

What can teachers do to involve children more fully in dramatic play? How might play centers be arranged and equipped? Should you be involved in the children's play? You may want to take a closer look at your classroom and teaching techniques with the principles suggested here for facilitating dramatic play.

David, Ruth, Shaun, and Ilene are Black kindergarten children playing in a research playroom in their school (Griffing 1980). There are three centers of interest for dramatic play—a home, grocery store, and doctor's office—and props for dramatic play including large boxes, ropes, and other unstructured materials as well as realistic toys.

The girls, wearing hats and carrying purses, shop at the grocery store with pretend money (gestures only) for food to take on a picnic. David, after trying out other roles briefly, crawls beneath the table in the home area with tools in hand. "I'm fixing the car. We got to fix the car before we can go anywhere." He is joined by Shaun, who began play as cashier at the store, and the two boys lie on their backs beneath the car using hammer, pliers, screw driver, and pretend screws on the imaginary vehicle.

Returning home with bags of food from the store, Ruth addresses Shaun and David. "Boys, let's get ready for the pic-- nic." David slides out from under the car. "Time to go now. We can fix the car later. You be the grandfather." He hands grocery bags to Shaun, then turns to Ilene, "I told you not to wear your new hat!" Ilene complies, "OK." She takes off the hat, then directs David to "pick up all the stuff and put it in the car." David picks up the doll, "OK, I'll take the baby."

All four children load things on the table (car), Ilene explaining to some invisible person still at home, "We'll be back tomorrow." David adds, "We're going to Hollywood." Ilene: "Here's a nice spot right here." David: "This is Hollywood." They begin to unload the car. Ruth: "Watch the eggs, they might break." (To David): "Don't put the baby on the table." (The table is now the picnic table.) "We're ready to eat now."

The boys depart for the grocery store, saying, "We'll be back." At the store David sits at the cash register. "I'm typing a letter to my wife." He punches the keys. "I love you."

Eventually the children return home again where the activity centers about another meal (although not everyone agrees to come and eat). They talk about their favorite foods, prepare corn dips for Shaun, to whom they refer as Grandpa, and wrap the food in pretend plastic wrap before storing it in the refrigerator.

Evidence is building that dramatic and sociodramatic play have important benefits for children (Fein 1981). This series of

Penelope Griffing, Ph.D., is Assistant Professor in the Department of Family Relations and Human Development at The Ohio State University, Columbus, Ohio.

play episodes illustrates some of these benefits. The play was rich in symbolic activity—the transformations of self, objects, and situations into characters, objects, and events that existed in imagination only. The play was cognitively complex in its organization, consisting of sequences of related ideas and events rather than isolated pretend behaviors. There was extensive social interaction and verbal communication with children taking roles and carrying them out cooperatively. In several instances, the children were flexible in adapting to the views of others, and thoughts and feelings of the characters were occasionally expressed. The children also displayed a high degree of persistence, interest, and involvement in their enactment of these familiar events in their lives. This type of play certainly provides children valuable opportunities to practice important cognitive, social, and emotional skills. It may do more by contributing *actively* to the development of these skills.

As teachers grow in awareness of the benefits of dramatic play for children, they are increasingly asking how such play can be encouraged. The purpose of this article is to make suggestions concerning ways in which early childhood teachers can enhance children's dramatic and sociodramatic play.

Observe children's play

"The problem of starting . . . is reduced to a minimum if we keep in mind that we are not attempting to add something new and strange—we are simply taking what already exists and working outwards from there" (Way 1966). It is only by observing that we can discover what exists already in children's play. Anecdotal descriptions either written or taped can give you much information about the extent and quality of children's dramatic play and about the roles and themes that interest them the most. In analyzing these observations it is helpful to ask the fol-

lowing questions regarding the play of each child:

1. Which activities and in what settings does the child most frequently use dramatic play?

2. In what types of pretend (types of symbolic transformations) does the child engage? Does the child pretend to be someone else or ascribe roles to toys or animals? Use actions to represent real action? Pretend with objects—substituting toys, other materials, or gestures for real objects? Use words to represent pretend situations or settings? Well-developed dramatic play usually involves all of these types of transformations.

3. How complex is the play? Does the child engage in the single, fleeting pretend acts characteristic of children just beginning to participate in pretend play, or does she or he combine actions and words into sequences or related make-believe events, or into themes?

4. What is the social context for dramatic play? Is it solitary, parallel, or socially interactive (sociodramatic) play? Sociodramatic play appears later and is more complex than nonsocial dramatic play.

5. To what extent does the child communicate with other children within the context of the pretend play situations? Increasingly, as children develop dramatic play skills, communication involves planning the play as well as engaging in role talk (speaking like an imaginary character).

6. What is the duration of the dramatic play? Does the child maintain play for increasingly longer periods of time? Is she or he persistent in play?

7. What is the content of the play? What themes and roles does the child undertake and how are these developed? Descriptions of the content of play as well as its form will provide clues not only about children's interests but also about their understanding of concepts expressed and of important concerns in their personal so-

Dramatic play provides children valuable opportunities to develop important cognitive, social, and emotional skills.

cial worlds. These may need special understanding if teachers are to help.

Describing children's play in terms of these characteristics can heighten your awareness of patterns or trends in the development of play among children of different ages, and at the same time can provide added appreciation of children's individuality in play styles, interests, abilities, and settings in which dramatic play is most likely to occur. This kind of understanding gives direction for the guidance of play.

For example, four-year-old Craig and Bethany pretended each day to be astronauts. They placed large blocks together to form a space ship, sat side by side on the space ship, but not speaking, for a brief period, then moved on to other activities. These children demonstrated imaginative play by pretending that the blocks were a space ship. However, the teacher had observed these and other four- and five-year-olds in the group develop themes and roles more extensively when the content of play was more familiar. She also wanted to encourage movement from parallel to socially interactive play. Using books, stories, and discussion to help the children acquire greater understanding of the space theme, making a few suggestions during play as to what astronauts might do next, and adding a few relevant props (special food containers,

Griffing

tools, and radio equipment to facilitate communication between space ships) resulted in enriched play. There was greater variety in types of pretend, more extensive theme development, more social interaction, greater persistence, and more use of language in play. In this instance the play was developed within a block play context. It was highly successful partly because the space ship interest originated with the children themselves.

Set the stage for play

Time for play

Free-play periods indoors and outdoors must, of course, be long enough for children to plan and carry out play ideas. Not as well recognized is the possible need, at least occasionally, to reduce the number of activities available during free play in order that there will be less distraction and greater opportunity for involvement in dramatic play. Tizard, Philps, and Plewis (1976a) hypothesized that distraction by the multitude of activities from which to choose was at least partially responsible for the low levels of play they observed. Rubin and Seibel (1979) found that sociodramatic play was inhibited by the presence of sand, water, puzzles, and art activities.

In planning the program, therefore, it might be wise to schedule free-play periods that emphasize dramatic play and related activities at different times from those periods in which activities that appear to cause distraction are the primary focus. Puppets, blocks, books, art, or woodworking projects in which play props are constructed are among the activities that have been found to stimulate or complement dramatic and sociodramatic play.

Another way to reduce distraction is to set up a separate pretend room with a home, store, and/or another play interest area (Griffing 1980). Children's play in this special playroom was found to be at a higher level than play in the classroom (Soiberg 1972), again possibly a result of less distraction from other activities.

Student teachers with whom I have worked have experimented with devoting an entire free-play period to dramatic play. On one such occasion three centers of interest—a home, post office, and airport—were set up. These centers had previously been available one or two at a time. During grouptime preceding the free-play period, the teachers prepared the children through stories and discussion for play and for integration of the home, post office, and airport. When play began the teachers participated in it for a short period of time, modeling family members going to the post office or airport, and taking letters from the post office to the airport. They were soon able to withdraw from active participation and to serve instead as interested resource people. They helped the children procure, for example, a second small wagon when one was needed at home for garbage pick up as well as for carrying luggage and mail to and from the airport. All but one or two children in this group of 16 three- to five-year-old preschoolers responded enthusiastically to this experience. They played actively at varying levels of social and cognitive complexity for a 40-minute period with minimum adult guidance.

Space and basic equipment

Housekeeping and block areas are among the play spaces in which dramatic play is most likely to occur, and both require continual attention and planning (see Hirsch 1974). It is important to examine these areas with a critical eye each week, if not each day. Are children becoming involved in dramatic or constructive play in these areas? If not, what could be done to make them more inviting and more likely to support sustained play?

Location of learning or interest centers also needs attention. Tizard, Philps, and

Plewis (1976a) and Field (1980) observed more imaginative play and/or more social interaction among children when rooms were partitioned into smaller play areas than when more open space designs were utilized. On the other hand, some opening up of space may be helpful, as when Kinsman and Berk (1979) joined block and housekeeping areas.

Use of other pretend areas can greatly expand the potential for dramatic play in many classrooms. Wood (1976) arranged dramatic play space in the gymnasium of her school for her class of 11 second graders. Four centers of interest were planned: a home and store, which were present every day for the six weeks of her research; two supplemental areas that varied each week; an occupation area (such as a doctor's office); and an area corresponding to the weekly social studies themes. During the first few sessions the teacher took an active part in play, helping the children to plan themes and roles. Soon, however, the children took charge, rearranging furniture and props according to their plans. The children also introduced new themes and centers of interest that had not been planned in advance.

It is advisable to keep the home center in operation even when dramatic play based upon other themes is planned. Playing house continues to be a preferred theme, and it provides familiar, meaningful roles that children can expand into new roles. In addition, home play increases the number of available roles and themes and makes play possible for several children. Finally, integrating the home center with other themes may help children begin to understand the relationship between home and other community activities. The home center and supplemental areas should be within view of each other and within good communication distance. Telephones in each center also encourage communication.

Outdoor settings offer extremely rich potentials for dramatic play, and provision of outdoor dramatic play oppor-tunities may be especially important for some children. Sanders and Harper (1976) found that imaginative play among boys occurred most often in conjunction with large muscle activity. Working-class British children also engaged more often in imaginative play outdoors than indoors (Tizard, Philps, and Plewis 1976b). Indoor large muscle areas are especially appropriate for physically active, boisterous dramatic play.

Props for play

Many teachers have found collections of props for enacting dramatic play themes to be valuable resources. Bender (1971) suggests constructing light but sturdy cardboard boxes in which props for a variety of themes can be easily carried and stored.

The effectiveness of systematic provision of theme-related props, at least on a short-term basis, was demonstrated by Stacker (1978). She found that preschool children who were provided each week for a five-week period with theme-related play materials doubled the amount of imaginative play in which they engaged and maintained this behavior consistently throughout the remainder of the research period. Control group children who were not regularly provided theme-related props did not develop a consistently high level of play even though they shared the same classroom and had the same teacher as the experimental group. Like the older children of Wood's study, the experimental children appeared to acquire favorable expectations associated with dramatic play, as evidenced by their going first to the dramatic play areas each morning.

In another study Friedrich-Cofer, Huston-Stein, Kipnes, Susman, and Clewett (1979) found that providing relevant materials together with selected fantasy segments from "Mister Rogers' Neighborhood" was a highly successful way of increasing children's imaginative play. Theme-related materials included props for play such as puppets from the program, a mock-up of King Friday's castle, clothes similar to those worn by program characters, and steering wheels placed within taped outlines on the floor representing the plane and rocket ship shown in the program.

The realistic props in these studies were selected because young children seem to need (Fein 1979) and prefer (Stern, Bragdon, and Gordon 1976) fairly realistic props. However, in research by Pulaski (1973), it was found that kindergarten and second grade children enacted a greater variety of themes when provided with unstructured props. The kindergarten children of my research were provided with realistic toys and unstructured materials, and used both types of materials extensively (Griffing 1980).

Playing house continues to be a preferred theme, and it provides familiar, meaningful roles which children can expand into new roles.

Extend and enrich ideas for play

Early childhood teachers have regularly employed field trips, stories, pictures, discussions, and visits of community helpers as learning experiences and as ways of stimulating imaginative play. Smilansky (1968) demonstrated the value of such enrichment. Although these activities alone were not sufficient to increase dramatic and sociodramatic play among Israeli children, enrichment combined with helping children learn dramatic play skills was more effective than teaching skills alone.

Participate in children's play? When and how?

If dramatic play activities are based on children's interests and experiences, and if the stage is set with time, space, and materials for play, relatively little in the way of adult involvement is usually necessary. The teacher's role is primarily that of an interested resource person (Kleiber and Barnett 1980) who can help solve problems or who offers an occasional suggestion or additional prop to extend play. Unobtrusive observation is necessary, of course, to know when such actions are likely to be helpful to the children.

More direct intervention methods may be appropriate if the children are inexperienced with dramatic play (although they may express imagination in other ways), if they appear ready to add new elements to play or themes to their play, or if relatively unfamiliar roles and themes are being enacted. Several researchers have been remarkably successful in increasing the extent and quality of children's play, at least for short periods of time (Smilansky 1968; Feitelson and Ross 1973; Freyberg 1973; Rosen 1974; Singer and Singer 1974; Fink 1976; Wood 1976; Saltz, Dixon, and Johnson 1977; and Dansky 1980). Their research provides clues as to what some of these more direct procedures may be. Although the methodology of these studies varied, they often introduced a play theme for each of several play sessions with small groups of children, encouraging children to take roles and enact themes, and modeling role-playing behavior while taking part in play with the children.

This intervention usually took place in the first few play sessions or in the first few minutes of each session. It was a common finding that the children quickly learned new play skills (or to express already existing skills), and the extent of adult involvement could then be greatly reduced.

The importance of phasing out teacher involvement as soon as children are ready to carry on by themselves is stressed by Kleiber and Barnett (1980) as well as by Singer and Singer (1977). "Your job as an adult should be to set the scene and to help suggest a story line. . . . You may need to provide props or simple costumes . . . but once you have indicated to the child how [she or] he can be the teacher, doctor, carwasher, move away . . . let [her or] him make believe in [her or] his own way with [her or] his own materials and ideas" (p. 97).

Teachers may find it helpful to determine their degree of involvement in play in terms of the following adaptation of Wolfgang's (1977) continuum of open to structured behavior. You may (1) show interest in play through open behavior such as unobtrusively observing the children; (2) ask questions, make relatively nondirective suggestions, or supply an occasional prop; (3) model the behavior by enacting a role with the children; (4) if necessary, as is sometimes the case with developmentally delayed children, give direct suggestions or an explicit demonstration of how to carry out a particular pretend act or type of social interaction. You will probably want to begin with the less structured approaches, move toward more direct involvement, if it is needed, then gradually, as the children begin to demonstrate the necessary play skills, phase out, using only the more open procedures. Remember that the objective is to foster not only imaginativeness and development of social skills but also independence, self-confidence, and joyful, intrinsically motivated play.

Adapt play facilitation methods to the players

Children's play will vary greatly depending upon factors such as age or developmental level, cultural background, play interests, and styles. For example, the play of four-year-olds will probably not be as advanced as that of the five- and six-year-olds described at the beginning of this article. Instead of carrying out roles using complementary speech and action, four-year-olds are more likely to enact roles independently of other children. Iwanaga (1973) found that four-year-olds playing train took on differentiated roles such as passenger and conductor, made train whistle sounds, and cooperated in getting on and off the train together. Other than that, however, there was little adjustment of behavior to that of a peer.

Teachers should not expect, therefore, a high level of socially interactive play among younger children. You can, however, provide a framework for play that permits children to enact similar roles such as bus, train, or space shuttle passenger; shopper; or homemaker; each in her or his own way. At the same time you can help children move toward more interactive play when they are ready for this step. Modeling interactive behavior in play with the children, or telling a story during grouptime that involves interactive behavior and having the children act out the story as it is being told are among the techniques that may be useful. Mandelbaum (1975) details imaginative activities that can complement and contribute to the development of spontaneous dramatic and sociodramatic play. Books by Sutton-Smith and Sutton-Smith (1974) and Singer and Singer (1977) are also useful resources.

The importance of becoming attuned to children's cultural backgrounds was underscored by Curry (1971), who reported how Navajo children suddenly began to play when housekeeping equipment was pushed back against the walls of their classroom for cleaning purposes. For the first time the furniture arrangement resembled that of their circular hogan homes. How often might the play of other children come to life if play materials and ideas were well related to their experiences!

Wolf and Gardner (1979) identify another source of variation in children's play—play style. In a study of very young children they observed some who were primarily interested in representing social experience in play. Other children found objects and their relationships more intriguing. When presented with a tea set and several dolls, for example, one child began to enact a feeding scene with the dolls and adults in the playroom. The second child, equally intelligent, became engrossed in stacking and rearranging the plates. As in the case of other types of individual differences it is probably wise to respect such differences in style and provide ways for children to express their individuality, but at the same time encourage all children to try out several kinds of play.

Make written plans

Quality dramatic play requires careful planning. It will be helpful to many teachers to prepare written plans for this activity. Table 1 illustrates an example of a plan for a supermarket theme that considers learning objectives, equipment and materials, and teaching techniques.

Enjoy the play

Just as play can enhance and enrich the lives of children, so too can our partnership in their play lift our spirits and heighten our own sense of joyfulness in living. Moreover, our own enjoyment of playful activity and our own creativity in developing it with children are probably the most influential factors of all in fostering playfulness, creativity, and learning.

Table 1. Dramatic play with a supermarket theme.

Objectives

The children will
1. play imaginatively—enact roles of shoppers, cashier, family members, grocery clerk; use toys and other objects to substitute for real items; use actions and gestures to represent real behavior; use language to describe make-believe situations.
2. demonstrate through their play understanding of what supermarkets sell, how produce is weighed, how purchases are made.
3. use related vocabulary: fruit, vegetables, meat, cleaning supplies, cashier, grocery clerk, family members, etc.
4. interact with each other as shoppers, cashiers, grocery clerk, family members.

Organization of space and equipment

The supermarket will face the housekeeping play space to increase communication between the two areas. Items for sale will be housed on two sets of shelves, one for groceries, one for household supplies. A cash register and bags for purchases will be placed on a table at the entrance. A small table with scales for weighing fruit and vegetables will be located nearby. The home center will be arranged with space and equipment for storing purchases as well as for cooking, eating, and other activities.

Materials

1. empty containers representing a variety of different kinds of groceries;
2. small bags of real potatoes to weigh on the scales;
3. empty detergent and cleaning powder cartons;
4. cash register, scales, grocery bags;
5. telephones for home and supermarket;
6. dress-up clothes, purses, wallets;
7. two wheels mounted on blocks with chairs behind for children who wish to drive to the store via car or bus.

Procedures

The supermarket theme will be developed
cont. on p. 46

Table 1. cont. from p. 45

over the period of one week with a supermarket field trip, pictures, stories, and poems. During grouptimes the teachers will show and discuss with the children some of the items that can be purchased at the supermarket and will develop role playing games in which groceries are weighed, purchases made, and different roles enacted.

The dramatic play activity will be introduced early in the week with the setting made increasingly complex as the children become ready for new steps such as weighing groceries. Each day the dramatic play will be introduced by means of a story (sometimes an original one) and/or game highlighting the new roles or procedures that children may carry out if they wish. Other activities available will also involve dramatic play or relate well to it.

These will include a table top house and store with human figures and other accessories for home and supermarket play, blocks, books, and articles for the home or store to be made from art materials.

During play the teacher will remain near the dramatic play activity, observing with interest, giving an occasional suggestion ("Do your potatoes need to be weighed, Mr. Bachman?") or possibly taking a role if the children need help starting or maintaining the play. The teacher will then withdraw as the children increasingly become involved. The teacher will be alert to and will support new ideas expressed by the children.

Suggestions for parents will be available regarding ways in which they can help children continue to develop the supermarket play at home.

References

Bender, J. "Have You Ever Thought of a Prop Box?" *Young Children* 26, no. 3 (January 1971): 164–169.

Curry, N. "Consideration of Current Basic Issues on Play." In *Play: The Child Strives for Self-Realization*, ed. G. Engstrom. Washington, D.C.: National Association for the Education of Young Children, 1971.

Dansky, J. L. "Cognitive Consequences of Sociodramatic Play and Exploration Training for Economically Disadvantaged Preschoolers." *Journal of Child Psychology and Psychiatry* 21 (1980): 47–58.

Fein, G. "Pretend Play: New Perspectives." *Young Children* 34, no. 5 (July 1979): 61–66.

Fein, G. "Pretend Play: An Integrative Review." *Child Development* 52 (December 1981): 1095–1118.

Feitelson, D., and Ross, G. "The Neglected Factor—Play." *Human Development* 16 (1973): 202–223.

Field, T. M. "Preschool Play: Effects of Teacher/Child Ratio and Organization of Classroom Space." *Child Study Journal* 10 (1980): 191–205.

Fink, R. S. "Role of Imaginative Play in Cognitive Development." *Psychological Reports* 39 (1976): 895–906.

Freyberg, J. T. "Increasing the Imaginative Play of Urban Disadvantaged Kindergarten Children Through Systematic Training." In *The Child's World of Make-Believe*, ed. J. L. Singer. New York: Academic Press, 1973.

Friedrich-Cofer, L. K.; Huston-Stein, A.; Kipnes, D. M.; Susman, E. J.; and Clewett, A. S. "Environmental Enhancement of Prosocial Television Content: Effects on Interpersonal Behavior, Imaginative Play, and Self-Regulation in a Natural Setting." *Developmental Psychology* 15 (1979): 637–646.

Griffing, P. "The Relationship Between Socioeconomic Status and Sociodramatic Play Among Black Kindergarten Children." *Genetic Psychology Monographs* 101 (1980): 3–34.

Hirsch, E. *The Block Book*. Washington, D.C.: National Association for the Education of Young Children, 1974.

Iwanaga, M. "Development of Interpersonal Play Structure in Three, Four, and Five Year Old Children." *Journal of Research and Development in Education* 6 (1973): 71–82.

Kinsman, C. A., and Berk, L. E. "Joining the Block and Housekeeping Areas: Changes in Play and Social Behavior." *Young Children* 35, no. 1 (November 1979): 66–75.

Kleiber, D. A., and Barnett, L. A. "Leisure in Childhood." *Young Children* 35, no. 5 (July 1980): 47–53.

Mandelbaum, J. "Creative Dramatics in Early Childhood." *Young Children* 30, no. 2 (January 1975): 84–92.

Pulaski, M. A. "Toys and Imaginative Play." In *The Child's World of Make-Believe*, ed. J. L. Singer. New York: Academic Press, 1973.

Rosen, C. E. "The Effects of Sociodramatic Play on Problem-Solving Behavior Among Culturally Disadvantaged Preschool Children." *Child Development* 45 (1974): 920–927.

Rubin, K. H., and Seibel, C. "The Effects of Ecological Setting on the Free Play Behaviors of Young Children." Paper presented at the annual meeting of the American Educational

Research Association, 1979. (ERIC Document Reproduction Service No. 168 691)

Saltz, E.; Dixon, D.; and Johnson, J. "Training Disadvantaged Preschoolers on Various Fantasy Activities: Effects on Cognitive Functioning and Impulse Control." *Child Development* 48 (1977): 369–380.

Sanders, K. M., and Harper, L. V. "Free-Play Fantasy Behavior in Preschool Children: Relations Among Gender, Age, Season, and Location." *Child Development* 47 (1976): 1182–1185.

Singer, J. L., and Singer, D. G. "Enhancing Imaginative Play in Preschoolers: Television and Live Adult Effects." 1974. (ERIC Document Reproduction Service No. 100 509)

Singer, J. L., and Singer, D. G. *Partners in Play.* New York: Harper & Row, 1977.

Smilansky, S. *The Effects of Sociodramatic Play on Disadvantaged Preschool Children.* New York: Wiley, 1968.

Soiberg, S. "A Comparative Study of the Sociodramatic Play of Black Kindergarten Children." Master's thesis, The Ohio State University, 1972.

Stacker, J. "The Effects of Altering the Physical Setting for Dramatic Play Upon Cognitive and Social Play Levels of Preschool Children." Master's thesis, The Ohio State University, 1978.

Stern, V.; Bragdon, N.; and Gordon, A. *Cognitive Aspects of Young Children's Symbolic Play. Final Report.* New York: Bank Street College of Education, 1976.

Sutton-Smith, B., and Sutton-Smith, S. *How to Play with Your Children (And When Not To).* New York: Hawthorn Books, 1974.

Tizard, B.; Philps, J.; and Plewis, I. "Play in Preschool Centres I: Play Measures and Their Relation to Age, Sex, and IQ." *Journal of Child Psychology and Psychiatry* 17 (1976a): 251–264.

Tizard, B.; Philps, J.; and Plewis, I. "Play in Preschool Centres II: Effects on Play of the Child's Social Class and Educational Orientation of the Centre." *Journal of Child Psychology and Psychiatry* 17 (1976b): 265–274.

Way, B. *Development Through Drama.* New York: Humanities Press, 1966.

Wolf, D., and Gardner, H. "Style and Sequence in Early Symbolic Play." In *Symbolic Functioning in Childhood,* ed. N. R. Smith and M. B. Franklin. Hillsdale, N.J.: Erlbaum, 1979.

Wolfgang, C. H. *Helping Aggressive and Passive Preschoolers Through Play.* Columbus, Ohio: Merrill, 1977.

Wood, J. K. "An Exploratory Study of the Effects of Intervention in Sociodramatic Play Upon Play Behavior and Upon the Social Structure of a Group of Second Grade Children." Master's thesis, The Ohio State University, 1976.

Joe L. Frost and Michael L. Henniger

Making Playgrounds Safe for Children and Children Safe for Playgrounds

Children's outdoor play spaces are in a state of transition. Exciting environments are being developed to replace the traditional concrete and asphalt-paved playgrounds equipped with jungle gyms, merry-go-rounds, swings, and slides. An example of such an environment is the *creative playground* (Frost 1978; Frost and Klein, forthcoming). This type of play space is constructed creatively from existing commercial equipment, a few purchased materials, and a wide variety of donated "junk" materials such as old tires, utility poles, railroad ties, and cable spools. It is often planned and constructed by parents, teachers, and children with the help of a playground specialist. Such an environment encourages a wide range of creative play from the children who use it.

A second example of an exciting play environment that is gaining popularity in this country is the *adventure playground.* Imported from European countries where it has been a huge success, the adventure playground is a highly informal play environment where tools, a wide range of scrap building materials, and modifiable climbing structures are provided for children to use in freely expressing themselves. In addition, the best adventure playgrounds in Europe accommodate a variety of farm animals and full-time adult play leaders to support and encourage children's play.

The American Adventure Play Association (Vance 1977) cited the following advantages for adventure playgrounds: (1) children use them more often than conventional playgrounds; (2) they are maintained less expensively; and (3) the community participates more actively through donations. In addition, other sources indicate the adventure playground stimulates a wider variety of play (Frost and Campbell 1977), a broader range of language, and more originality in play themes (Hayward, Rothenburg, and Beasley 1974).

As these new types of playgrounds gain popularity in this country, concerns are frequently expressed about their safety. Can such play environments, constructed from junk and surplus materials by parents, teachers and children, be as functional and safe as the traditional commercially-equipped playgrounds? The data now available show that traditional playgrounds are unduly hazardous. Accidents and injuries are encouraged by slipshod equipment manufacturing, improper installation, and lack of maintenance.

Joe L. Frost, Ph.D., is Professor of Curriculum and Instruction, The University of Texas, Austin, Texas 78746. He is a former public school teacher. Dr. Frost is President-Elect of the Association for Childhood Education International.

Michael L. Henniger, Ph.D., is Assistant Professor of Early Childhood Education, Department of Curriculum, Instruction, and Media, Southern Illinois University, Carbondale, Illinois 62901. He has taught preschool, primary grades, and secondary mathematics.

Traditional American playgrounds are also inappropriate for the wide range of developmental play needs of children. Our personal observations and those of playground colleagues in North America and Europe make it clear that many American children are unsafe for any playground because they spend too little time on playgrounds of sufficient challenge and variety to allow optimal development of perceptual-motor skills.

Playground Hazards

What kinds of hazards exist on typical American playgrounds? (See Vernon 1976; Wilkinson and Lockhart 1976; National Recreation and Park Association 1975; McConnell, Parks, and Knapp 1973; Bureau of Product Safety 1972.) The most serious hazard is the **surface** under and around children's play equipment. Hard-packed earth, rocks, asphalt, and concrete are commonly found beneath swings, slides, and climbing structures. Children falling from equipment onto this type of ground cover can receive bruises, sprains, broken bones, concussions, or even a fatal injury.

Exposed bolts, sharp or rough edges, and protruding corners on outdoor equipment are a second common source of injuries. Cuts and scrapes, many of which require more than just a bandage to repair, are a frequent result. The **openings and angles** found on certain pieces of equipment present another hazard for children playing outdoors. Some of these openings allow children to get their fingers, hands, feet, or heads trapped in the equipment. In addition to the discomfort and fear of being unable to move a limb, serious injuries can result from such entrapments.

Improper installation and infrequent maintenance of playground equipment create additional hazards for children. Installation of equipment with inadequate footings, weak braces, and minimal surrounding play space can lead to a variety of unnecessary injuries. Without periodic examination and maintenance of moving parts, bolts, screws, ropes, paint, wood, and metal, other potential hazards gradually develop.

A less obvious but potentially dangerous situation is created on many playgrounds when the available equipment is **inappropriate for the developmental levels of the children** using it. A frequent problem arises when kindergarten and preschool children are enrolled in schools where the play equipment is designed for older children. Another serious problem exists when children have thoroughly mastered all of the equipment available to them. It is then that they begin experimenting and using the equipment in ways for which it was never designed. The risk of injury in such situations increases markedly.

Antiquated, poorly maintained equipment, installed on hard surfaces, is a common cause of injury on playgrounds.

Photographs © Joe L. Frost

Hazards such as these can be dramatically reduced. They are not an inherent part of any playground and should never be used as an excuse for avoiding the outdoor environment or for not providing a challenging playground. With careful planning, the hazards described can be reduced far below their present intolerable levels as evidenced by statistics on the extent and seriousness of playground injuries.

Playground Injuries

Although data on playground injuries are incomplete, British researchers (International Playground Association 1977) have estimated that as many as 150,000 children a year are treated by doctors and hospitals for playground-related accidents in their country. These researchers indicated that the leading cause of injuries was the surface onto which a child fell.

The Consumer Product Safety Commission (CPSC 1975) has reported playground injuries in the United States. The National Electronic Injury Surveillance System (NEISS 1977) data, taken from a statistically selected sample of hospital emergency rooms, revealed that an estimated 118,000 playground-related injuries were incurred during 1974. Seventy-eight percent of the injured children were under ten years of age. The injuries, reported in rank order, included lacerations, contusions/abrasions, fractures, strains/sprains, concussions, and hematomas. Twenty-four death certificates were issued from July 1973 to October 1974 for fatal injuries related to playground equipment. Thirteen of the injured children were between the ages of five and nine.

More recent statistics from the Consumer Product Safety Commission (Desbordes 1976) indicate that an estimated 125,000 playground-related injuries occurred during 1975. During the twelve-month period ending November 1977, an estimated 150,773 injuries related to swings, slides, seesaws, and climbing apparatus resulted in emergency room treat-

ment in the United States (NEISS 1977). An in-depth analysis of these statistics has yet to be completed.

The Consumer Product Safety Commission (1975) also analyzed the causes of playground injuries and deaths. As in England, falling from a piece of equipment was found to be the leading cause of accidents. Other major causes, listed in rank order, included being struck by a moving piece of equipment, entrapment of an extremity, and contact with rough edges and protruding bolts. The leading cause of deaths on public playgrounds was falling onto hard surfaces; hanging was the leading cause of home playground deaths.

The major cause of serious and fatal injuries on public playgrounds, falling onto hard surfaces, can be alleviated by providing eight to twelve inches of sand under climbing and moving equipment.

Frost and Henniger

The statistical analyses to date have many shortcomings. One is the lack of any serious attempt to compare the number and severity of injuries on different types of playgrounds. Because of the commonly held belief that the more creative, stimulating play environments such as adventure playgrounds are more dangerous than traditional playgrounds, this is an important area for research. Several informal investigations indicate that such environments are no more dangerous than traditional playgrounds (Nicholson 1974; Vance 1977). The American Adventure Play Association (Vance 1977) received complete information from fourteen agencies with adventure playgrounds in five states. The number of injuries was "about the same" or "fewer" than at conventional playgrounds. Officials in the Swedish Playground Society, the Scandinavian Playground Council, and the London Adventure Playground Association have reported to us that no injury resulting in permanent impairment or death has been reported on any of their adventure playgrounds.

Standards for Playground Safety

Steps are being taken to improve the safety of children's playgrounds. At least one country (Swedish Council for Children's Play 1976) has established a set of safety standards for the installation and maintenance of playground equipment, while England, Canada, and the United States appear to be moving in a similar direction.

Presently, there are no mandatory standards for the manufacture of playground equipment in the United States. At least two manufacturers (Miracle and Game Time) are operating under a set of voluntary standards developed by industry in conjunction with the Consumer Product Safety Commission (1973). Despite many limitations, these standards laid the foundation for a more comprehensive set of proposed standards developed by the National Recreation and Park Association (1976), under an agreement with the CPSC. The major thrusts of these standards are as follows:

1. Equipment designed for a specific age group shall be so labeled, and it shall be designed with an understanding of developmental characteristics of that specific age group.

2. The materials used in constructing playground equipment shall be durable, structurally sound, and stable following assembly and installation, and shall be assembled using connecting and covering devices (bolts, hooks, rings, etc.) that shall not open during specified tests.

3. Equipment, shall be free of sharp edges, dangerous protrusions (including exposed ends of bolts), points where children's extremeties could be pinched or crushed, and openings or angles that could trap part of the child's body.

4. Moving equipment such as swings and merry-go-rounds shall not exceed certain impact and velocity limits described in the standards.

5. Falls from equipment will be controlled by increasing the degree of enclosure of the surface as the height of the structure increases (4 to 8 feet: railings; 8 to 12 feet: protective barrier; over 12 feet: totally enclosed).

6. Slide exits and inclines, side protection on the slide surface, ladder and stairway inclines, and slide heights will be regulated by the standards.

7. A statement recommending appropriate surfacing materials must be included in all equipment catalogs and with all installation instructions for new equipment.

8. Manufacturers will be required to furnish complete instructions for the installation and maintenance of the equipment they sell. These instructions shall include a facsimile of the checklist in the table.

9. Recommended minimum space requirements for varying pieces of equipment are outlined in the standards.

Table: Suggested Playground Equipment
Maintenance Safety Checklist

Item	Look for . . .*
Structure	Bending, warping, cracking, loosening, breaking, etc.
Surface finish	No protective coating, rust, other corrosion, cracks, splinters, harmful preservatives or paints, etc.
Hardware	Missing, bent, broken, loosened, open hooks, etc.
Edges	Sharp points or edges, protruding bolts, or other protrusions, etc.
Pinch or Crush Points	Exposed mechanisms, junctures of moving components, etc.
Mechanical Devices and Other Moving Parts	Worn bearings, lubrication needed, missing protective covers, etc.
Guard or Hand Rails	Missing, bent, broken, loosened, etc.
Ladders and Steps	Missing rungs or steps, broken, loosened, etc.
Swing seats	Missing, damaged, loosened, sharp corners, etc.
Footings	Exposed, cracked, loose in ground, etc.
Protective Surfacing under Equipment	Compacted, displaced to ineffective level, does not extend to potential impact area, unsanitary, poor drainage, etc.

* Reprinted, by permission, from *Proposed Safety Standards for Public Playground Equipment* by the National Recreation and Park Association.

Making Children Safe for Playgrounds

It is neither possible nor desirable to create a totally safe playground. Children would find such an environment sterile and uninviting. Challenging tasks that require some degree of risk-taking are an important ingredient of children's play. We can, however, eliminate the unnecessary hazards on playgrounds and help prepare children to deal sensibly and safely with the challenges the outdoor environment provides.

What can be done to "make children safe" for the playgrounds on which they play? One important step is to teach children the proper and safe uses of the playground equipment available to them. There is a reciprocal relationship between the amount of preparation children receive in using playgrounds and the amount of playground protection necessary for safe use (Wilkinson and Lockhart 1976). As the

Frost and Henniger

preparation for safety increases, the necessity for protection decreases.

Teachers can take an active role in understanding and facilitating children's outdoor play. Skillful, sensitive adults make a difference in the safe play of children. They can provide the following support to help children develop important skills for safe outdoor play:

Cooperative Planning

Discussions of playground safety during group time are effective ways for children to identify safety needs for themselves. Important ideas and insights can be gathered from the children, and a workable list of "Safety Hints for the Playground" can be developed. Such activity also contributes to language, reading, evaluation, and decision making.

Adult-Child Interaction

Adults must take an active role if children are to be made safe for playgrounds. The time spent outdoors cannot be considered a break time for teachers, but rather a new and exciting setting for stimulating children's learning and development. The kinds of direction and guidance traditionally given children indoors are often appropriate outdoors as well. Adult-child interaction should take place naturally and informally as children move about the playground and engage in the play of their choice. Through informal comments and modeling by a teacher or child, the safe use of equipment can be demonstrated. Stopping a child momentarily to discuss a better way to climb the steps to the slide or the problems of running too near the swings is usually all that is needed to shape safe behavior.

Capabilities and Limitations

Another aspect of making children safe for the playground is to help them realize their own capabilities and limitations. For many young children, the preschool setting is their first extended exposure to the

Skillful, sensitive adults help to make children safe for playgrounds.

equipment found on playgrounds. They need adult guidance in determining their own levels of competence. Words of encouragement and praise along with comfort and support when needed can help children strengthen knowledge of their own capabilities.

Challenge and Interest

A wide array of challenges provides needed diversity on playgrounds and encourages safe play outdoors. A stimulating mix of different kinds of equipment is needed to keep children's interests high and to help prevent misuse of equipment. Using a basic concept from adventure playgrounds, children should have boards, sawhorses, cable spools, old tires, boxes, blocks, lumber, ladders, and so on to build creatively the structures needed in their play.

Developmental Needs

Providing an outdoor play environment with equipment designed for use at increasing levels of complexity also makes good sense. We are constantly reminded that children vary in their levels of development. In terms of outdoor play, this means that children will have different climbing abilities, running skills, balancing skills, coordination, and strength. The play environment then is equipped and arranged to present graduated challenges appropriate to the skills of all children playing there. In addition, the equipment should be sufficiently varied to allow children to engage in all of the cognitive forms of play (exercise, dramatic, construction, and games with rules), to develop social skills through interaction with peers, and to allow for quiet solitude and reflection.

Time to Play

Providing the finest play environment is of no consequence unless children are allowed time to play there. Extraordinary perceptual-motor skills are exhibited by children on some of the finest adventure playgrounds of Europe and the United States. On these sites children spend up to four hours per day in environments rich in challenge, complexity, and variety. Full-time play leaders, animals, and gardening further enrich experiences.

Wise teachers view the outdoor environment as a natural extension of the indoor environment. Each of these environments provides for unique experiences not readily available in the other. Indoor space tends to restrict noise, movement, and types of equipment, while the outdoor environment allows almost unlimited sound and movement and greater freedom with raw materials such as water, dirt, construction materials, and large play structures. Consequently, the types of play occurring in the outdoor environment are significantly different from those types occurring indoors (Henniger 1977). Both spaces are needed for a complete play/learning environment.

When loose parts are made available, children create challenge and variety for themselves.

Summary and Conclusions

Conventional American playgrounds are hazardous and ill-suited for the developmental needs of children. Such play environments are now being rebuilt or replaced by more exciting creative or adventure playgrounds.

Many serious and fatal injuries on playgrounds can be eliminated by attention to two major factors: (1) reducing or eliminating hazards such as hard fall surfaces and poorly manufactured, installed, and maintained equipment, and (2) assisting children in learning to play safely.

Standards for the manufacture of play equipment are now being developed, but the major responsibility for safety lies with adults who work daily with children. Adults' roles are varied and complex, ranging from informal personal interaction with children to assistance in the design and use of exciting, varied, challenging play environments.

There is little argument that playgrounds created by adults and children working together are more stimulating and developmentally appropriate than conventional ones. The claim that creative or adventure playgrounds are more hazardous than conventional playgrounds is unsubstantiated.

References

Bureau of Product Safety. *Public Playground Equipment.* Washington, D.C.: Food and Drug Administration, September 12, 1972.

Consumer Product Safety Commission. *Hazard Analysis—Playground Equipment.* Washington, D.C.: Consumer Product Safety Commission, 1975.

Consumer Product Safety Commission. *Proposed Technical Requirements for Heavy Duty Playground Equipment Regulations.* Washington, D.C.: Consumer Product Safety Commission, 1973.

Desbordes, L. G., 1976: personal communication.

Frost, J. L. "The American Playground Movement." *Childhood Education* 54, no. 4 (1978): 176-182.

Frost, J. L., and Campbell, S. D. "Play and Equipment Choices of Conserving and Preconserving Children on Two Types of Playgrounds." Unpublished paper, The University of Texas at Austin, 1977.

Frost, J. L., and Klein, B. L. *Children's Play and Playgrounds.* Boston: Allyn and Bacon, forthcoming.

Hayward, D.; Rothenburg, M.; and Beasley, R. "Children's Play and Urban Playground Environments: A Comparison of Traditional, Contemporary and Adventure Playground Types." *Environment and Behavior* 6, no. 2 (1974): 131-168.

Henniger, M. L. "Free Play Behaviors of Nursery School Children in an Indoor and Outdoor Environment." Doctoral dissertation, The University of Texas at Austin, 1977.

International Playground Association. "Children's Playgrounds." *Newsletter* 6 (1977): 8-12.

McConnell, W. H.; Parks, J. T.; and Knapp, L. W. *Public Playground Equipment.* Iowa City: University of Iowa, College of Medicine, 1973.

National Electronic Injury Surveillance System (NEISS). *NEISS Data Highlights* 5, no. 1 (1977).

National Recreation and Park Association. *Proposed Safety Standards for Public Playground Equipment.* Arlington, Va.: National Recreation and Park Association, 1976.

National Recreation and Park Association. "Summary of In-Depth Accident Studies Received from 1/9/74 to 6/17/75." Arlington, Va.: National Recreation and Park Association, 1975. Mimeographed.

Nicholson, M. *Adventure Playgrounds.* London: The National Playing Fields Association, 1974.

Swedish Council on Children's Play. *Annual Report.* Stockholm: Swedish Council on Children's Play, 1975-76.

Vance, B. "The President's Message." *American Adventure Play Association News* 1, no. 4 (Fall 1977): 1.

Vernon, E. A. "A Survey of Preprimary and Primary Outdoor Learning Centers/Playgrounds in Texas Public Schools." Doctoral dissertation, The University of Texas at Austin, 1976.

Wilkinson, P. F., and Lockhart, R. *Safety in Children's Formal Play Environments.* Ontario, Canada: Ontario Ministry of Culture and Recreation, 1976.

3

Learning to communicate

What is "reading readiness"? Worksheets, flash cards, the alphabet song, magnetic letters, fat pencils? While play is basically seen as *how* young children learn, reading is often viewed as *what* young children are expected to learn. Identifying the skills and experiences that can lead to the development of avid communicators is a difficult and more involved process than just learning to read, as evidenced in the diversity of ideas in Part 3.

Three articles deal with how children read, and each takes a slightly different focus based on research and current practices. Jensen and Hanson, Schickedanz, and Goetz each offer ideas that will help you answer questions such as: "Is alphabet recognition essential to learning to read?"

How does bilingualism affect children's language acquisition? Model programs, research, and recommendations based on what we know are highlighted by Garcia in an article valuable to *all* teachers.

Children's experiences with books can also enrich their lives, especially if those books are literature and teachers set goals such as those proposed by Williamson. You may want to reevaluate the books in your classroom and how you use them with children.

Another aspect of communicating is handwriting. When should it begin? How should it be taught? Children who are ready to write will profit from any methods you implement after reading Lamme's article.

research in review

by Mary A. Jensen and Bette A. Hanson

Helping Young Children Learn to Read: What Research Says to Teachers

Language experience instruction is a popular method for beginning reading activities with young children (Goetz 1979; Nurss 1980; "Reading and Pre-First Grade" 1977; Spodek 1979). Early childhood teachers have several reasons for favoring language experience instruction as a way to introduce young children to reading:

(1) The language experience approach uses the child's own experiences and oral language as the basis for development of reading behaviors.

(2) The flexibility of the language experience approach is well-suited to the diverse needs and abilities of young children.

(3) The language experience approach can be incorporated into most programs in a gradual, meaningful, and natural manner.

Nevertheless, implementation of language experience instruction in preschool and kindergarten settings is often limited to occasionally recording children's dictation, labeling objects, writing captions for paintings, making name tags, or writing thank you letters. Once dictation is recorded, teachers of young children seem hesitant in deciding on their next move. Some responsibility for this apparent dilemma rests with teacher education programs that have not given early childhood

teachers adequate preparation in the language experience approach. However, it is also true that less systematic research and analysis of teaching practices and materials have been conducted for language experience instruction than for decoding instruction (Glaser 1979).

Approaches to teaching reading

A survey of reading programs and literature about learning to read indicates that teaching practices in beginning reading generally reflect one of two orientations for instruction: skill (Smith, Otto, and Hansen 1978) or ideational (Bloomfield and Barnhart 1961; Feldman 1977; Halliday 1970). These two orientations are outlined in Figure 1.

The **skill orientation** embodies the belief that reading is related to alphabetic writing as tokens of speech forms or aspects of linguistics. The emphasis in teaching is on developing skillful behaviors for a set of mechanical, highly

Mary A. Jensen, Ph.D., is Assistant Professor of Early Childhood Education at the State University College of Arts and Science, Geneseo, New York.

Bette A. Hanson, Ph.D., is Professor of Early Childhood Education and Human Development at the University of Wisconsin-Stout, Menomonie, Wisconsin. She is also Program Director for Early Childhood Education, Child Development, and Family Life at the University of Wisconsin-Stout.

This is one of a regular series of columns edited by Joseph H. Stevens, Ph.D., Professor, Department of Early Childhood Education, Georgia State University, Atlanta, Georgia.

Figure 1

Common Approaches to Beginning Reading Instruction

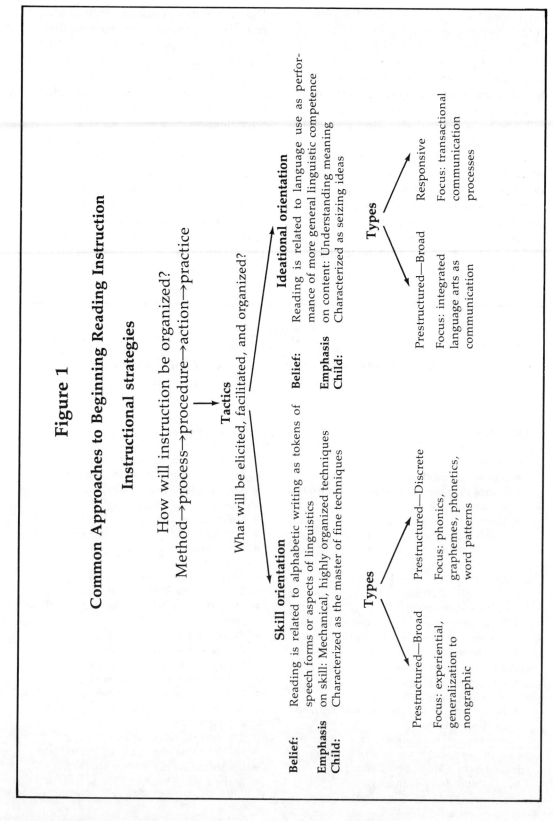

Instructional strategies

How will instruction be organized?

Method→process→procedure→action→practice

Tactics

What will be elicited, facilitated, and organized?

Skill orientation

Belief: Reading is related to alphabetic writing as tokens of speech forms or aspects of linguistics

Emphasis on skill: Mechanical, highly organized techniques

Child: Characterized as the master of fine techniques

Types

Prestructured—Broad

Focus: experiential, generalization to nongraphic

Prestructured—Discrete

Focus: phonics, graphemes, phonetics, word patterns

Ideational orientation

Belief: Reading is related to language use as performance of more general linguistic competence

Emphasis on content: Understanding meaning

Child: Characterized as seizing ideas

Types

Prestructured—Broad

Focus: integrated language arts as communication

Responsive

Focus: transactional communication processes

organized techniques. The skill orientation to beginning reading views the child as the potential master of these fine techniques. Included within this orientation are child behaviors such as learning letter names. Having been historically popular, the skill orientation is still the basis for the television program *Sesame Street.*

In contrast to the skill orientation, the **ideational orientation** reflects the belief that reading is related to language use as performance of a more general linguistic competence. Teaching emphasizes content and meaning. The child is viewed as one who seizes ideas.

This orientation provides experiences and discussions that incorporate the child's own language and ideas which then assist the child in learning to read fluently and with comprehension. Advocates of an ideational orientation often call for use of language experience activities.

Specific child behaviors can be linked to teaching tactics of both the skill and ideational orientations of reading. Loban (1978) suggested that language experience instruction can include behaviors of the skill orientation as well as behaviors of the ideational orientation. These behaviors are outlined in Figure 2.

Figure 2

Child Behaviors Linked with Teaching Tactics for Language Experience Instruction

Skill tactics

Visual discrimination of letters and words
- Match words by initial letter(s)
- Sort words by initial letter(s)
- Locate all examples of a letter in a word or in a line of print
- Identify word boundaries
- Match letters to a word on a story chart
- Locate words beginning with various letters in a story

Reproduction of letters and words
- Print letters (trace, copy, type, or use rubber letter stamps)
- Reconstruct words (use letter cards, rubber letter stamps, or a typewriter)
- Write words

Identification of letter names
- Recognize letter names

Use of spelling patterns
- Recognize similarities and differences in spelling patterns

Use of prompted mediation to map from one system of representation to another sytem of representation (Gibson and Levin 1975)
- Map print to oral language

Ideational tactics

Use of connotative recall cues
- Make personal illustrations for ideas
- Attach photographs of the experience
- Attach objects from the experience

Comparison of meaning units
- Match sentences
- Match phrases
- Match words

Use of contextual cues
- Complete sentences or phrases
- Respond correctly to recall questions
- Identify repeated or redundant words or phrases
- Sequence ideas or sentences

Classification of words into concept categories
- Group words into concept categories

Use of stress and intonation signals
- Interpret meaning expressed by stress and intonation signals

Intersecting tactics

Use of conventional organizers
- Follow a line of print from left to right
- Underline words as they are read
- Make a word bank

Skill tactics

The first category of skill tactics, visual discrimination of letters and words, involves matching words by initial letter(s), sorting words by initial letter(s), locating all examples of a letter in a word or in a line of print, identifying word boundaries, matching letters to a word on a story chart, and locating words beginning with various letters in a story. An example of the first target behavior, *match words by initial letter(s)*, would be to ask children to take the word card *sizzle* and match it to other words in a language experience story that begin with the letter "s". The second target behavior, *sort words by initial letter(s)*, is illustrated by the child who, given word cards beginning with the letter "p" or "s" from a popcorn story, sorts the cards by initial letter into two groups. Beginning readers use the initial part of a word as a cue in word identification (Marchbanks and Levin 1965; Pick 1978; Williams, Blumberg, and Williams 1970; Weber 1970).

The third target behavior is *locate all examples of a letter in a word or in a line of print*. In this situation, the child given a letter card searches a word or line of print for matching letters. Garner (1962) estimated that letters are more redundant and predictable than words. Thus, letter redundancy can also be a valuable word identification cue. Hall (1976) recommended that beginning readers practice this target behavior.

The fourth target behavior for visual discrimination of print is *identify word boundaries*. Although young children often have difficulty separating orally presented words (Huttenlocher 1964), they apparently can identify word boundaries in print (in some instances after brief instruction) (Holden and MacGinitie 1972; Kelly 1977). A developmental study by Meltzer and Herse (1969), however, suggested that young children equate letters with words before they discover space as a word boundary cue.

The fifth target behavior, *match letters to a word on a story chart*, calls for placing matching letter cards below a word in a language experience story. Gibson (1965) advocated discrimination practice focusing on characteristic differences in print. Samuels (1973) suggested matching-to-sample practice as the first step in learning characteristic differences among letters. Hall (1976) included this target behavior among the recommended practices for beginning reading instruction.

The final target behavior in the visual discrimination category is *locate words in the story beginning with various letters*. Here, the child given a letter card finds words on a story chart beginning with that letter (Hall 1976). Gibson (1965), Marchbanks and Levin (1965), Samuels (1973), and Weber (1970) supported this target behavior, indicating that initial letters are salient cues for novice readers.

The second category of skill tactics, reproduction of letters and words, contains the following target behaviors: print letters, reconstruct words, and write words. *Print letters* includes a range of associated behaviors such as tracing over letters, copying or typing letters from a story chart, and using rubber letter stamps. Durkin (1966) found that early readers were interested in learning to print. The relationship between the constructive act of printing and early interest or ability in reading, however, remains unclear. Williams (1969) noted that letter reproduction training was as effective as simple letter discrimination training, but not as effective as contrastive letter discrimination training. Methods of writing and reading instruction developed by Montessori (1912) systematically guide young children in printing letters. For example, to introduce printing, young children trace sandpaper letters with their fingers.

The second target behavior, *reconstruct words*, entails use of individual letters to

The child given a letter card finds words on a story chart beginning with that letter. Objects from the experience can be attached to a language experience story to aid recall.

build words printed on a story chart. For this purpose, a child might use letter cards, rubber letter stamps, or a typewriter. Gough (1972) argued that reading is a letter-by-letter process. Other support for this activity comes from Chomsky's (1971) report of the efforts of a young child to compose words using individual letter shapes before being able to read. Montessori (1912) included word construction with letter cards among her writing and reading methods.

The last target behavior for reproduction of letters and words is to *write words* from a language experience story. Early readers often copy words or ask questions about how to spell a particular word (Durkin 1966). Preschool and kindergarten spellers have also used letter names to invent their own spellings for familiar words (Paul 1976; Read 1971).

The third category of skill tactics is identification of letter names. The corresponding target behavior is to *recognize letter names*. For this target behavior, a teacher might either ask the child to name a letter in print or name a letter and ask the child to find it on a story chart. Teaching letter names to beginning readers is a controversial, though common, practice, but if naming letters is an intended aim of instruction, then features in those letters should be used in prior discrimination training (Samuels 1973). Some support for learning letter names appears in the literature. Chisholm and Knafle (1975) found that learning letter names facilitates learning words more quickly than letter discrimination training or control conditions. Most research evidence, however, favors letter naming only as a predictor or correlate of reading achievement. On reading readiness

Jensen and Hanson

tests, recognition of letter names is a strong predictor of first-grade achievement (Barrett 1965; Silberberg, Iverson, and Silberberg 1968). In literature on reading methods, Bloomfield and Barnhart (1961) called for learning letter names in their linguistic reading materials and Hall (1976) described this practice as part of language experience instruction.

The fourth category of skill tactics is use of spelling patterns. The target behavior in this category is to *recognize similarities and differences in spelling patterns* of words in a language experience story. Numerous studies have related spelling pattern recognition to reading. Bloomfield (1942) suggested using words with simple spelling patterns for beginning reading instruction. Only such words were included in his published reading materials (Bloomfield and Barnhart 1961). Based on analyses of spelling patterns, Gibson (1965), Venezky (1970), and Chomsky (1970) argued the importance of spelling pattern recognition in skillful reading and in understanding word relationships represented by the orthography. The ability of five-year-old children to transfer perceived spelling pattern similarities and differences to the decoding of new words was confirmed in a study by Baron (1977). Other support for use of spelling patterns appears in accounts of the spontaneous spelling efforts of preschoolers (Chomsky 1971; Read 1971).

The last category of skill tactics is use of prompted mediation to map from one system of representation to another system of representation. The key target behavior is to *map print to oral language.* Gibson and Levin (1975) discussed the reading stage of relating print with appropriate oral language responses. Questions remain about the development of this learning. Durrell and Murphy (1963) and Muehl (1962) hypothesized that children use letter names as mediators in initially learning to hook up print with oral language. If letter names are learned more readily by young children than are grapheme-phoneme relations, then letter names provide a more accessible cue than phonemes (Jenkins, Bausell, and Jenkins 1972). Nevertheless, only 16 of the 26 letter names correspond closely with oral language sounds (Venezky 1975). Therefore, use of letter names can only be a temporary or partial cue in the hook-up stage. Young children's rudimentary ability to use mediation can be improved by training or prompting (Muehl 1962; Flavell 1970).

Ideational tactics

The first category of ideational tactics is use of connotative recall cues. Various environmental or pictorial cues can prompt the young child's recall of a language experience story or related activities.

The first target behavior is *make personal illustrations for ideas,* through which children can capture and organize personally meaningful aspects of their experience. Stauffer (1970) included this target behavior among recommended practices for language experience instruction. Semantic information (related to sentence meaning rather than sentence grammar) dominates a child's recall and processing of a language experience story (Tyler and Marslen-Wilson 1978). Personally meaningful illustrations can also help a child to later recall and understand the meaning of the story.

The second target behavior is to *attach photographs of the experience* to a language experience story (Hall 1976). Photographs or slides can help the child to make sense of accompanying written material (Hiebert 1978). Photographs of settings and situations chosen by the child (in contrast to photographs of objects) increase the child's language production for descriptions of the pictures (Strandberg and Griffith 1969).

To *attach objects from the experience* is

the third target behavior for use of connotative recall cues. An example of this behavior is attaching dried leaves to a story about a nature walk, because the use of the environmental context can help a child to decipher print (Hiebert 1978). Moreover, an object can evoke more language production than can a picture of the object (Strandberg 1969). In traditional language experience instruction, objects were used to aid recall of past experiences and ideas (Lamoreaux and Lee 1943).

The second category for ideational tactics is comparison of meaning units. The three target behaviors for this category are *match sentences, match phrases,* and *match words.* Cutting up a story into sentence strips, next into phrase strips, and finally into word strips and reconstructing the story after each cutting to match the original story is a traditional language experience practice

(Lamoreaux and Lee 1943). More recently, Hall (1976) mentioned this practice as part of language experience instruction. This holistic practice proceeds from larger meaning units to smaller meaning units. Based on their review of reading research, Ryan and Semmel (1969) advocated early development of hypothesis-testing strategies such as matching or making use of equivalence relations. If only particular words from the story are matched, practice and research suggest that these words should be chosen by the child (Ashton-Warner 1963; Holman 1973).

The third category of ideational tactics, use of contextual cues, includes four target behaviors. Using contextual cues to *complete sentences or phrases* or to *respond correctly to recall questions* drawn from a language experience story are behaviors supported by a number of research studies and reviews. Contextual

If particular words from the story are matched, these words should be chosen by the child.

Jensen and Hanson

richness and contextual word associations can benefit young readers in word identification, comprehension, and reading achievement (Pearson and Studt 1975; Samuels, Dahl, and Archwamety 1974; Samuels and Wittrock 1969). Goodman (1965) found that beginning readers could read more words in context than in lists. Ryan and Semmel (1969) advocated the practice of completing interrupted passages for development of hypothesis-testing strategies in beginning reading.

The third target behavior is to *identify repeated or redundant words or phrases.* From miscue analysis, Goodman (1967) identified the use of redundancy as a reading cue. Wales and Marshall (1966) and Ryan and Semmel (1969) noted the contribution of redundancy in language and reading. Thus, Ryan and Semmel as well as Loban (1978) advocated development of games and beginning reading materials that provide opportunities to use the redundancy of language as an aid to reading and comprehension. Hall (1976) also recognized this reading behavior in describing methods for language experience instruction.

The final target behavior for use of contextual cues is *sequence ideas or sentences.* To elicit this behavior, a teacher can, for example, mix up sentence strips from a story and ask the child to arrange them in the correct order. The abilities of young children to sequence ideas or sentences of simple narratives and to recall simple narratives is well documented (Brown 1975; Brown 1976; Clay 1968; Mandler and Johnson 1977; Stein and Glenn 1978; Tyler and Marslen-Wilson 1978).

The fourth category of ideational tactics is classification of words into concept categories. The corresponding target behavior is *group words into concept categories.* For example, given word cards from a language experience story, the child forms groupings. Young children rely on immediate context and per-

ceptual features rather than on functional or abstract qualities in making groupings (Saltz, Soller, and Sigel 1972). Integrating analytic features for vocabulary or lexical concepts is important to reading attainment and language development (Clark 1973; Serafica and Sigel 1970).

The last category of ideational tactics is use of stress and intonation signals. For this category, the child must learn to *interpret meaning expressed by stress and intonation signals.* Support for the influence of this target behavior in reading comes from oral reading research by Clay and Imlach (1971) and from practice recommendations by Loban (1978).

Intersecting tactics

Three conventional organizing behaviors which relate to beginning reading and language experience instruction can be incorporated into either skill or ideational practices: *follow a line of print from left to right, underline words as they are read,* and *make a word bank* (Bates, Bethke, Dieden, and Hanson 1979; Hall 1976; Stauffer 1970). Each of these target behaviors is self-explanatory.

Decisions about teaching strategies

Some young children may benefit more either from skill or ideational instruction when first learning to read. Not only must the teacher decide which orientation best matches the child's needs, but within either orientation, the teacher must make choices from a repertoire of possible teaching tactics. Patterns of these teacher behaviors make more of a difference in reading outcomes than does the type of instructional program (Chall and Feldman 1966; Malmquist 1973; McDonald and Elias 1976). Responsive language experience instruction provides more opportunities for the teacher to make instructional decisions about teaching strategies than do prestructured instructional programs.

Decisions about teaching tactics and teaching strategies for language experience instruction can be guided by knowledge about early reading acquisition and development. With a comprehensive and developmental view of reading acquisition, teachers will be better able to select and organize appropriate teaching methods for helping young children learn to read.

References

Ashton-Warner, S. *Teacher*. New York: Simon & Schuster, 1963.

Baron, J. "Mechanisms for Pronouncing Printed Words: Use and Acquisition." In *Basic Processes in Reading: Perception and Comprehension,* eds. D. LaBerge, and S. J. Samuels. Hillsdale, N.J.: Lawrence Erlbaum Associates, 1977.

Barrett, T. C. "Visual Discrimination Tasks as Predictors of First Grade Reading Achievement." *The Reading Teacher* 18 (1965): 276-282.

Bates, S. A.; Bethke, E.; Dieden, R.; and Hanson, B A. *Kindergarten Curriculum Issues: Reading*. Madison, Wis.: Wisconsin Department of Public Instruction, 1979.

Bloomfield, L. "Linguistics and Reading." *Elementary English* 19 (1942): 125-130.

Bloomfield, L., and Barnhart, C. L. *Let's Read: A Linguistic Approach*. Detroit: Wayne State University Press, 1961.

Brown, A. L. "Recognition, Reconstruction, and Recall of Narrative Sequences by Preoperational Children." *Child Development* 46, no. 1 (1975): 156-166.

Brown, A. L. "Semantic Integration in Children's Reconstruction of Narrative Sequences." *Cognitive Psychology* 8 (1976): 247-262.

Chall, J., and Feldman, S. "First Grade Reading: An Analysis of the Interactions of Professed Methods, Teacher Implementation and Child Background." *The Reading Teacher* 19 (1966): 569-575.

Chisholm, D., and Knafle, J. D. *Letter-Name Knowledge as a Prerequisite to Learning to Read,* 1975. (ERIC Document Reproduction Service, No. ED102 536)

Chomsky, C. "Reading, Writing, and Phonology." *Harvard Educational Review* 40 (1970): 287-309.

Chomsky, C. "Write First, Read Later." *Childhood Education* 47 (1971): 296-299.

Clark, E. V. "What's in a Word? On the Child's Acquisition of Semantics in His First Language." In *Cognitive Development and the Acquisition of Language,* ed. T. E. Moore. New York: Academic Press, 1973.

Clay, M. M. "A Syntactic Analysis of Reading Errors." *Journal of Verbal Learning and Verbal Behavior* 7 (1968): 434-438.

Clay, M. M., and Imlach, R. H. "Juncture, Pitch, and Stress as Reading Behavior Variables." *Journal of Verbal Learning and Verbal Behavior* 10 (1971): 133-139.

Durkin, D. *Children Who Read Early*. New York: Teachers College Press, 1966.

Durrell, D. D., and Murphy, H. A. "Boston University Research in Elementary School Reading 1933-1963: Reading Readiness." *Journal of Education* 146 (1963): 3-10.

Feldman, C. F. "Two Functions of Language." *Harvard Educational Review* 47 (August 1977): 282-293.

Flavell, J. H. "Developmental Studies of Mediated Memory." In *Advances in Child Development and Behavior,* eds. H. W. Reese, and L. P. Lipsitt. New York: Academic Press, 1970.

Garner, W. R. *Uncertainty and Structure as Psychological Concepts*. New York: Wiley, 1962.

Gibson, E. J. "Learning to Read." *Science* 148 (May 1965): 1066-1072.

Gibson, E. J., and Levin, H. *The Psychology of Reading*. Cambridge, Mass.: MIT Press, 1975.

Glaser, R. "Trends and Research Questions in Psychological Research on Learning and Schooling." *Educational Researcher* 8 (November 1979): 6-13.

Goetz, E. M. "Early Reading: A Developmental Approach." *Young Children* 34, no. 5 (July 1979): 4-11.

Goodman, K. S. "A Linguistic Study of Cues and Miscues in Reading." *Elementary English* 42 (1965): 639-643.

Goodman, K. S. "Reading: A Psycholinguistic Guessing Game." *Journal of the Reading Specialist* 6 (1967): 126-135.

Jensen and Hanson

Gough, P. B. "One Second of Reading." In *Language by Ear and by Eye*, eds. J. F. Kavanagh, and I. G. Mattingly. Cambridge, Mass.: MIT Press, 1972.

Hall, M. *Teaching Reading as a Language Experience*. 2nd ed. Columbus, Ohio: Merrill, 1976.

Halliday, M. A. K. "Language Structure and Language Function." In *New Horizons in Linguistics*, ed. J. Lyons. Baltimore: Penguin, 1970.

Hiebert, E. H. "Preschool Children's Understanding of Written Language." *Child Development* 49, no. 4 (1978): 1231-1234.

Holden, M. H., and MacGinitie, W. H. "Children's Conceptions of Word Boundaries in Speech and Print." *Journal of Educational Psychology* 63 (1972): 551-557.

Holman, G. C., Jr. *Interest and Evaluative Meaning as Factors in the Acquisition of a Sight Vocabulary*, 1973. (ERIC Document Reproduction Service, No. ED 078 937)

Huttenlocher, J. "Children's Language: Word-Phrase Relationship." *Science* 143 (January 1964): 264-265.

Jenkins, J. R.; Bausell, R. B.; and Jenkins, L. M. "Comparisons of Letter Name and Letter Sound Training as Transfer Variables." *American Educational Research Journal* 9 (1972): 75-85.

Kelly, A. M. *Children's Ability to Segment Oral Language*, 1977. (ERIC Document Reproduction Service, No. ED 145 402)

Lamoreaux, L. A., and Lee, D. M. *Learning to Read Through Experience*. New York: Appleton-Century, 1943.

Loban, W. "Our Expanding Vision of Reading." *Claremont Reading Conference 42nd Yearbook*. Claremont, Calif.: The Claremont Reading Conference, 1978.

Malmquist, E. "Perspectives on Reading Research." In *Reading for All*, ed. R. Karlin. Newark, Del.: International Reading Association, 1973.

Mandler, J. M., and Johnson, N. S. "Remembrance of Things Passed: Story Structure and Recall." *Cognitive Psychology* 9 (1977): 111-151.

Marchbanks, G., and Levin, H. "Cues by Which Children Recognize Words." *Journal of Educational Psychology* 56 (1965): 57-61.

McDonald, F. J., and Elias, P. *Beginning Teacher Evaluation Study, Phase II, 1973-74. Executive Summary Report*. Princeton, N.J.: Educational Testing Service, 1976.

Meltzer, N. S., and Herse, R. "The Boundaries of Written Words as Seen by First Graders." *Journal of Reading Behavior* 1 (1969): 3-14.

Montessori, M. *The Montessori Method*. New York: Frederick A. Stokes, 1912.

Muehl, S. "The Effects of Letter-Name Knowledge on Learning to Read a Word List in Kindergarten Children." *Journal of Educational Psychology* 53 (1962): 181-186.

Nurss, J. R. "Research in Review. Linguistic Awareness and Learning to Read." *Young Children* 35, no. 3 (March 1980): 57-66.

Paul, R. "Invented Spelling in Kindergarten." *Young Children* 31, no. 3 (March 1976): 195-200.

Pearson, P. D., and Studt, A. "Effects of Word Frequency and Contextual Richness on Children's Word Identification Abilities." *Journal of Educational Psychology* 67 (1975): 89-95.

Pick, A. D. "Perception in the Acquisition of Reading." In *The Acquisition of Reading*, eds. F. B. Murray, and J. J. Pikalski. Baltimore: University Park Press, 1978.

Read, C. "Pre-School Children's Knowledge of English Phonology." *Harvard Educational Review* 41 (1971): 1-34.

"Reading and Pre-First Grade." *Young Children* 32, no. 6 (September 1977): 25-26.

Ryan, E. B., and Semmel, M. I. "Reading as a Constructive Language Process." *Reading Research Quarterly* 5 (1969): 59-83.

Saltz, E.; Soller, E.; and Sigel, I. E. "The Development of Natural Language Concepts." *Child Development* 43, no. 4 (1972): 1191-1202.

Samuels, S. J. "Effect of Distinctive Feature Training on Paired-Associate Learning." *Journal of Educational Psychology* 64 (1973): 164-170.

Samuels, S. J.; Dahl, P.; and Archwamety, T. "Effect of Hypothesis/Test Training on Reading Skill." *Journal of Educational Psychology* 66 (1974): 835-844.

Samuels, S. J., and Wittrock, M. C. "Word-Association Strength and Learning to Read." *Journal of Educational Psychology* 60 (1969): 248-252.

Serafica, F. C., and Sigel, I. E. "Styles of Categorization and Reading Disability." *Journal of Reading Behavior* 2 (1970): 105-115.

Silberberg, N.; Iverson, I.; and Silberberg, M. "The Predictive Efficiency of the Gates Reading Readiness Tests." *Elementary School Journal* 68 (1968): 213-218.

Smith, R. J.; Otto, W.; and Hansen, L. *The School Reading Program*. Boston: Houghton Mifflin, 1978.

Spodek, B. "Early Reading and Preprimary Education." Paper presented at the annual meeting of the American Educational Research Association, San Francisco, April 1979.

Stauffer, R. G. *The Language-Experience Approach to the Teaching of Reading*. New York: Harper & Row, 1970.

Stein, N. L., and Glenn, C. G. "An Analysis of Story Comprehension in Elementary School Children." In *New Directions in Discourse Comprehension*, ed. R. O. Freedle. Hillsdale, N.J.: Ablex, 1978.

Strandberg, T. E. "An Evaluation of Three Stimulus Media for Evoking Verbalizations for Preschool Children." (M.S. thesis, Eastern Illinois University, 1969).

Strandberg, T. E., and Griffith, J. "A Study of the Effects of Training in Visual Literacy on Verbal Language Behavior." *Journal of Communication Disorders* 2 (1969): 252-263.

Tyler, L. K., and Marslen-Wilson, W. "Some Developmental Aspects of Sentence Processing and Memory." *Journal of Child Language* 5 (1978): 113-129.

Venezky, R. L. "Regularity in Reading and Spelling." In *Basic Studies on Reading*, eds. H. Levin, and J. P. Williams. New York: Basic Books, 1970.

Venezky, R. L. "The Curious Role of Letter Names in Reading Instruction." *Visible Language* 9 (1975): 7-23.

Wales, R. J., and Marshall, J. C. "The Organization of Linguistic Performance." In *Psycholinguistic Papers*, eds. J. Lyons, and R. J. Wales. Edinburgh: Edinburgh University Press, 1966.

Weber, R. "A Linguistic Analysis of First-Grade Reading Errors." *Reading Research Quarterly* 5 (1970): 427-451.

Williams, J. P. "Training Kindergarten Children to Discriminate Letter-Like Forms." *American Educational Research Journal* 6 (1969): 501-514.

Williams, J. P.; Blumberg, E. L.; and Williams, D. V. "Cues Used in Visual Word Recognition." *Journal of Educational Psychology* 61 (1970): 310-315.

Judith A. Schickedanz

"Hey! This Book's Not Working Right."

Four-year-old Robbie was trying to read the title *Where the Wild Things Are* (Sendak 1963). But each time he said the title, which he had memorized, he exaggerated the pronunciation of the word *wild,* making it into a word with two, rather than one, syllables:

Where	the	Wild	Things	Are		(text)
↑	↑	↑	↑	↑	↑	
Where	the	wi	ld	things	are	(speech
						with
						finger
						pointing
						to print)

Clearly, speech and print were not matching up evenly, and Robbie knew it. "This book's not working right," he said.

After his eleventh attempt, I decided to offer some help, "When you say the word *wild,* make sure your finger ends up on the *d* at the end of the word," I explained. "See, you do it like this." Robbie watched and listened with great interest. "Oh," he said, and then he tried to do it. "That worked!" he announced, and it had. Then he did it correctly once again before pausing for a moment to stare at the words in the title, as if thinking hard about how printed words are made and how they can be matched up with spoken words.

Judith A. Schickedanz, Ph.D., is Associate Professor, Early Childhood Education, Boston University. She is the current director of the Boston University Preelementary Reading Improvement Project.

Children cannot hear what we know

Robbie was in the process of making some very important discoveries about the relationship between oral language and print, relationships which are very difficult for children to understand.

With an alphabetic orthography such as we have in English, the child must at some point become aware that letters represent individual sounds, not syllables or some larger unit of the stream of speech. The difficulty involved in becoming "phonemically aware" (Mattingly 1979) seems to be due to the fact that the speech we utter does not really contain any individual sounds in a physical, acoustical sense (Liberman, Cooper, Shankweiler, and Studdert-Kennedy 1967). Perceiving three individual sounds in a word such as *cat* is more a *cognitive*-perceptual than a *physical*-perceptual task. In other words, we learn to think about what we hear when the word *cat* is said in terms of three sounds, even though the physical phenomenon is more like one complete sound.

To make matters even more difficult for the naïve child, even being able to perceive language at the sound level does not solve the problems encountered with print. A single *phonemic* category, the smallest meaningful unit of sound, is actually a collection of several physically distinct sounds (*phones*) (Gleitman and Rozin 1977; Golinkoff 1978). Phonemes are abstractions which are created through interactions with print. They exist in our heads, and are not out there to be objectively heard (Savin and Bever 1970; McNeill and Lindig 1973). For example, the sound represented by a *t* can vary somewhat depending on its context in words (compare the *t*'s in *tar*, *grater*, and *trade*). Recognizing phonemes is not so much a matter of hearing sounds as knowing which differences are attended to for purposes of being represented in our spelling system.

Typical phonics instruction and teacher behavior during such instruction often attempt the impossible—getting children to hear what the teachers know. Children who do hear what the teachers say in such situations are, no doubt, children who come to school already knowing what the teachers mean. I would guess that they are children like Robbie who have been read to a great deal since infancy, or who have had labels on food containers pointed out to them, and have begun to experiment with trying to map speech to print. Perhaps we should not be surprised that children who have been read to extensively before they enter school are the children who often are the highest achievers in reading (Durkin 1966; Sutton 1964).

Becoming aware of phonemes: constructing knowledge

Actually, no one knows for sure how children become aware of phonemes, or what set of experiences lead children to this awareness. But we do know that oral language play alone, such as in learning rhyming verses, tapping out syllables of words heard, or saying verses containing alliteration, is not sufficient (Savin 1972). We know, too, that knowledge of the orthography, for example, having some visual awareness of the letter combinations which are permissible in words, is correlated with phonemic awareness (Ehri and Wilce 1979; Valtin 1979); and that reading instruction (of any kind) is, too (Ehri and Wilce 1979; Golinkoff 1978). This information would suggest that there is something about experiences with print, and bringing oral language and print together, that are crucial.

It would appear that the development of phonemic awareness depends on experience in situations analogous to those required for the development of logico-mathematical knowledge. For example, with logico-mathematical knowledge, what is learned comes from actions on objects (objects to be classified, seriated, or counted), not from the objects themselves (Kamii and DeVries 1977). For example, it is not one particular object from among a group of three or five objects which has the characteristic of threeness or fiveness; it is our actions on objects which result in number. Similarly, a classification scheme based on color, size, or shape, does not reside in the objects, but in our heads; we impose it onto various objects. (Obviously the characteristics of objects determine the specific schemes we can create.) In other words, when it comes to knowledge which does not exist in external reality, but which must be constructed (i.e., abstracted) from it, we cannot tell it to children, or transfer it ready-made. Instead, we must create situations from which they can discover this information through their own interactions.

The concept of phonemic awareness would seem to depend on actions performed on print and speech together, for phonemes are not objective characteristics of speech, nor do all orthographies represent single speech sounds as opposed to syllables or words. Phonemic awareness may be knowledge that is constructed in the unique situation of trying to match speech to an alphabetic orthography. Robbie, then, would have been in the ideal situation for making sense out of print and sounds.

Children who have been read to extensively before they enter school are the children who often are the highest achievers in reading.

Emily Siroka

"This Book's Not Working Right."

The focus of this article on the role of phonemic awareness in learning to read is not meant to suggest that this is the only, or the primary, understanding required. Language and cognitive abilities, as well as general knowledge of the world, are also essential. The role of phonemic awareness was selected for discussion because it is often the skill of concern in instruction, and because such instruction, I feel, is often poorly suited to the young child.

Possible stages of learning about print

At four, Robbie already knew a lot. For example, he knew that the print, not the pictures, determines what one reads aloud. This surely is a prerequisite to understanding how print itself works (how it represents speech). But at first, children ignore the words in books and attend only to the pictures (Clay 1972; Rossman 1980). If asked where on the page the adult reader must look in order to read the book, the young child is quite likely to point to the pictures, not to the print. Often, if a child who has this notion is holding the book while the adult reads, the child may unknowingly cover the print with a thumb, making it necessary occasionally for the adult to request that it be moved so that the story can be read. In contrast, a four- or five-year-old who has been read to extensively will sometimes cover the print on purpose to tease the reader.

In addition, children who think that readers read the pictures often want to skip pages which have no pictures; and conversely want the adult to read pages which have pictures, but no print. For example, in *Where the Wild Things Are*, the last page reads "and it was still hot," but there is no illustration on this page. Young children will often not turn to this page but wait instead for the adult to say this phrase while still looking at the picture on the previous page. Similarly, if the adult is silent, or merely strikes up a conversation about the pictures of the wild rumpus on the pages where there are illustrations but no print, a young child is likely to insist that the adult read these pages. An explanation that the pages cannot be read because there are no words often does not convince a child who thinks that a reader reads pictures. It helps (in time) to turn to a page containing print and explain, while pointing to it, that this is what a reader must look at to know what a story says.

But even after children have grasped the basic notion about the symbolic nature of print, they still have a great deal to learn about the exact way in which print functions. Fortunately, children seem able to use what they know to help them figure out how print works. Apparently, many children like Robbie use their knowledge of what a title or part of a story says to guide their investigations into the mysteries of print.

Even though young children can use what they know to figure out how print works, the process of discovery is a lengthy one. When observing children trying to map speech to print, we can see their tentative and growing understandings reflected in their behavior. For example, one three-year-old tried to read the title *Frosty the Snowman* (Nelson and Rollins 1975), like this:

F r o s t y t h e S n o w m a n	(text)	
Fro sty the snow man What does this one say?	(ignored)	(speech with finger pointing to print)

This child was aware of speech at the syllable, not the phonemic, level and she assumed that the orthography was syllabic (that each letter stood for a syllable). But even this rudimentary understanding showed a degree of sophistication. Often, before children even begin to be this accurate, they merely make broad sweeps, or back and forth motions, at the print.

Another child whose name was Deborah, read "Deborah, Deborah, Deborah," etc., as she pointed to each letter of her name which I had written. Obviously, this four-year-old thought that each letter in print stood for a whole spoken word. (Such a notion may explain why many young children initially use only a few letters found in their name when they write it: perhaps they think each one, and, therefore, any one, can stand for the entire name.) I demonstrated for Deborah how I would read her name, sweeping my finger under all of the letters. I noticed somewhat later that she was reading her name over and over, sweeping her finger under all of the letters just as I had. I do not think she had an accurate understanding of the relationship between speech and print at this point, but she had seemed to understand that all of those letters were needed to be able to say Deborah.

Another variation of children's behavior when they match speech to print is illustrated by the following example provided by another four-year-old who was trying to read the book, *The Very Hungry Caterpillar* (Carle 1969):

On Monday, he ate one apple. But he was still hungry.	(text)
On Mon day, he ate one ap ple. But he was still hungry.	(speech with finger pointing to print)

In this instance, the child knew what a word in print was (a collection of letters separated from other letters by space), but did not understand the difference between a syllable and a word in speech, or that some words contain more than one syllable. Because some of the words in this story are multisyllabic, the child could not get the speech and print to come out right using her hypotheses.

These are some of the main variations in behavior that one can observe as young children attempt to map speech to print. As they test out hypotheses and find that they do not always work, they stumble onto other ways to do it, or receive a little help from someone the way Robbie did. Sometimes children cannot solve the problems involved in mapping speech to print and they revert back to an earlier strategy that worked for them. For example, they may merely say the words they have memorized, and not try to match these to print. Doake (1979) has studied preschool children's reading behavior, and tells about a discussion he had with a child named Gillian, concerning whether one must look at words or just say them when reading. The child tells Doake that she just says the words, "cos if I point I get all mixed up." Gillian had been attempting to match syllables in speech to words in print despite the fact that some of the words were multisyllabic. This caused her to run out of print to point to before running out of words to say. This mixed her up as she explained, so she stopped doing it for awhile and just read her stories by looking at the pictures and repeating the storyline which she had memorized from hours of listening to an adult reader.

At such points, children may also insist that the adult read to them. Rossman (1980), for example, found that children go in and out of nonresponse stages (stages in which they do not want to tell the adult what the book says, but do want the adult to read to them) throughout the years when they are having storybook experiences. She suggests that these may be points at which children realize that a previous hypothesis about what reading entails will not work. Children then want the adult to read, perhaps so that the children can observe and formulate new ideas which they can later test.

How can adults help children learn about written language?

When we assume that learning is a matter of knowledge construction, rather than knowledge transference, the adult's role includes helping children learn about written language from experiences which place children in a good position to construct the essential knowledge. This means first of all that the adult provides an environment which is rich with print and tools for creating it. In addition, when it comes to language, whether oral or written, an essential aspect of experience involves a social component: hearing someone talk in meaningful situations and hearing and seeing someone read meaningful print. Children, it seems, cannot get into a position to discover how print works if they do not first have the opportunity to learn what some representative samples of print say (e.g., their name posted on a cubby, the name of a favorite cereal and where it appears on the cereal box, the title and storyline of a favorite book). It takes a considerable amount of interaction with adults for children to come to know these samples. In a sense, the adult's reading is the object of the child's interaction. Furthermore, the interactions must have certain characteristics if they are to be effective. For example, one-to-one story reading such as that done by many parents at home allows children to see the pictures and print, to ask ques-

tions, to turn the pages, etc., while the group story reading which occurs in many preschool settings allows for none of these. What children learn in the two situations is likely to be very different, with the home reading situation being the more effective (Schickedanz 1978).

Adults also provide essential feedback to children as they test their hypotheses. For example, when reading *Where the Wild Things Are,* the adult can say, "We have to turn the page to read the last part. See, here is where it says 'and it was still hot.'" Or, when a child who has been playing with a set of manipulative alphabet materials places several letters in a row and comes to us to ask, "What does this word say?" We need to be there to say, "You're right, we do put letters together to make words, but some combinations of letters don't make a word. But if we put this letter over here and that one over there, we can make the word *cane.* Do you know what a cane is?"

Children will not understand such explanations immediately, and they do not serve the purpose of directly transferring to children what adults know. Children take the feedback with them to new explorations, and gradually they do understand what the adult has been saying. The situation may be compared to the oral language situation in which a child calls a horse a doggie. The adult says "That's not a doggie; that's a horse." Perhaps it will take awhile (and several more clarifications in context from an adult) for the child to consistently refer to the two animals with different labels, but we surely would not say that the adult's feedback had not been helpful or vital.

In short, adult interaction with children and with print is absolutely necessary if children are to learn about written language. But the adult's role is not one of telling children about reading. Instead, it is one of engaging children in meaningful interactions with print in an environment which contains many such opportunities, and then providing guidance and feedback in ways which make sense to children, which means at points when children are actively engaged in trying to make print make sense.

The roles of alphabet recognition and perceptual-motor skills in learning to read

Reading is not largely a matter of perceptual-motor or alphabet recognition skills (Mason 1980; Menyuk 1976; Williams 1976). Instead, it is a matter of coming to know about how written language works. Obviously, basic perceptual-motor skills are required when one reads, but children's perceptual skills are very keen from early infancy. Perceptual problems seem not to be at the heart of reading problems, though teachers often think they are. For example, consider the situation in which a child has written letters of the alphabet or perhaps a word on a piece of paper and has reversed several of the letters. The teacher refers to an alphabet chart while asking the child if her or his letter looks like the one the teacher has pointed out. The child says yes. The teacher instructs the child to look carefully. But again, the child says the letters are the same. (Some children would catch on at this point that their first answer was wrong and change it to no, though they would not know why.) Again (assuming the answer was yes) the teacher says "Look carefully. You're not looking closely enough. Look again."

The teacher in this case does not understand that the problem is not with seeing anything, but with knowing the meaning of what we see. This child has learned from experiences with the three-dimensional world that orientation is not a meaningful feature: a dog is a dog is a dog regardless of the direction it faces. Of course, with print, orientation is a meaningful or distinctive feature. A teacher who understands this problem might say "Well, they don't look the same to me. They are made from

Recognition of the letters of the alphabet is of little use in learning to read, but knowing about letters and how they function seems to be important.

the same lines, but one is facing this way and one is facing the other, and that makes them different."

Similar confusions can be made with regard to phonics. Perhaps a child is not doing well. The teacher may assume that the child is not paying close enough attention to how letters sound, or that the child is not hearing how things sound. But as was pointed out earlier, learning phonemes requires knowing about phonemes, just as seeing differences in some letters requires knowing that orientation matters with print. Children may hear perfectly well what we are saying, but if they do not know what we are talking about, what we say will make little sense.

But what about alphabet recognition? Is this essential to learning to read? The answer seems to be yes and no. Recognition per se is of little use, but knowing about letters and how they function seems to be important. For example, it was useful (probably essential) in helping Robbie read the title *Where the Wild Things Are*, to be able to refer to the letter *d*. Children must have a vocabulary relating to written language if they are to understand what we are talking about.

Many children, even by the time they enter school, do not have this basic vocabulary, and this may be the basis for a great deal of confusion (Downing 1973–1974). Clay (1975) gives a good example of how such confusion can come about:

> Suppose a teacher has placed an attractive picture on the wall and has asked her children for a story which she will record under it. They offer the text "Mother is cooking" which the teacher alters slightly to introduce some features she wishes to teach. She writes.
>
> > Mother said,
> > "I am baking." . . .
>
> Perhaps the children read in unison "Mother is . . ." and the teacher tries to sort this out. Pointing to *said* she asks, "Does this say is?" Half agree it does because it has "s" in it. "What *letter* does it start with?" Now the teacher is really in trouble. She assumes that children *know* that a word is built out of letters, but 50 percent of children still confuse the verbal labels "word" and "letter" after six months of instruction. . . .
> The lesson continues and the class makes a final unison statement "Mother said, 'I am cooking.' " Many have focussed on the quaint letter "k" in the middle. The teacher says, "Does it say cooking? Look carefully. Look at the beginning. Tell me what the first letter says." Many of the children may not locate the first letter. "Does it say c-c-c-c?" Children with an intuitive awareness of the phonetic identity "k" agree heartily. . . . (pp. 3–4)

Obviously, such a lesson is not very effective, but not because children do not listen or do not know phonics. The basic problem is that they lack a vocabulary for dealing with written language in the way the teacher chose to present it.

But how might children go about learning the vocabulary we use to talk about written language? I would suggest they can learn it in the same way they learn the names of other objects and actions in their world—in context, as they interact with written language. For example, a teacher might write a child's name on a piece of artwork and say, "What is this word? That's right. It is your name; the word is *Amy*." A teacher might also point out words in the environment which contain the same letters as a child's name: "That word is *exit*, and it has two letters that your name has, Matthew. See the *e* and the *t*?" Or, a child may be playing with felt letters and a teacher might say, "Oh, I see you've put all the letters that are alike together. There are two *a*'s up there, two *s*'s over here, and two *o*'s down here. And I see that you've made a word down here. What does it spell? Yes, it says *Tracy*. That's your name. Do you know how to make any other words?"

It is not difficult to imagine how children involved in such situations might learn the vocabulary of written language quite naturally. It is also not difficult to understand why children whose parents read to them, provide manipulative alphabet materials, small chalkboards, and paper and pencils, (in short, materials relating to written language) do well in reading when they reach school. They would surely know the vocabulary of written language from the countless interactions they have had with their parents or older brothers and sisters. And they would be the ones who would understand what a teacher is talking about in situations such as the one described by Clay. But it is important to note that it is not so much that these children know the alphabet (which they usually do), but that they know a great deal more as a result of the way in which they learned the alphabet.

Summary

Learning to read is largely a matter of coming to know about written language. In order for children to construct knowl-

Schickedanz

Stephanie H. Meyer

Children who are successful in reading in elementary school typically are children who have a history of meaningful interactions with print.

edge about written language, they must be provided meaningful print with which to interact. Children who are successful in reading in elementary school typically are children who have a history of such interaction. We need to be certain that children who are in early childhood centers have an opportunity for this interaction so that they will have the long period of exploration and discovery that seems to serve as the backbone of a good reader's success. There is no such thing as starting too early with appropriate reading experiences. We generally agree that children start to talk when they are around one year of age. But we would think it foolish not to talk to them until they start, because we know that their starting depends a great deal on the talking we have done to them since they were born. Similarly, children generally start to read when they are between five and seven years of age. We need to start using written language with

them years before this age. When we do use it in ways suggested above, written language becomes as interesting to young children as any other part of the environment. It is just something else to explore and to learn about, right along with the blocks and the paint.

References

Carle, E. *The Very Hungry Caterpillar.* Cleveland, Ohio: Collins-World, 1969.

Clay, M. *Reading: The Patterning of Complex Behavior.* Auckland, New Zealand: Heinemann Educational Books, 1972.

Clay, M. *What Did I Write?* Auckland, New Zealand: Heinemann Educational Books, 1975.

Doake, D. "Preschool Book Handling Knowledge." Paper presented at the Annual Meeting of the International Reading Association, May 1979, Atlanta, Georgia.

Downing, J. "The Child's Conception of 'A Word.'" *Reading Research Quarterly* 9, no. 4 (1973–1974): 568–582.

Durkin, D. *Children Who Read Early.* New York: Teachers College Press, 1966.

Ehri, L. C., and Wilce, L. S. "Does Orthography Influence a Reader's Metalinguistic Awareness of Syllabic and Phonemic Segments in Words?" Paper presented at the International Reading Association/University of Victoria International Reading Research Seminar on Linguistic Awareness and Learning to Read, June 1979, Victoria, British Columbia, Canada.

Gleitman, L. R., and Rozin, P. "The Structure and Acquisition of Reading I: Relations Between Orthographies and the Structure of Language." In *Toward a Psychology of Reading,* ed. A. S. Reber and D. L. Scarborough. Hillsdale, N.J.: Lawrence Erlbaum Associates, 1977.

Golinkoff, R. M. "Critique: Phonemic Awareness Skills and Reading Achievement." In *The Acquisition of Reading,* ed. F. Murray and J. Pikulski. Baltimore: University Park Press, 1978.

Kamii, C., and DeVries, R. "Piaget for Early Education." In *The Preschool in Action,* ed. M. C. Day and R. K. Parker. Boston: Allyn & Bacon, 1977.

Liberman, A. M.; Cooper, F. S.; Shankweiler, D.; and Studdert-Kennedy, M. "Perception of the Speech Code." *Psychological Review* 74 (1967): 431–461.

Mason, J. "When Do Children Begin to Read: An Explanation of Four Year Old Children's

"This Book's Not Working Right."

Letter and Word-Reading Competencies."
Reading Research Quarterly 15, no. 2 (1980):
203–277.

Mattingly, I. G. "Reading, Linguistic Awareness and Language Acquisition." Paper written for IRA/University of Victoria International Reading Research Seminar on Linguistic Awareness and Learning to Read, June 1979, Victoria, British Columbia, Canada.

McNeill, D., and Lindig, K. "The Perceptual Reality of Phonemes, Syllables, Words, and Sentences." *Journal of Verbal Learning and Verbal Behavior* 12 (1973): 419–430.

Menyuk, P. "Relations Between Acquisition of Phonology and Reading." In *Aspects of Reading Acquisition*, ed. J. R. Guthrie. Baltimore: Johns Hopkins University Press, 1976.

Nelson, S., and Rollins, J. *Frosty the Snowman.* New York: Golden Press, 1975.

Rossman, F. P. "Preschoolers' Knowledge of the Symbolic Function of Written Language in Storybooks." Unpublished doctoral dissertation, Boston University, 1980.

Savin, H. "What the Child Knows About Speech When He Starts to Learn to Read." In *Language By Ear and By Eye: The Relationship Between Speech and Reading*, ed. J. F. Kavanagh and I. G. Mattingly. Cambridge, Mass.: MIT Press, 1972.

Savin, H. B., and Bever, T. G. "The Nonperceptual Reality of the Phoneme." *Journal of Verbal Learning and Verbal Behavior* 9 (1970): 295–302.

Schickedanz, J. "'Please Read that Story Again!': Exploring Relationships Between Story Reading and Learning to Read." *Young Children* 33, no. 5 (July 1978): 48–55.

Sendak, M. *Where the Wild Things Are.* New York: Harper & Row, 1963.

Sutton, M. "Readiness for Reading at the Kindergarten Level." *The Reading Teacher* 22 (1964): 234–239.

Valtin, R. "Increasing Awareness of Linguistic Awareness in Research on Beginning Reading and Dyslexia." Paper presented at the International Reading Association/University of Victoria International Reading Research Seminar on Linguistic Awareness and Learning to Read, June 1979, Victoria, British Columbia, Canada.

Williams, J. "Commentary on Research in Reading Acquisition." In *Aspects of Reading Acquisition*, ed. J. T. Guthrie. Baltimore: Johns Hopkins University Press, 1976.

Preparation of this article was supported in part by Grant No. G6007-605-403 from the U.S. Office of Education, Right to Read Effort, to the Boston University Preelementary Reading Improvement Collaborative.

Elizabeth M. Goetz

Early Reading
A Developmental Approach

Teachers have known for years that very young children sometimes begin to read on their own or with help from family members. This common knowledge has been verified by research (Durkin 1966). Early readers—whether self-taught or trained—who have the same IQ's as nonreading peers maintain their head start in reading throughout the elementary years, given appropriate curriculum adjustment (Durkin 1966; McKee and Brezinski 1966). This acceleration in reading, in turn, enhances their performance in other school subjects. The University of Kansas Child Development Laboratory therefore concluded that, if feasible, early reading might be a desirable curriculum option for children as young as three or four years old, provided they are ready.

Any program for teaching children to read at these early ages is likely to raise some eyebrows. Two points must be emphasized: Participation in the program is strictly voluntary with each child and is carefully geared to the readiness of the particular child. It is not our objective to promote the teaching of reading in early

Elizabeth M. Goetz, Ph.D., is Director, Child Development Laboratory, and Associate Professor, Department of Human Development, University of Kansas, Lawrence, Kansas.

childhood programs generally or to induce others to accelerate satisfactory existing schedules for reading instruction. Instead, we are simply interested in finding out what, if anything, might be done to assist the young child who manifests a readiness for reading by self-instruction or requested instruction. Since the effectiveness of such programs is still in the exploratory stage (Robison 1977, p. 139), we feel that a laboratory such as ours is making a contribution.

Interest in early reading has been developing rapidly (Allen 1978; Hunsberger 1982; Popp 1975) and probably will accelerate with the federal mandate (P.L. 94-142) that individualized education programs (IEP's) be designed for the gifted as well as the handicapped. Preschool teachers have been advised to handle the teaching of reading in a responsible manner ("Reading and Pre-First Grade" 1977). They also have been warned to provide reading instruction befitting each child's developmental stage rather than blindly following commercial reading programs that do not consider the individual child's learning style, deficits, and assets.

Unfortunately, few early childhood specialists have been trained to assess reading readiness or teach beginning reading in a manner suited to the developmental level of very young children. The instruction of these children has concentrated on enhancing the child's total development: social, physical, intellectual, and emotional (Leeper, Dales, Skipper, and Witherspoon 1971; Robison 1977; Stevens and King 1976). Intellectual development is a part of the total child at an early age, not something to be set aside for later years. From the beginning, one ought to teach as much as each child, as an individual, is comfortably, naturally, and rightfully ready for—even reading (Hymes 1973). Care must be taken of course to avoid any threats, punishment, or emotional pressures to induce a child to learn to read (Smethurst 1975).

Children are never totally ready or unready to read. Reading "readiness," after all, is nothing more than reading instruction in its early stages. Consequently, reading "readiness" and beginning reading are taught simultaneously (Durkin 1976). The same activity may be used as a readiness activity for one child and as a reading activity for another. This versatile method of teaching reading is seldom part of formal early childhood teacher training (see Emery 1975, p. 51).

Research on appropriate reading methods has dealt primarily with children of kindergarten age and older (Chall 1967; Goetz 1977; Stauffer 1967). The purpose of this article is to describe recommended procedures for assessing reading readiness and the teaching of beginning reading for three- and four-year-olds that have been used successfully at the University of Kansas Child Development Laboratory. These procedures might provide the basis for future research that may ultimately provide a data-based methodology.

Reading Readiness Assessment

Commercial tests do not adequately assess reading readiness, in part because they do not take into account the developmental level of very young children: (1) their need for informality; (2) their need for praise; (3) their need for active involvement; (4) their limited language skills; (5) their need for individualized instruction; (6) their lack of pencil and paper test-taking skills; and (7) their inability to process complex stimuli on a complex background.

Readiness tests are generally given to children in groups and focus on vocabulary, visual discrimination, and auditory discrimination. These three abilities usually are assessed by having the children mark the correct picture on a page with several rows of pictures, some of which may be foreign to the very young child's experience. The child may be asked to mark the correct picture for a spoken word, for a match of an original picture, or for a picture's label that rhymes with or has the same beginning sound as the original picture (Durkin 1976, p. 70). Such tests results predict future reading achievement only 16 to 34 percent better than chance (Ladd 1978; Olson and Rosen 1971).

Teacher judgment often may be more reliable than such test scores for predicting reading achievement (Sparberg 1973). Emery (1975, Chapter 6) has suggested an informal reading readiness assessment that we have used along with several innovations of our own. His primary indicators of reading readiness are: (1) oral vocabulary; (2) reading curiosity; (3) auditory discrimination as it relates to clear speech and learning letter sounds; and (4) visual discrimination of letters.

Vocabulary may be assessed by observing and listening to the child in the natural early childhood setting for several weeks. While Emery considers a good working vocabulary to consist of 1,540 words, teachers are not expected to count the words but just to get an overall impression. A child who talks freely and has a good oral vocabulary is easily recognized by an experienced teacher. Reading curiosity is judged by observing the child during the school day: Does the child seem interested in books, look at books, and ask questions about letters and words? The environment, of course, should provide opportunities for reading curiosity to occur.

Auditory discrimination is assessed informally, in part, through everyday conversation. If a child's speech is clear, it is an indication that the child is hearing exact sounds and can reproduce them. A short test is conducted on an individual basis to determine if a child can learn the correct sounds for single letters and groups of letters. For visual discrimination, another short test is conducted on an individual basis to determine if the child can determine whether two letters are the

The teacher works with the child on a one-to-one basis, thereby stimulating a feeling of success and excitement about reading for each child.

same or different. Usually, auditory discrimination tests on sounds and the visual discrimination tests on letters are conducted within a regular activity involving letters (e.g., grocery store with numerous foods labeled, storytime with books, etc.).

To Emery's (1975) primary indicators, our staff added tests for left-to-right and top-to-bottom visual tracking of words printed on a page and for sound blending. For tracking, the child is asked to show with his or her finger in what direction words are read on a printed page. For blending, the child is given two sounds accompanied by matching letters and asked what sound is made when the two sounds are put together.

All these readiness tests are either observations in the natural environment of the program or individual tests that do not require pencil and paper test-taking skills. In the case of individual tests, there is much teacher help and encouragement. When the child does not know, the answer is given and rehearsed, and the assessment then becomes a learning activity. Observation-type tests and individual tests given by friendly, helpful teachers eliminate test anxiety and provide the child with relaxed opportunities to demonstrate knowledge while actively involved in situations that tend to keep motivational level high. Individual tests also allow the teacher to note subtle characteristics that might not be apparent in groups.

Emery (1975) also listed secondary indicators of reading readiness: (1) attention; (2) compliance; (3) memory as it relates to the general idea of a story; (4) concepts such as top/bottom, up/down, open/closed, etc.; (5) writing in terms of copying straight lines, circles, etc.; and (6) page turning. Our staff found it is not necessary to test specifically for these secondary indicators. Instead, with these indicators in mind, we observe the children during typical activities that provide opportunities to demonstrate these skills.

After considering these observations and tests for primary and secondary indicators and conferring with parents who contribute their own observations, our teaching team can intelligently decide what type of reading instruction a child is best-suited for.

Reading Instruction

During the assessment for reading readiness, all children are introduced to our organic reading center, one of the free-play options along with the blocks, art, concepts, science, and house centers. This reading center is a modified version of Ashton-Warner's organic reading program with Maori children in New Zealand which is described in *Teacher* (1963). It is based on the reading of words that grow out of the child's own life experience. Each child selects the key vocabulary to learn to read; thus, the words were *organic* or *natural* for that child.

There have been two doctoral dissertations on the key vocabulary (Barnette 1971; Duquette 1970), and research is currently being conducted with five- to seven-year-olds in Vancouver, British Columbia (Wassermann 1978). Not only do key vocabulary children learn to read and show growth in language skill development, but compared to control subjects, they show a more favorable attitude toward reading. The positive results of Ashton-Warner's (1963) experience and the subsequent research, along with Durkin's (1976) advice that the same activity could be used either for reading "readiness" or instruction, inspired us to devise

an organic reading program that would be appropriate for three- and four-year-old children.

The organic reading center, tucked in a quiet corner of our classroom, consists of an electric primary (large type) typewriter on a child-sized table, two small chairs (one for the child and one for the teacher), a pack of 3″ × 5″ cards, crayons, each child's reading envelope, and a data collection notebook in which the teacher records each child's words, sentences, and performance in reviewing them along with anecdotal notes. The teacher works with the child on a one-to-one basis, thereby stimulating a feeling of success and excitement about reading for each child. Children are free to come into the area or not, but only one child may be there at a time. The reading procedure involves the following steps:

1. The child is asked, "What word would you like to learn to read today?"
2. The teacher types the word given by the child on the middle-top of the 3″ × 5″ card.
3. The teacher and child read this word together with the child underlining from left to right.
4. The child is asked, "What can you tell me about this word?" (The teacher may help the child make a sentence using that word.)
5. The teacher types the sentence in the middle of another 3″ × 5″ card with the words four spaces apart.
6. The teacher and child read this sentence together, with the child underlining the words from left to right. The period at the end of the sentence is pointed out to help the child understand its significance as marking a completion of thought.
7. The child is asked to take the card with the word only and slide it under

Goetz

the sentence to find the matching word.

8. When the child finds the matching words, the words are read and then framed with the child's hands.

9. The teacher asks follow-up, open-ended questions related to the sentence to help build inferential and analytical comprehension skills in the child.

10. The child is asked to draw a picture on the front or back of each card to remind the child of the word.

11. Finally, the cards are put in the child's reading envelope to be reviewed before beginning a new word the next time the child comes into the center.

12. When a child has four words, the teacher and child make up a story with them. The story is typed, and they read it together with the child underlining from left to right. Individual words that have been incorporated into the story are no longer reviewed, but the story may be reviewed if the child chooses.

13. The child takes the reading packet home over the weekend every other week and returns it the following Monday.

As Durkin has advised, this reading procedure is carried out with many variations depending on the child's developmental level determined from skills evaluated informally during the first few weeks in the program. For a child with a sparse vocabulary, this procedure becomes primarily a language activity since emphasis is on oral expression rather than reading typed words. A child who hesitates to provide a word with an accompanying sentence is helped with such questions as, "What is your favorite color? What things are that color?" or perhaps a more thought-provoking question such as, "What did you do over the weekend?"

or "Did you hear the thunderstorm last night?" If a child is having difficulty reading the typed words, the teacher reads the words for the child to prevent the situation from becoming embarrassing or painful. But even a child with a poor vocabulary in this oral variation of organic reading is learning something about reading. Words are simply speech written down.

A child with normal language development who readily says words and sentences to be typed and read is allowed to have as many words and sentences as desired—within reason, of course. Unlike the child with weak language, this child often says, "Let me read it myself."

Though organic reading for these three- and four-year-olds is basically sight word recognition, some children are beginning to learn phonic sounds selected from their organic words and the blending of sounds. The teacher tries to direct these children to learn very different consonant phonic sounds first and then short vowels. Long vowels are taught last with the rationale that this is another way of pronouncing those letters that formerly were learned as short vowels. Yet, the basic rules of phonics have not been taught since these children have not seemed ready for such structured activities.

Some children ask to type their own words, sentences, and stories and are allowed to do so. Some ask to write their words, by hand, and this also is allowed with the teacher providing a handwritten model. Some children stop the matching, framing, and underlining of words on their own, without any adverse effect on learning. Some type messages to take home such as "Keep out, this room is private." Some children even use their reading for therapeutic purposes. For example, one said, "My sister isn't nice because she kicks and bites me." These situations are supported by talking about it as well as reading the typed sentence.

Whatever the child's developmental level, an appropriate variation of organic reading can expose each child to concepts of a word, a sentence, a story, and left-to-right and top-to-bottom tracking. All children are encouraged to increase their attention span through an activity that entices them to continue. What is more interesting than talking and reading about topics of one's own choice? Most important, all children are introduced to the reading process as meaningful communication, since organic reading is based on each child's language aptitude, rather than on rote learning of isolated word and phonics sounds. This approach is supported by findings of reading specialists (e.g., Giordano 1978; Goodman 1976; Pflaum-Connor 1978; Smith 1971) that it is especially important for beginning readers to understand the communication aspect of reading.

Although our reading program probably could have been implemented with handwritten words and sentences, we found that use of the electric primary typewriter has significant advantages. Typing words and sentences can be accomplished quickly to avoid having the young child wait around without active involvement. Since the type is more legible than some teacher's handwriting, reading is not hampered by variations in lettering. Children who want to type their words can do so easily (whereas individual handwriting skills might otherwise rule out writing) which is very helpful in learning letter order.

Conclusion

The teaching of reading to young children should be an important concern. The informal reading assessment and organic reading procedure presented here represent a modest proposal for such instruction of three- and four-year-olds. Looking

© Gary Mason

What is more interesting than talking and reading about topics of one's own choice? Most important, all children are introduced to the reading process as meaningful communication.

Goetz

back on our experience, it seems that Emery's (1975) informal readiness assessment combined with our own innovations provide a reliable guide for determining each child's developmental level in reading. And Durkin's (1976) advice was sound—the same type of reading activity may be used in a competent manner for "readiness" or reading instruction by varying it to match each child's stage of development.

For us, the procedure seems to be working extremely well, but research is needed to affirm its validity. To date, such research has been hampered by unavailability of standardized reading tests appropriate for very young children and the difficulty of making certain that each organic word chosen by the child is not already in the child's reading vocabulary; apparent reading progress could be contaminated by known words. But despite the present lack of supporting data, we know our children enjoy coming to the organic reading center and are becoming readers by their own choice. They look forward to taking their reading envelopes home to share with their parents. In fact, we need more reading teachers and typewriters to handle all the children all the time they want to participate. It is hoped that other practitioners will find these procedures useful and will share their techniques for assessing and teaching reading.

References

Allen, K. E. "Reading and the Young Child: Ancient and Recent History." Paper presented at the annual meeting of the Midwest Association for the Education of Young Children, Dearborn, Mich., March 1978.

Ashton-Warner, S. *Teacher*. New York: Simon and Schuster, 1963.

Barnette, E. "The Effect of Key Vocabulary upon Attitudes Toward Reading and Self." Doctoral dissertation, Arizona State University, 1971.

Chall, J. *Learning to Read: The Great Debate*. New York: McGraw-Hill, 1967.

Duquette, R. "An Experimental Study Comparing the Effects of a Specific Program of Sight Vocabulary upon Reading and Writing Achievement of Selected First and Second Grade Children." Doctoral dissertation, Arizona State University, 1970.

Durkin, D. *Children Who Read Early*. New York: Teachers College Press, 1966.

Durkin, D. *Teaching Young Children to Read*. Boston: Allyn and Bacon, 1976.

Emery, D. G. *Teach Your Preschooler to Read*. New York: Simon and Schuster, 1975.

Giordano, G. "Convergent Research on Language and Teaching Reading." *Exceptional Children* 44, no. 8 (1978): 604-613.

Goetz, E. M. "The Traditional and Operant Approaches to Reading Research." Unpublished manuscript, University of Kansas, 1977.

Goodman, K. S. "Behind the Eye: What Happens in Reading." In *Theoretical Models and Processes in Reading*, ed. H. Singer and R. B. Ruddell. 2nd ed. Newark, Del.: International Reading Association, 1976.

Hunsberger, M. "Reading Investigations: What Directions?" *Journal of Reading* 25, no. 7 (April 1982): 629–633.

Hymes, J. L. "Teaching Reading to the Under-Six Age: A Child Development Point of View." In *Perspectives on Elementary Reading*, ed. R. Karlin. New York: Harcourt Brace Jovanovich, 1973.

Ladd, E. M. "Informal and Formal Screening and Assessment." Paper presented at the annual meeting of the International Reading Association, Houston, Tx., May 1978.

Leeper, S. H.; Dales, R. J.; Skipper, D. S.; and Witherspoon, R. L. *Good Schools for Young Children*. New York: Macmillan, 1971.

McKee, P., and Brezinski, J. E. "The Effectiveness of Teaching Reading in Kindergarten." Cooperative Research Project No. 5-0371. Denver, Colo.: Denver Public Schools, 1966.

Olson, A. V., and Rosen, C. L. "Exploration of the Structure of Selected Reading Readiness Tests." Paper presented at the annual meeting of the American Educational Research Association, New York, February 1971.

Pflaum-Conner, S. *The Development of Language and Reading in Young Children*. Columbus, Ohio: Merrill, 1978.

Popp, H. M. "Current Practices in the Teaching of Beginning Reading." In *Towards a Literate*

Society, ed. J. B. Carroll and J. S. Chall. New York: McGraw-Hill, 1975.

"Reading and Pre-First Grade." A joint statement of concerns about present practices in pre-first grade reading instruction and recommendations for improvement. Newark, Del.: International Reading Association, 1977.

Robison, H. F. *Exploring Teaching in Early Childhood Education.* Boston: Allyn and Bacon, 1977.

Smethurst, W. *Teaching Young Children to Read at Home.* New York: McGraw-Hill, 1975.

Smith, F. *Understanding Reading: A Psycholinguistic Analysis of Reading and Learning.* New York: Holt, Rinehart & Winston, 1971.

Sparberg, N. Z. "A Quick Teacher-Administered Screening Test to Predict Future Academic Failure in Kindergarten Children." Paper presented at the annual meeting of American Educational Research Association, New Orleans, February/March 1973.

Stauffer, R. O. *The First Grade Reading Studies Findings of Individual Investigations.* Newark, Del.: International Reading Association, 1967.

Stevens, J. H., and King, E. W. *Administering Early Childhood Education Programs.* Boston: Little Brown, 1976.

Wassermann, S. "Key Vocabulary: Impact on Beginning Reading." *Young Children* 33, no. 4 (1978): 33-38.

Bilingualism in Early Childhood
by Eugene E. Garcia

To a large bilingual segment (Mexican-American, Chinese, Haitian, Native American, Puerto Rican, Cajun, Vietnamese, etc.) of this nation's population (U.S. Commission on Civil Rights 1975), the issues surrounding bilingualism are of specific interest; to teachers and those individuals studying language acquisition (McNeil 1966), such issues are of more general interest. Other reviews of bilingualism and second language acquisition have dealt with definitions, linguistic overlap or "interference," cognitive interaction, and theoretical issues related to these areas (see MacNamara 1967; Riegel 1968; John and Horner 1971; Vildomec 1971; McLaughlin 1977; Cummins 1979). This review will discuss some of the same issues in light of more recent research and applied information specific to bilingual development in young children.

Early childhood bilingualism

Any definition of bilingualism must address our existing linguistic diversity (Valdes-Fallis 1979), but to consider only the linguistic domain would be an error. Thorough definitions of bilingualism must also consider the cognitive and social domains because the acquisition of language(s) coincides with identifiable

This is one of a regular series of columns edited by Joseph H. Stevens, Ph.D., Associate Professor, Department of Early Childhood Education, Georgia State University, Atlanta.

periods of cognitive development within significant social contexts.

Early childhood bilingualism suggests the acquisition of two languages during the first five years of life and includes the following conditions:

(1) Children are able to *comprehend and/or produce* some aspects of each language beyond the ability to discriminate that either one language or another is being spoken. Many combinations of linguistic competence fall within the boundaries of bilingualism from the child who has memorized one or more lexical utterances in a second language to the child fluent in two or more languages.

(2) Children are *exposed naturally to the two systems of languages* as they are used in the form of social interaction during early childhood. This condition requires a substantive bilingual environment in the child's first three to five years of life. In many cases, such exposure comes from within a nuclear or an extended family network, but this need not be the case (visitors and extended visits to foreign countries are examples of alternative environments).

(3) The *simultaneous character of development* must be apparent in both languages as contrasted with the case of a native speaker of one language who, after mastery of that language, begins to acquire a second language.

Bilingual development

Developmental research

Within the first few years of life, drastic changes in linguistic competence can clearly be identified (Menyuk 1971). Research in this field has been voluminous and theoretically varied (Lenneberg and Lenneberg 1975; DeVilliers and DeVilliers 1978). The main focus has centered on acquisition of a single language (Brown 1973) although more recent research has employed comparative linguistic analysis of children who are learning different languages (Bowerman 1975; Braine 1976). However, very little systematic investigation has been undertaken of children who are acquiring more than one language simultaneously during the early part of their lives.

In many societies throughout the world, children learn more than one language form. Sorensen (1967) described the acquisition of three to four languages by young children who live in the northwest Amazon area of South America. In this Brazilian-Colombian border region, the Tukano tribal language serves as the *lingua franca*, but there continue to exist some 25 clearly distinguishable linguistic groups. In the United States, Skrabanek (1970) noted the continued acquisition and support of both English and Spanish among young children in the Southwest for the last hundred years.

Research with bilinguals is not a recent subarea of linguistic or psychological interest. Ronjat (1913) studied the

Eugene E. Garcia, Ph.D., is Associate Professor of Psychology and Chicano Studies at the University of California, Santa Barbara, California. A former Associate Professor of Psychology at the University of Utah, Dr. Garcia has done research with Spanish/English-speaking bilingual children and further research in language development.

development of French and German in his son. Finding few deleterious effects of bilingual development, he attributed such positive outcomes to the fact that one parent consistently spoke French and the other German. Pavlovitch (1920) also recorded the development of two languages, French and Serbian, in his son. Similarly, languages were separated across individuals and reportedly developed simultaneously with minimal confusion. Geissler (1938), a teacher of foreign languages, observed young children acquire up to four languages simultaneously without apparent difficulty. However, Smith's study (1935) of missionary families who spoke English and Chinese noted difficulty during simultaneous acquisition. This difficulty was most apparent in the language-mixing character of some children's speech.

Leopold conducted one of the first systematic investigations of bilingual acquisition in young children (1939, 1947, 1949a, 1949b), by studying his daughter's simultaneous acquisition of English and German. Exposed to both languages during infancy, she seemed to weld them into one system during initial language production periods. For instance, early language forms were characterized by free mixing. As she grew older, the use of English and German grammatical forms developed independently.

More recent studies have addressed several issues relevant to bilingual acquisition. Carrow (1971 and 1972) restricted her study to the receptive domain of young bilingual Mexican-American children in the Southwest. In one analysis children aged three years, ten months to six years, nine months from bilingual Spanish/English home environments were administered the Auditory Test for Language Comprehension. The test consists of a series of pictures representing referential categories that can be signaled by words, morphological constructions, grammatical categories, and syntactic structures, including verbs, adjectives, adverbs, nouns, pronouns, morphological endings, prepositions, interrogatives, and syntax complexity in both languages. Carrow (1971) reported the following results:

(1) Linguistically, children were heterogeneous; some scored better in one language than another; others were equal in both.

(2) A greater proportion of children scored higher in English than in Spanish.

(3) Older children scored higher on these measures in both languages. (Spanish was not used as a medium of instruction for children who were in educational programs.)

In a cross-sectional comparison of English comprehension among monolingual English and bilingual Spanish/English children aged three years, ten months to six years, nine months, Carrow (1972) found a positive developmental trend for both Spanish and English in the bilingual children. Additionally, the bilingual children tended to score lower than the monolingual children on measures of English from age three years, ten months to age five years, nine months. For the final age comparison group (six years, nine months), bilingual and monolingual children did not differ significantly on these same measures. The combined results seem to indicate that at the receptive level, Spanish/English bilingual children were (a) increasing their competence in both Spanish and English; (b) heterogeneous as a group with most favoring one language (typically English) over another; and (c) lagging behind monolingual children in their early acquisition of English but eventually catching up. Carrow's studies were only at the receptive level, used specific test procedures, and restricted the popula-

tion of study to one regional population. While the conclusions are necessarily limited, they do offer some initial empirical information relevant to the study of early childhood bilingual development.

With respect to expressive development, Padilla and Liebman (1975) studied Spanish/English acquisition in two 3-year-old bilingual children and recorded linguistic interactions of the children over a five-month period (see Brown 1973). An analysis of several dependent linguistic variables (phonological, grammatical, syntactic, and semantic characteristics) showed gains in both languages although several English forms were in evidence while similar Spanish forms were not. Padilla and Liebman also discussed the differentiation of linguistic systems at phonological, vocabulary, and syntactic levels:

> (T)he appropriate use of both languages even in mixed utterances was evident; that is, correct word order was preserved. For example, there were no occurrences of "raining esta" or "a es baby," but there was evidence for such utterances as "esta raining" and "es a baby." There was also an absence of the redundance of unnecessary words which might tend to confuse meaning. (p. 51)

Garcia (1980a) analyzed developmental data related to the acquisition of Spanish and English for Spanish/English bilingual three- and four-year-old children and the acquisition of English for a group of matched English-only speakers. The results of that study can be summarized as follows:

(1) Acquisition of both Spanish and English was evident at complex morphological (grammatical) and syntactic levels for Spanish/English four-year-old children.

(2) For the bilingual children studied, English was more advanced, based on the quantity and quality of obtained morphological and syntactic instances of language productions.

(3) There was no quantitative or qualitative difference between Spanish/English bilingual children and matched English-only controls on English language productions.

Huerta (1977), in making a longitudinal analysis of a Spanish/English bilingual two-year-old child, found a similar pattern of continuous Spanish/English development, although identifiable stages appeared in which one language forged ahead of the other. Moreover, Huerta noted the significant occurrence of mixed language utterances which made use of both Spanish and English lexicon as well as Spanish and English morphology. In all such cases, these mixed linguistic utterances were well formed and communicative.

Garcia (1980b), in a national study of bilingual children four, five, and six years of age, discovered regional differences in the relative occurrence of switched language utterances. Bilingual Spanish/English children from Texas, Arizona, Colorado, and New Mexico showed higher (15 to 20 percent) incidences of language-switched utterances than children from California, Illinois, New York, or Florida, especially at prekindergarten levels. These findings suggest that some children may very well develop an "interlanguage" before the acquisition of two independent language systems later in development.

Although the specific nature of bilingual development and its links to environmental variables remain unavailable, tentative findings are capsulized here:

(1) The acquisition of more than one language during early childhood is a documented phenomenon.

(2) The acquisition of two languages can be parallel but need not be. The qualitative character of one language may lag behind, surge

Does learning more than one language influence the rate and/or quality of acquisition of each language?

Michael D. Sullivan

Garcia

ahead, or develop equally with the other language.

(3) The acquisition of two languages may very well result in the child's development of an interlanguage, incorporating the aspects (lexicon, morphology, and syntax) of both languages.

(4) The acquisition of two languages does not developmentally hamper the acquisition of either language.

Research on linguistic interference

Does learning more than one language influence the rate and/or quality of acquisition of each language? A second popular form of research has considered the interactive influence of multiple language acquisition. When referring to the interactive phenomenon between languages of the bilingual person, the term *linguistic transfer* is often used. The term has gained multiple meanings as shown by its various modifiers: linguistic interference, psychological interference, and educational interference (Saville and Troike 1971). Experimental studies of specific instances of transfer or lack of it are available with bilingual children.

Evans (1974) compared word-pair discriminations and word imitations in Spanish and English for monolingual English and bilingual Spanish/English children. Elementary school children were asked to discriminate between words containing English phonemes considered difficult for Spanish speakers. (Examples are the phonemes /b/ and /v/ which are clearly separate in English but not so clearly separate in Spanish.) Additionally, children were requested to imitate a series of words in each language which were also considered difficult. The bilingual children did not differ from the monolingual children on any of the English tasks, but as expected, the bilingual children scored significantly higher than the monolingual children on all Spanish-language tasks.

Garcia and Trujillo (1979) found similar results when they compared bilingual (Spanish/English) and monolingual (English) three- through seven-year-old children on high-error risk phonemes in Spanish that adult Spanish speakers mispronounce and simple to complex syntactic forms (sentences containing plural and possessive morphemes). The bilingual children did not differ from the monolingual children on English imitation tasks where both groups scored near 100 percent correct; but they made significantly fewer errors than English speakers on Spanish tasks. This was the case across all age levels. These studies suggest that negative transfer at the phonological level in young bilingual children is nonexistent.

In the same study (Garcia and Trujillo 1979), however, complex Spanish sentences which involved adjective placement were not imitated correctly by the bilingual subjects. Complex English sentences of this type presented no significant problem for either bilingual or English-only children. [Adjective placement in Spanish (pato *azul*) differs from adjective placement in English (*blue* duck). Therefore, it is likely that transfer (positive and/or negative) is a possibility as syntactic complexity increases and as differences in syntactic structure are involved across the languages of the bilingual person.]

An earlier report (Garcia 1977) indicated transfer in the form of language substitution during the acquisition of prepositional labels in the weaker language of the bilingual. In this study, Spanish/English bilingual children could provide the correct prepositional label in one language (first language) but not the other (second language). Language substitution occurred when subjects were taught to label prepositions in the second language. Therefore, transfer may be an indication of failure to discriminate the language deemed socially appropriate. Such transfer effects are more sociolinguistic than linguistic in character.

On the other hand, Dulay and Burt (1972 and 1973) found few linguistic errors in English that could be attributed to children's first language even when the child's first language varied from an Asian to a Western European derivative. Dulay and Burt concluded that identifiable English linguistic errors were much like those of young children acquiring English as a first and only language.

Studies in the field of linguistic transfer with young bilingual children can be used to support one or more of the following contradictory conclusions concerning the acquisition of two languages during early childhood:

(1) A linguistic transfer phenomenon is evident in which the specific structures of the dominant language influence the developmental quality of the less dominant language.

(2) A linguistic transfer phenomenon is evident in which the structures of the two independent languages influence the developmental quality of both languages, frequently producing a third identifiable interlanguage.

(3) The developmental character of the bilingual person is not significantly influenced by the simultaneous linguistic development of two languages; the developmental character of each language is similar to that of a native speaker of either language.

The specific character of transfer between the languages of the bilingual person continues to be an area of significant research interest and controversy. It would appear inappropriate at this time to make any other conclusion.

Linguistic input and social context

As Riegel (1968) suggests, any chronological record of children's linguistic output coupled with linguistic input information would allow an important correlational analysis of language development. Although extensive information remains unavailable, some systematic data are becoming available for monolingual English children (Brown and Fraser 1964; Schacter, Kirshner, Klips, Friedericks, and Sanders 1974). Unfortunately, little information of this caliber is available for young bilingual children.

Although empirical data are minimal, some cautious notions of bilingual input seem justifiable. If one considers the eventual bilingual character of the child, it seems appropriate to suggest that some percentage of the child's linguistic information is in one language and some other percentage is in a second language. The acquisition of either language is probably tied to the degree of linguistic input for each language.

This simple relationship must be qualified due to several theoretical and empirical considerations. Edelman (1969) analyzed the differential use of Spanish and English vocabulary in Puerto Rican children on a word-naming task as a function of the different contexts (school, home, neighborhood, church) the children were asked to describe. Skrabanek (1970) in a study of Spanish maintenance among Mexican-Americans, found that the use of Spanish differed as a function of the age of the speaker. Older subjects spoke more often in Spanish although both young and old alike used Spanish a substantial proportion of the time. Kuo (1974) concluded that the differential use of language by Chinese-American children was related to age and other socialization variables.

These data imply that linguistic input may differ for each language across both physical and social settings. Of course, the quality of the input may also differ. This variability of input may predictably influence bilingual development. For instance, Harris and Hassemer (1972)

Garcia

found that sentence length among bilingual children was affected by models who used different levels of syntactic complexity.

Recent sociolinguistic formulations of code-switching (the alternating use of more than one language by the bilingual person), further elucidate the importance of considering more than the simple notion of linguistic input. Zentella (1978) found that eight-year-old Puerto Rican children were already proficient in using switched utterances to provide emphasis and elaboration. Lindholm and Padilla (1979) have reported similar findings for three- and four-year-old bilingual Mexican-American children.

Useful accounts of early childhood bilingualism must therefore address more than the child's linguistic ability by considering certain determinants in the child's surrounding environment:

(1) linguistic and metalinguistic information important for the development of each language
(2) rules of social language use for each language
(3) linguistic and sociolinguistic rules governing code-switching
(4) the prestige of the language and consequently the motivation to learn-maintain or ignore-dissipate languages differentially

Such an analysis is most needed within the bilingual arena, for it holds much promise in providing information about bilingual acquisition and is important to the understanding of language acquisition in general. As McNeil (1966) has indicated, differential development of specific language features in bilingual children may very well signal important relationships between that development and the cognitive and environmental variables related to development.

How do the child's environment and culture affect language acquisition?

Fred Forbes

Intelligence, cognition, and bilingualism

Based on information relating childhood bilingualism to decreased performance on standardized intelligence tests, it is tempting to make a causal statement linking bilingualism to depressed intelligence. Although this pervasive negative relationship characterizes much early work (Darcy 1953), the methodological problems of such studies are serious; and thus any conclusions concerning bilingualism and intellectual functioning as measured by standardized individual or group intelligence tests are extremely tentative in nature (Darcy 1963).

With the general shift away from standardized measures of intelligence, the information processing of bilingual children as it relates to specific areas of cognitive development has received attention. Leopold (1939), in one of the first investigations of bilingual acquisition, noticed a general cognitive plasticity in his young bilingual subject. He suggested that linguistic flexibility (in the form of bilingualism) generalized to nonlinguistic, cognitive tasks. Peal and Lambert (1962) in a summary of their work with French/English bilingual subjects and English monolingual subjects suggested that the intellectual experience of acquiring two languages contributed to an advantageous mental flexibility, superior concept formation, and a generally diversified set of mental abilities.

Padilla (1977) reasoned that bilinguals must be cognitively advanced because they are able to process information in more than one language. Additionally, many bilinguals are capable of understanding a problem statement in one language, solving that problem, and producing the answer in a second language. For example, Keats and Keats (1974) observed that German/English bilingual subjects who did not exemplify weight conservation were trained to conserve in one of the two languages. Results from English and German post-tests indicated that the concept was acquired in both languages. This suggests the possible increased flexibility of bilingual people during conceptual acquisition.

Other relevant evidence is provided by Feldman and Shen (1971), who studied different responses between Spanish/English bilingual and English monolingual subjects across three separate cognitive tasks. An object constancy task required subjects to identify a cup after it had been smashed in their presence. The second task required the subjects either to label familiar items with nonsense words or to switch the names of the items. The third, an associative sentence task, required the subjects to use familiar, nonsense, and switched labels from the second task in a sentence describing a relationship between the items. Results indicated significantly increased cognitive flexibility for the bilingual subjects.

Ianco-Worral (1972) compared matched bilingual subjects (Afrikanos/English) and monolingual (either Afrikanos or English) subjects on separation of word-sound, word-meaning tasks. Comparison of scores indicated that the bilingual subjects concentrated more on attaching meaning to words rather than sounds. Other work in this area has been conducted by Carringer (1974) and Cummins and Gulatson (1974).

In an attempt to identify more specifically the relationship between cognition and bilingualism, Cummins (1979) proposed that children who achieve balance proficiency in two languages are cognitively advantaged in comparison with monolingual children and that children who do not achieve balance proficiency (but who are immersed in a bilingual environment) are cognitively disadvantaged in comparison to monolingual and balanced-proficient bilinguals. This interactionist position attempts to account for the success of French immersion bilingual programs for English-speaking children in Canada and the failure of English immersion programs for Spanish-speaking children in the United States.

MacNab (1979) took issue with this interactionist conceptualization on several grounds. First, the data are primarily Canadian and have been criticized for subject selection criteria. It is likely that only high achieving and highly intelligent children were selected for inclusion in the bilingual education groupings. Therefore, cognitive advantages already existed prior to bilingual instruction and most likely contributed to the success of bilingual development, not vice versa. Moreover, the successful subjects came from majority, middle, or high socioeconomic strata where education is valued, and learning a second language is openly rewarded. Learning a second language under such conditions is quite different from learning under conditions dictated by economic depression as well as social and psychological repression of a minority language and culture. Individual differences in intellectual functioning, combined with the support/nonsupport of the social context for acquiring linguistic and academic skills, appear to be the primary factors for differences in bilingual and monolingual performance on cognitive measures.

An additional note of caution is warranted in attempting to make direct causal statements between bilingualism and cognition. Ramirez and Castañeda's work (1974) highlighted the potentially strong relationship between specific cultural experiences and cognitive style. In young children, bilingualism and biculturalism are easily confounded. The study of the relationship of cultural differences to psychological processes has only begun (Price-Williams 1975); yet any researcher concerned with bilingualism and cognition must be aware of this relationship. Any detailed conclusions concerning the bilingual character of children and their cognitive functioning must remain tentative. It is true that

(1) bilingual children have been found to score both higher and lower than monolingual children on specific and general measures of cognitive development, intelligence, and school achievement;

(2) balanced bilingual children have outperformed monolingual children and unbalanced bilingual children on specific cognitive tasks; and

(3) hypotheses relating bilingualism to cognitive and intellectual functioning have been proposed (Darcy 1953 and 1963; Cummins 1979).

Bilingual education in early childhood

Educational programs for linguistic minority children have taken various forms. Two extreme categories of bilingual education endeavors can be identified by the nonexistence or existence of two languages within the formal curriculum.

Immersion programs

These programs are exemplified by the Canadian model (Lambert and Tucker 1972), which involved the exclusive use of the student's second language within the formal educational curriculum. The students were treated as if they were native speakers of the second language. According to Lambert and Tucker, this program (in French for English speakers), was an overall educational success as measured by common academic indices: The children acquired both English and French linguistic skills and did not differ from monolingual English children (attending English language schools) or monolingual French children (attending French language schools) on various measures of linguistic, academic, and intellectual functioning. These results are clearly in conflict with the findings of similar immersion efforts in the United States. Prior to the 1967 bilingual legislation (P.L. 90-247), the United States educational policy with respect to linguistic minority groups could be described as immersion.

Non-immersion programs

These programs use both the native language and the second language (English) in the curriculum. Most often, instruction begins in the native language and is faded over a number of years into the second language. Both languages are generally valued, although the specific quantity and quality of bilingual instruction may differ dramatically in these programs.

Two models of non-immersion programs will be described here as an indication of their variability. (See Fishman and Lovaas 1970; Pacheco 1973; and Holguin 1977 for further detailed descriptions.)

Transition/ESL (English as a Second Language) programs concentrate on using the native language as a bridge to the eventual immersion of the non-English speaker in an English curriculum. Such programs have the following characteristics:

(1) A specific concern is shown for the teaching of English language in a formal sense.
(2) A remedial/compensatory (catch up) perspective is exemplified.
(3) Native language-speaking aides are extensively used in lieu of bilingual teaching staff.
(4) Native language instruction in a formal sense is nonexistent.
(5) The overall curriculum does not integrate aspects of the ESL Program. ESL instruction is taught as a separate curricular unit.

Transition/maintenance programs concern themselves with the development of two linguistic systems. They are also most likely to place importance on the general cultural attributes of the non-English-speaking community. The objectives of the programs may be (1) an eventual total English immersion, or (2) the continued development of both languages in future grades. Such programs have the following characteristics:

(1) Team teaching is employed through the pairing of monolingual English and bilingual professional staff or through single bilingual professional classroom staffing.
(2) The native language is used extensively in subject content areas.

(3) Instruction of language (both aspects of the native language and English) is most likely integrated into various subject content areas.
(4) An extensive effort is made to incorporate relevant cultural learning activities in the curriculum. These activities usually take on a multicultural characteristic.
(5) Monolingual English children are included in the class and are given instruction in the non-English-speaking children's language.
(6) Monolingual English children that are of the same ethnic group as the non-English-speaking children are encouraged to participate in an attempt to restore their native language.

The heterogeneity of bilingual programs is common to other educational curriculum areas such as language arts, mathematics, and social studies. What makes the heterogeneity significantly different is the compounded relevancy of the language(s) of instruction. Such increased diversity is most likely a function of the children themselves; interpretation of federal, state, and local mandates; school district staffing; availability of resources; and the specific prevailing community attitude toward these programs. In the United States, immersion programs are rare while both transition/ESL and transition/maintenance programs share equal popularity. Because of this heterogeneity, the evaluation of elementary bilingual programs has been a herculean task although heated discussion has been generated at the policy level (Epstein 1977).

Almost all the basic linguistic skills (phonology, morphology, syntax) of adult language as well as important personal and social attributes (self-concept, social identity, social interaction styles) are significantly influenced during the early childhood years. Consequently, one motive for early educational intervention has been the removal of potential barriers related to the development of important linguistic, psychological, and social attributes. Early childhood programs for bilingual children must recognize the linguistic and cultural character of these children. In 1975, the U.S. Commission on Civil Rights stressed that instructional staff must be able to communicate in the child's native language, and the instructional curriculum must also significantly reflect the child's native tongue:

> When language is recognized as the means for representing thought, and as the vehicle for complex thinking, the importance of allowing children to use and develop the language they know best becomes obvious. (U.S. Commission on Civil Rights 1975, p. 44)

In line with the above recommendation, the Administration for Children, Youth and Families has initiated a national effort to assist local Head Start centers to "implement sound developmental, bilingual-bicultural programs (Arenas 1978)." Efforts are under way in four areas: curriculum development, staff training, resource network development, and research and evaluation. Evaluation of these significant undertakings is not yet available, but their presence is indicative of the educational relevancy of bilingualism to early childhood. As Williams (1978) concluded, bilingual education is a natural extension of the maturing of early childhood education and will hold a prominent position in the field in future years.

Implications for early childhood education

McLaughlin's review of research (1978) led him to conclude that many **misconceptions** are prevalent with respect to language and bilingual acquisition in early childhood:

(1) The young child acquires a language more quickly and easily than an adult because the child is biologically programmed to acquire language whereas the adult is not.

(2) The younger the child, the more skilled the child will be in acquiring a second language.

(3) Second language acquisition is a qualitatively different process from first language acquisition.

(4) Interference between first and second language is an inevitable and ubiquitous part of second language acquisition.

(5) There is a single method of second language instruction that is most effective with all children.

(6) The experience of bilingualism negatively (or positively) affects the child's intellectual development, language skills, educational attainment, emotional adjustment, and/or cognitive functioning. (McLaughlin 1978, pp. 197-205)

In concluding that the above propositions are false, McLaughlin followed the strategy of any good scientist: Propositions which are extracted from empirical observation and experimentation are to be handled with extreme caution. It is possible that some or all of the above propositions are true, but to claim their truth at a time when empirical support is limited is clearly not in the best interest of future research and the applied technology of education.

Is it possible to address any bilingual education concerns? With the above caution in mind, there are some questions related to bilingual education in early childhood which deserve discussion, based on available research.

Will bilingual education efforts in early childhood negatively affect children's linguistic and cognitive development?

The research discussed here reveals that exposure to two language systems and subsequent proficiency in these two languages does not retard linguistic or cognitive development. Children who were operating at complex levels in Spanish were not retarded in English as compared to other matched monolingual English-speaking children. Moreover, bilingual preschool children did not score lower than their matched monolingual English peers on measures of cognitive development. Therefore, a bilingual experience in early childhood alone does not necessarily retard linguistic or cognitive development and may foster cognitive flexibility. Two important questions still remain: (1) How are differences in the qualitative nature of the bilingual experience related to linguistic and cognitive development? (2) How are cognitive process variables related to bilingual development?

Do bilingual education efforts in early childhood positively influence linguistic and cognitive development?

Although there is evidence of the lack of negative effects of bilingual acquisition on general linguistic development, there is no evidence of advanced linguistic development for bilingual children when compared to matched monolingual children. There is evidence that bilingual children score significantly higher on several cognitive measures than matched monolingual peers. Such measures tend to be those reflecting the ability to consider properties of the environment in a more flexible manner. Critical questions remain, however: (1) Are these advantages related to bilingualism or other potentially cultural variables associated with bilingualism? (2) Are these advantages related to proficiency levels of bilingualism? (3) Are these advantages related to the specific languages involved and specific cognitive tasks?

Should bilingual education efforts in early childhood be through *immersion, transition/ESL,* or *transition/ maintenance* programs?

There is very little evidence on which to base even the most cautious answer to this question. Certainly, previous immersion efforts have been evaluated positively for elementary school children in French/English schools in Canada (Lambert and Tucker 1972). A similar conclusion for Spanish/English elementary school children in the United States is not warranted. Prior to the formal funding of bilingual education at the national level in 1968, the English immersion program was the model for the education of language-minority children in U.S. public schools. That program has proved disastrous for those children (Carter 1970).

Data from empirical research in bilingual and cognitive development shed some light on this question. Dulay and Burt (1972 and 1973), acknowledging the low incidence of second-language errors related to native language structure, suggested that incidental teaching of a second language might prove most beneficial. That is, an immersion or transition effort which allows the child to be exposed to the second language as naturally as possible without formal language instruction seems the most effective strategy for second-language acquisition. Data presented by Garcia (1977) suggest that a formal maintenance instruction system that reinforces the native language while at the same time formally teaching a second language produces parallel development in both languages. Cummins (1979) reviewed several studies which indicated that cognitive flexibility is an attribute of only the proficient bilingual. Monolingual and unbalanced bilingual children scored significantly lower than proficient preschool bilingual children on Piagetian and traditional tests of cognitive development. Therefore, *transition/ maintenance* bilingual efforts may both enhance the acquisition of new language structures and provide advantageous cognitive benefits. Of course, sound evaluations of immersion, transition, and maintenance bilingual programs in early childhood are needed prior to reaching any conclusions concerning the adequacy or relative effectiveness of these strategies.

Still remaining are other curriculum questions: (1) Should languages be temporally and contextually separated (e.g., teacher A speaks L_1, teacher B speaks L_2; Monday and Friday L_1, Tuesday and Thursday L_2). (2) Should content areas be repeated in both languages? (3) What is the role of using transition as a curricular tool?

In conclusion, it remains difficult to speculate on the implications of bilingual research for bilingual education in early childhood. It does seem clear that bilingual experiences need not produce negative effects and may even produce positive effects. More specific conclusions have been suggested based on the research literature throughout this article. Unfortunately, more questions than answers have been generated by research. That is not as discouraging as it might seem, for such challenges will undoubtedly benefit all children who acquire the language(s) of their society during early childhood.

References

Arenas, S. "Bilingual/Bicultural Programs for Preschool Children." *Children Today* 12 (July/Aug. 1978):43-48.

Bowerman, M. "Crosslinguistic Similarities at Two Stages of Syntactic Development." In *Foundations of Language Development*, ed. E. Lenneberg and E. Lenneberg. London: UNESCO Press, 1975.

Braine, M. D. S. "Children's First Word Combinations." *Monographs of the Society for Research in Child Development*, 1976.

Brown, R. A. *A First Language: The Early Stages*. Cambridge, Mass.: Harvard University Press, 1973.

Brown, R., and Fraser, R. "The Acquisition of Syntax." In *The Acquisition of Language*, ed. U. Bellugi and R. Brown. Topeka, Kans.: Society for Research in Child Development, 1964.

Carringer, D. C. "Creative Thinking Abilities of Mexican Youth: The Relationship of Bilingualism." *Journal of Cross-Cultural Psychology* 5 (1974):492-504.

Carrow, E. "Comprehension of English and Spanish by Preschool Mexican-American Children." *Modern Language Journal* 55 (1971): 299-306.

Carrow, E. "Auditory Comprehension of English by Monolingual and Bilingual Preschool Children." *Journal of Speech and Hearing Research* 15 (1972):407-457.

Carter, T. *Mexican Americans in School: A History of Educational Neglect*. New York: College Entrance Examination Board, 1970.

Cummins, J. "Linguistic Interdependence and the Educational Development of Bilingual Children." *Review of Educational Research* 49 (1979):222-251.

Cummins, J., and Gulatson, M. "Bilingual Education and Cognition." *Alberta Journal of Educational Research* 20 (1974):259-269.

Darcy, N. T. "A Review of the Literature of the Effects of Bilingualism upon the Measurement of Intelligence." *Journal of Genetic Psychology* 82 (1953):21-57.

Darcy, N. T. "Bilingualism and the Measurement of Intelligence: Review of a Decade of Research." *Journal of Genetic Psychology* 103 (1963):259-282.

DeVilliers, J., and DeVilliers, P. *Language Acquisition*. Cambridge, Mass.: Harvard University Press, 1978.

Dulay, H. C., and Burt, M. K. "Goofing: An Indication of Children's Second Language Learning Strategies." *Language Learning* 22 (1972):235-252.

Dulay, H. E., and Burt, M. K. "Should We Teach Children Syntax?" *Language Learning* 23 (1973):245-258.

Edelman, M. "The Contextualization of School Children's Bilingualism." *Modern Language Journal* 53 (1969):179-182.

Epstein, N. *Language, Ethnicity and Schools: Policy Alternatives for Bilingual-Bicultural Education*. Washington, D. C.: The George Washington University Institute for Educational Leadership, 1977.

Evans, J. S. "Word Pair Discrimination and Imitation Abilities of Preschool Spanish-Speaking Children." *Journal of Learning Disabilities* 7 (1974):573-584.

Feldman, C., and Shen, M. "Some Language-Related Cognitive Advantages of Bilingual

Five-Year-Olds." *Journal of Genetic Psychology* 118 (1971):235-244.

Fishman, S. A., and Lovaas, J. "Bilingual Education in Sociological Perspective." *TESOL Quarterly* 4 (1970):215-222.

Garcia, E. "The Study of Early Childhood Bilingualism: Strategies for Linguistic Transfer Research." In *Chicano Psychology*, ed. J. L. Martinez, Jr. New York: Academic Press, 1977.

Garcia, E. "Mother-Child Bilingual Interaction: A Developmental Analysis." *Journal of Discourse Processes*, in press (1980a).

Garcia, E. "Language Switching in Bilingual Children: A National Perspective." In *The Mexican American Child: Language, Cognitive and Social Development*, ed. E. Garcia and M. S. Vargas. South Bend, Ind.: Notre Dame University Press, forthcoming (1980b).

Garcia, E., and Trujillo, A. "A Developmental Comparison of English and Spanish Imitation Between Bilingual and Monolingual Children." *Journal of Educational Psychology* 21 (1979):161-168.

Geissler, H. *Zweisprachigkeit Deuscher Kinder im Aushland.* Stuttgart: Kohlhammas, 1938.

Harris, M. B., and Hassemer, W. G. "Some Factors Affecting the Complexity of Children's Sentences: The Effect of Modeling, Age, Sex, and Bilingualism." *Journal of Experimental Child Psychology* 13 (1972):447-455.

Holguin, R. *Curriculum and Instruction: A Handbook for Teaching in a Bilingual Setting.* Pomona, Calif.: Multilingual Multicultural Materials Development Center, 1977.

Huerta, A. "The Development of Codeswitching in a Young Bilingual." *Working Papers in Sociolinguistics*, no. 21, June 1977.

Ianco-Worall, A. "Bilingualism and Cognitive Development." *Child Development* 43 (1972): 1390-1400.

John, V. P., and Horner, V. M. *Early Childhood Bilingual Education.* New York: Modern Language Association of America, 1971.

Keats, D. M., and Keats, J. A. "The Effect of Language on Concept Acquisition in Bilingual Children." *Journal of Cross-Cultural Psychology* 5 (1974):80-99.

Kuo, E. C. "The Family and Bilingual Socialization: A Sociolinguistic Study of a Sample of Chinese Children in the United States." *Journal of Social Psychology* 92 (1974):181-191.

Lambert, W., and Tucker, G. *Bilingual Education of Children: The St. Lambert Experiment.* Rowley, Mass.: Newbury House, 1972.

Lenneberg, E., and Lenneberg, E. *Foundations of Language Development*, Vol. I and Vol. II. London: UNESCO Press, 1975.

Leopold, W. F. *Speech Development of a Bilingual Child: A Linguist's Record, Vol. I, Vocab-ulary Growth in the First Two Years.* Evanston, Ill.: Northwestern University Press, 1939.

Leopold, W. F. *Speech Development of a Bilingual Child: A Linguist's Record, Vol. II, Sound Learning in the First Two Years.* Evanston, Ill.: Northwestern University Press, 1947.

Leopold, W. F. *Speech Development of a Bilingual Child: A Linguist's Record, Vol. III, Grammars and General Problems in the First Two Years.* Evanston, Ill.: Northwestern University Press, 1949a.

Leopold, W. F. *Speech Development of a Bilingual Child: A Linguist's Record, Vol. IV, Diary from Age Two.* Evanston, Ill.: Northwestern University Press, 1949b.

Lindholm, K. J., and Padilla, A. M. "Child Bilingualism: Report on Language Mixing, Switching and Translations." *Linguistics* 211 (1979):23-44.

MacNab, G. C. "Cognition and Bilingualism: A Re-analysis of Studies." *Linguistics* 17 (1979):231-255.

MacNamara, J. "Bilingualism in the Modern World." *Journal of Social Issues* 23 (1967):1-7.

McLaughlin, B. "Second Language Learning in Children." *Psychological Bulletin* 84 (1977): 438-459.

McLaughlin, B. *Second Language Acquisition in Childhood.* Hillsdale, N. J.: Lawrence Erlbaum Associates, 1978.

McNeil, D. "Developmental Psycholinguistics." In *The Genesis of Language: A Psycholinguistic Approach*, ed. F. Smith and G. Miller. Cambridge, Mass.: M.I.T. Press, 1966.

Menyuk, P. *The Acquisition and Development of Language.* New York: Prentice-Hall, 1971.

Pacheco, M. T. "Approaches to Bilingualism: Recognition of a Multilingual Society." In *Pluralism in Foreign Language Education*, ed. D. C. Lange, Skokie, Ill.: National Textbook, Inc., 1973.

Padilla, A. "Child Bilingualism: Insights to Issues." In *Chicano Psychology*, ed. J. Martinez. New York: Academic Press, 1977.

Padilla, A., and Liebman, E. "Language Acquisition in the Bilingual Child." *The Bilingual Review/La Revista Bilingue* 2 (1975) 34-55.

Pavlovitch, M. *Le Langage Enfantin: Acquisition du Serbe et du Francais par un Enfant Serbe.* Paris: Champion, 1920.

Peal, E., and Lambert, W. "The Relation of Bilingualism to Intelligence." *Psychological Monograph* 72 (1962) 1-23.

Price-Williams, D. R. *Explorations in Cross-Cultural Psychology.* San Franciso: Chandler and Sharp, 1975.

Ramirez, M., and Castañeda, A. *Cultural Democracy, Bicognitive Development and Education*. New York: Academic Press, 1974.

Riegel, K. F. "Some Theoretical Considerations of Bilingual Development." *Psychological Bulletin* 70 (1968):647-670.

Ronjat, J. *Le Development du Langage Observe Chez un Enfant Bilingue*. Paris: Champion, 1913.

Saville, M. R., and Troike, R. "Interference Phenomenon in Language Teaching: Their Nature, Extent, and Significance in the Acquisition of Standard English." *Elementary English* (March 1971):396-405.

Schacter, F. F.; Kirshner, D.; Klips, B.; Friedericks, M.; and Sanders, K. "Everyday Preschool Interpersonal Speech Usage: Methodological Development and Sociolinguistic Studies." *Monographs of the Society for Research in Child Development*, 1974.

Skrabanek, R. L., "Language Maintenance among Mexican-Americans." *International Journal of Comparative Sociology* 11 (1970): 272-282.

Smith, M. D., "A Study of the Speech of Eight Bilingual Children of the Same Family." *Child Development* 6 (1935):19-25.

Sorensen, A. P., "Multilingualism in the Northwest Amazon." *American Anthropologist* 69 (1967):670-684.

U.S. Commission on Civil Rights. *Toward Quality Education for Mexican Americans. Report IV: Mexican American Education Study*. Washington, D.C.: U.S. Commission on Civil Rights, 1975.

Valdes-Fallia, G. "Language Diversity in Chicano Speech Communities: Implications for Language Teaching." *Working Papers in Sociolinguistics*, no. 54, January 1979.

Vildomec, V. *Multilingualism*. Leyden: A. W. Sijthoff, 1971.

Williams, L. R., "Early Childhood Education in the 1970's: Some Reflections on Reaching Adulthood." *Teachers College Record* 79 (1978):529-538.

Zentella, M. "Codeswitching in Elementary Level Puerto Rican Children." *Working Papers in Sociolinguistics*, no. 43, September 1978.

Paul M. Williamson

Literature Goals and Activities for Young Children

What is the place of literature in the curriculum for the very young? What should children from three to seven years old be learning from their experiences with literature? Teachers of young children often select literature for its content or its didactic possibilities. *The Snowy Day* (Keats 1962) may be read at the time of the first snowfall. *Count and See* (Hoban 1972) is popular for those with an interest in learning numbers. The teacher of a fractious group may select *No Fighting, No Biting!* (Minarik 1958). Similarly, *My Doctor* (Rockwell 1973) may be chosen for the contribution it can make to children's dramatic play. Other books may be chosen because they are old favorites, because they are available, or because of their colorful illustrations or simple vocabulary. Frequently books are enjoyed and read aloud once and then returned to the bookshelf.

Young children's experiences with literature should be enjoyable, but the experiences can also be planned and enriched to develop children's knowledge and appreciation of language and literature. Five goals are developed in this article to give direction to a program of literature experiences for three- to seven-year-old children. These goals are illustrated with examples of activities drawn from my ex-

periences as a librarian and teacher for various groups of children.

Recognize, enjoy, and value literature

The teacher of a class of three-year-old children asked for help because the children in her class showed little interest in books or stories. The children could not sit still for a story, even in a small group. A book corner went unused. What could be done? Together we planned to focus on literature for three weeks in an effort to involve children with books. The teacher arranged a new book corner with large bulletin board spaces, a soft rug, some pillows, and a display rack for books.

On the first day I entered the classroom, I sat down in the book corner with oaktag and felt pen and quietly began to make enlarged drawings of the animal characters in *Mushroom in the Rain* (Ginsburg 1974). As expected, an audience soon appeared. "What are you doing?"—"I'm drawing. This is going to be an ant."—"I got bit by ants once."—"Oh, I'll bet that hurt. This ant is part of a story. . . . " As I worked, we talked about the animals, and I told them parts of the story. A child who wanted to help was given the drawing of an animal and shown how to apply colored chalk and then rub with the hand to produce an evenly-colored figure. The children came and went for a short time daily until all the characters were finished: ant, butterfly, mouse, sparrow, rabbit, fox, frog, and, of course, the mushroom. Some came to color while others came to talk and find out about the man drawing in the corner. Some children merely

Paul M. Williamson, M.Ed. is a doctoral candidate at the University of Massachusetts, Amherst, in the Center for Curriculum Studies, School of Education. He was formerly a teacher and librarian at the Smith College Campus School, Northampton, Massachusetts, where the ideas presented here were developed.

watched and sucked their thumbs. All of them found out something about the drawings and heard at least part of the story.

When all the characters had been drawn, colored, and cut out, the group assembled near the book corner. As I told the entire story, I displayed the drawings on the bulletin board. Because many of the children had helped make the figures and most of them knew at least part of the story, it made sense, and the children participated willingly. Many had comments like, "I made that one!" or "There's the rabbit!"

On the following day, I finally brought out the book to read and show the pictures. Before long, several children realized that the animals illustrated in the book were the same as those on the bulletin board. This discovery provoked excitement and pleasure over pointing out in the display each animal as it appeared in the story. When the story was finished, the book was placed in the display rack in the book corner. Several children immediately went to the book corner to pore over the book and again compare the illustrations with the display.

This sequence of activities was designed to get children involved with one book. Why were these activities so successful?

During the first few years of a child's life, vocabulary and ability to use language increase phenomenally, but words are often elusive. The three-year-old learns mostly through observation and manipulation of physical objects, and "language is just beginning to serve as a mediator between the environment and action" (Elkind 1978, p. 60). For a child recently enrolled in a group, prior experiences with books or stories probably occurred at home in a highly personalized setting where the appeal was as much the chance to cuddle and share a private time with a parent as the story itself. Understandably, three-year-olds often show little interest in group stories or in books

Steve Herzog

Children who learn to value literature from a very early age do not need to be convinced to learn to read; they know it will be worth the effort.

when sand, paints, blocks, dress-up clothes, and other things compete for their attention in the classroom.

In this example, the literature experiences were organized to overcome these obstacles. The first highly personal encounters gave children opportunities to watch the illustrations being created and talk about them. They could then give meaning to these drawings by relating them to previous experiences. Often, displays appear in the classroom as if by magic and therefore lack meaning for the children. By providing a series of experiences based on the same story, children can develop a greater understanding of the story each time. Often, a large part of a story's appeal is that it is already known. Children frequently request familiar stories, even ones they can recite from memory!

I chose *Mushroom in the Rain* for several reasons. The simple text and colorful illustrations are well integrated. There is also the intriguing problem of how an ant, butterfly, sparrow, mouse, and rabbit all fit under one mushroom. On a deeper level, the book discusses meeting and solving problems out in the world. This is a significant issue to the three-year-old, especially one just starting school. The three-year-old child is rapidly gaining independence but often finds coping with the larger world difficult (Elkind 1978, pp. 60-61).

The activities with this one book were directed toward a longer-range literature goal for the three- to seven-year-old: to *recognize, enjoy, and value many kinds of literature*. Involvement is a first step toward this goal.

Develop a strong sense of story

This example involves the same class as the previous example and follows it by about two weeks. This time, the sequence began with a free telling of *The Great Big Enormous Turnip* (Tolstoy 1968) in which an old man requires the cumulative assistance of first the old woman, and then her granddaughter, the dog, the cat, and the mouse to pull up a turnip. Each time "they pulled and pulled again, but they could not pull it up," the children were invited to join in pulling. Naturally, when the turnip finally did come out, the children enjoyed tumbling along with all the story characters.

Next, the story was read aloud from the book while showing the illustrations. Knowing the story and having tried to pull out the turnip themselves, the children eagerly listened and looked.

As a final activity, the class visited the school library. After initial exploration, they watched the sound-filmstrip based on the book (Weston Woods, n.d.).

These experiences were intended to enable children to recognize a story presented in different formats and contexts. The notion of a "story" as a telling of some

event or series of events is an abstract and difficult concept. There are no obvious physical examples of stories as there are for concepts like "dog," "car," or "book." Stories are often found in books; but not all books are stories, and not all stories are in books. A story exists apart from the specific form in which it is embodied. To separate "the story" from the specific format and situation in which it is presented can be difficult for a young child. The importance of being able to do so is revealed in a child's joyous comment after seeing the filmstrip: "We have that story at our school, too!" This is part of a larger literature goal: *to develop a strong sense of story*.

It is for the purpose of developing a sense of story that a series of experiences with a single story is valuable for young children, for it enables them to extract what is common to the experiences: the story. Do not disrupt the flow of a story in the telling or reading of it. For example, teachers, intending to check on understanding or maintain attention, often intersperse questions in their telling or reading of a story. For young children, this may defeat the purpose by breaking up the continuity of the story and posing the danger of being sidetracked. The teacher who asks, "And what do you think happens next?" may be answered, "I've got new shoes!"

In contrast to the first example, this series began with a free telling of the story because the children in the class had come to expect that a story would be enjoyable and make sense. Also, telling a story is a more personal experience than reading it aloud. Baker and Greene (1978) and Sherman (1979) provide many suggestions for developing storytelling skills.

Respond to literature

The activities described in both examples are directed toward another literature goal for the young: *to respond actively and*

Young children should be given plenty of opportunities to relate their own lives and experiences to those of characters in literature.

appropriately to literature in a variety of ways. The young child must have many experiences which give meaning *to* the literature and provide expression for the meaning taken *from* the literature. For this purpose a wide range of creative and expressive activities is available: dramatic play, painting, choral speaking, puppetry, flannel board presentations, cooking, and so on. Such experiences heighten enjoyment and enrich the meaning of literature for children. The following example further illustrates this notion of active and appropriate responses to literature and will bring out other goals.

Appreciating words and characters

A teacher of four-year-old children designed a series of activities around the book *Where the Wild Things Are* (Sendak 1963), beginning with reading the book aloud and showing the pictures. Next, the class saw the sound-filmstrip version of the story (Weston Woods, n.d.). Later, the teacher retold the story, with the class supplying appropriate sound effects for the wild things. In the art center of the classroom, materials were set out for making paper bag puppets, and each child made a wild thing. When all the puppets were finished, the class brought them to the library where I could narrate a puppet performance. Exhibiting extraordinary self-control, the children kept their puppets at their sides as the story began. Right on cue, however, the wild things made their entrance and "roared their terrible roars and gnashed their terrible teeth." There is the possibility for absolute chaos in saying to a group of four-year-old

Literature Goals and Activities

wild things, "Let the wild rumpus start!" Yet, so strong was the spell cast by this story that when Max said, "Stop!" the wild things were tamed immediately.

The children in the above example became totally involved with the story. They were wild things. The remarkable effect of such a story attests partly to the artistry of the story's language. Children often object strenuously if the language of this story is altered in retelling. Such children are on their way toward another literature goal: *to become aware of and appreciate the magic and power of words.* As Anderson and Groff state "literature is the art form of language" (1972, p. 221). An awareness and appreciation of the special way language is used in good literature is a valuable outcome of any literature program.

In addition to masterful use of language, the book appeals to children for another reason. Children are subject to intense and often unstable emotions (Elkind 1978, p. 37). They are often afraid of losing their self-control. They need a chance to be wild, but within secure boundaries. Max's encounter with the wild things has significance for children who are attempting to tame their own sometimes wild feelings. Max meets the wild things and tames them with words! Choosing books to which children can develop strong responses helps them to achieve another goal: *to identify, and identify with, characters in literature.*

The examples described above are based on extensive and intensive experiences with well-known children's books. Other types of literature, such as finger plays, poems, nursery rhymes, and songs, are also excellent sources. One teacher even adapted an old joke into a popular story for five-year-olds. In the story, a monster plagues an old man by appearing under his bed each night. The old man seeks advice from several wise men, without success. Despite his efforts, the monster always reappears. Finally, a wise man whispers a suggestion. That night, when the monster appears, the man gets up quietly, tiptoes downstairs to his toolbox, comes back with a saw, and quickly saws the legs off the bed. This not only squashes the monster, but also leaves no room for others to take up residence. Several activities focused on this story, including making a large mural, an overhead projector show, and reading a printed version. Many parents found a carefully crafted paper monster under their children's beds.

Review of goals

Literature learnings can be an important part of the curriculum for young children. These long-range goals may give your program direction. Children will—

• *Recognize, enjoy, and value many kinds of literature.* Huck said that "the long-term goal of a literature program is the development of a life-time pattern of preference for reading quality literature" (1976, p. 711). During the early years, help children know some literature well and enjoy it so much that they feel it "belongs" to them. Children who learn early to value literature know learning to read will be worth the effort.

• *Develop a strong sense of story.* Children need opportunities to develop a concept of what a story is. For the very young, it is often enough to recognize the same story when it is presented in different ways or to recall the events of a story in their right order. Somewhat older children enjoy comparing different versions of a story or book. An extension of this goal in later study of literature includes recognizing basic plot structures and recurring themes.

• *Respond actively and appropriately to literature in a variety of ways.* Young children must learn to bring meaning to and take meaning from literature:

Literature offers new ways of exploring the world and new worlds to explore—the stuff a child's brain thrives on. Children can immerse themselves in novels, plays,

Williamson

Creative activities help children bring meaning to and take meaning from literature.

Diane Wasserman

and poetry with the same enthusiasm with which they immerse themselves in the world, and learn accordingly. (Smith 1979, p. 124)

Children may be helped to achieve this goal through dramatization, art projects, field trips, cooking, performances, puppetry, and other creative and expressive activities.

• *Be aware of and appreciate the magic and power of words.* Words are powerful, and people have power over words. Young children should have many experiences with words used well. This not only contributes to the child's language development, but also supports later study of how writers convey and enhance their meaning by artful use of language.

• *Identify and identify with characters in literature.* Young children should be given many opportunities to relate their own lives and experiences to those of charac-

ters in literature. Many excellent children's books now available address issues important to children. Their ability to do so partly explains the appeal of certain books.

These goals relate to both the special characteristics of the young child and to the broader study of literature. To meet these goals, the literature program must be as carefully planned as any other part of the curriculum. Provide experiences both before and after the reading to deepen the child's involvement and understanding. In planning for the literature curriculum, the teacher will have to draw on knowledge of children and child development, of literature, and of effective teaching techniques. Remember that "the first step in any literature program is to discover delight in books" (Huck 1976, p. 708), especially for the very young. The art of

Literature Goals and Activities

teaching literature to the young is to structure the experiences to develop understandings and appreciations while maintaining the sense of spontaneity, pleasure, and sheer exuberance which comes from sharing literature. Such experiences enrich the lives of both children and teachers.

References

Anderson, W. and Groff, P. *A New Look at Children's Literature.* Belmont, Calif.: Wadsworth, 1972.

Baker, A., and Greene, E. "Storytelling: Preparation and Presentation." *School Library Journal* 24, no. 7 (March 1978): 93-96.

Elkind, D. *A Sympathetic Understanding of the Child,* 2nd ed. Boston: Allyn and Bacon, 1978.

Ginsburg, M. *Mushroom in the Rain.* New York: Macmillan, 1974.

Hoban, T. *Count and See.* New York: Macmillan, 1972.

Huck, C. S. *Children's Literature in the Elementary School,* 3rd ed. New York: Holt, Rinehart and Winston, 1976.

Keats, E. J. *The Snowy Day.* New York: Viking, 1962.

Minarik, E. H. *No Fighting, No Biting!* New York: Harper & Row, 1958.

Rockwell, H. *My Doctor.* New York: Macmillan, 1973.

Sendak, M. *Where the Wild Things Are.* New York: Harper & Row, 1963.

Sherman, J. L. "Storytelling with Young Children." *Young Children* 34, no. 2 (January 1979): 20-27.

Smith, F. "The Language Arts and the Learner's Mind." *Language Arts* 56, no. 2 (February 1979): 118-125.

Tolstoy, A. *The Great Big Enormous Turnip.* New York: Franklin Watts, 1968.

Sound-Filmstrips

Weston Woods Studios. Sound-Filmstrip 140. *The Great Big Enormous Turnip,* by Alexei Tolstoy. Weston Woods, Conn., n.d.

Weston Woods Studios. Sound-Filmstrip 84. *Where the Wild Things Are,* by Maurice Sendak. Weston Woods, Conn., n.d.

Linda Leonard Lamme

Handwriting
In an Early Childhood Curriculum

What are the skills prerequisite for handwriting, and how can we help children acquire them? When should formal writing instruction begin?

Handwriting is being taught to young children today in more and more kindergartens and early childhood programs. Children have long been taught to write their names (usually in upper case letters) at home by eager parents who find them highly motivated to acquire this skill. But to assume that children who can write their names are ready to write all letters and words may be a fallacy. Some children are being pushed into handwriting before they have acquired adequate prehandwriting skills. Handwriting is difficult for these children, causing them to become discouraged. They overcompensate for the prehandwriting skills they lack, thus causing poor writing habits that are very difficult to correct later.

What are the skills prerequisite for handwriting, and how can we help children acquire them? When should formal writing instruction begin? Until recently development and assessment of children's readiness for handwriting have received little attention in instructional programs or in professional literature. Barbe (1974) states that "the readiness phase of instruction in handwriting is as important as a sound readiness program in reading" (p. 209). There appear to be six prerequisite skill areas for handwriting: small muscle development, eye-hand coordination, holding a writing tool, basic strokes, letter perception, and orientation to printed language.

Small Muscle Development

The first skill children need to develop is small muscle coordination. Those who have difficulty holding a pencil properly often lack a high degree of small muscle control. Although small muscle activities are rarely thought of as prerequisite skills for handwriting in an early childhood curriculum, motor development clearly is needed prior to using a writing tool.

Activities that enhance small muscle development include many manipulative tasks. Jigsaw puzzles can be graded from easy (with a few large pieces) to complex (with many small pieces). Manipulative toys such as Legos, Tinker Toys, and snap beads are excellent for small muscle development. Play with small motor vehicles,

Linda Leonard Lamme, Ph.D., is Assistant Professor, General Teacher Education (Early Childhood Program Area), University of Florida, Gainesville. She is a former elementary teacher.

miniature gas stations, dollhouses, etc., gives children experience in using small muscles with precision.

Molding opportunities are indispensable. Clay, sand, play dough, real dough (for baking), putty, sawdust, oatmeal, and papier maché offer children a variety of molding experiences.

Children can also participate in activities common in daily experiences to promote small muscle coordination — zipping, buttoning, sewing, screwing caps on small jars, screwing nuts and bolts, typing, tying knots and bows, and playing a piano. The art curriculum can enhance small muscle development with activities such as painting (with easel or larger brushes), coloring, drawing, sketching, tearing paper, folding paper, and for older children, cutting paper with scissors. Scissors are often introduced into the curriculum too early. Children can be seen struggling with scissors when tearing would be a more appropriate activity. A

Constructing with blocks promotes small muscle development and eye-hand coordination—two skills necessary prior to writing.

child who can cut easily with small scissors is very likely ready for handwriting instruction.

A word is in order about the left-handed child. Approximately ten percent of the population is left-handed (Foerster 1975). The small muscle activities listed above will help each child develop hand dominance as well as provide opportunities for teachers to observe and respect the child's handedness. As instruction in letter formation is begun, it is recommended that left-handers be grouped together for instruction (Enstrom 1969).

Eye-Hand Coordination

The second series of handwriting skills in a good early childhood curriculum consists of eye-hand coordination skills. These skills are clearly related to the small muscle development skills, for one must have the muscle control to accomplish what the eye and brain wish to be done. Many of the small muscle activities mentioned above also enhance eye-hand coordination.

Any of the manipulative activities requiring utensils develop eye-hand coordination. Constructing with Legos, blocks, or popsicle sticks builds eye-hand coordination. Balancing objects such as blocks requires precise hand motions. Other precision motor activities include playing the piano, playing with a cash register, pushing buttons, typing, working puzzles, stringing beads, weaving, and sewing. Even large muscle activities such as climbing a ladder, playing Simon Says, and jumping rope help build eye-hand coordination.

Numerous paper-oriented tasks can refine eye-hand coordination skills. Coloring, painting, and drawing are commonly part of an early childhood curriculum. Following dots and completing mazes are enjoyable games for most children. Pasting and finger painting can also enhance eye-hand coordination.

Lamme

Copying is often part of a handwriting program. However, young children frequently have difficulty with far-to-near copying such as from a chalkboard or chart paper. Children's immature eyes have difficulty translating distant images to closeup images. It is better to have young children copy on paper with the same size letters as the model, first copying directly below the model, then copying from a model placed nearby.

Tracing likewise appears in some early childhood curriculums. At least two research studies have shown that copying is more effective than tracing for initial handwriting instruction (Hirsch and Niedermeyer 1973; Askov and Greff 1975). When tracing, children focus more on staying on the line (or dots) than on visually perceiving what the overall letter or word looks like (Foerster 1972). Tracing actually can inhibit the development of strong basic handwriting strokes.

To observe how well developed eye-hand coordination is, look for children who can consistently hammer nails straight into wood; build a tall building out of blocks without knocking it down; copy sophisticated designs in Legos constructions; follow mazes without touching exterior lines. These children would have the prerequisite eye-hand coordination skills to begin handwriting.

Holding Utensils or Tools

There is a hierarchy of difficulty in using tools or utensils for writing. Pencils are one of the most difficult tools to manipulate effectively; therefore pencils should be the last tools given to children. If you doubt that pencils are the most difficult writing tools, try this experiment: Give young children an opportunity to write their names with four writing tools—chalk, a felt-tip marker, a pencil, and a crayon. Then ask the children which tool was the easiest and which was the most difficult utensil to write with. In most

early childhood classrooms where this test has been tried, children overwhelmingly chose markers as the easiest tools to use, followed by chalk, crayon, and pencil, in that order. When asked which tool they enjoyed the most, markers again headed the list.

Children enjoy playing with utensils before they are ready to write. Children need to manipulate tools as part of their early childhood curriculum. A water table with sponges, funnels, straws, and squeeze bottles is essential. Likewise, a sand table with sieves, strainers, containers of various sizes and shapes, sticks, shovels, and pails gives children opportunities to use tools. Gardening adds raking, hoeing, watering, digging, and weeding. Kitchen utensils such as beaters, spoons for stirring, spatulas, and pancake turners make cooking a vital part of the curriculum. Prior to writing, children need many experiences drawing and painting with paint brushes, markers, sponges, chalk, crayons, and pencils. Charcoal is less suitable because it crumbles easily.

Actual handwriting experiences can begin with markers and felt-tip pens. After the child gains confidence in making firm strokes while holding the tools in a relaxed manner (since they require little pressure), crayons and eventually pencils can be introduced. Crayons, often used as beginning writing tools, require more pressure than markers in order to produce the brighter colors to which children have become accustomed. There is no particular advantage to the large child-sized pencils. In fact, some children write better using regular adult-sized pencils from the start. Although no research studies have involved preschoolers, there is evidence that older children write better with felt-tip and ballpoint pens than with pencils (Krzesni 1971).

It is important that children learn how to hold the writing tool properly from the beginning, because incorrect habits are difficult to break later. The pencil should be loosely gripped with the fingers above the shaved tip to about an inch from the tip. Only the index finger should remain on top of the pencil, not two or three fingers. Left-handers should be encouraged not to "hook" (Enstrom 1969). However, do not stress position of the pencil to such a degree that you discourage the young writer. Rather, simply provide a variety of tools for writing. The child naturally will select those that are easier. Children who select pencils are ready for instruction on the correct position for holding that tool.

There are two indicators that determine if children are holding a pencil correctly. Children who are experiencing stress will grip the pencil too tightly and tire easily and thus will not be able to write for long periods of time. You should be able to easily pull the pencil from the writer's hand as he or she is writing. Look at the child's teeth. Are they clenched, or is the child relaxed? A second indicator of correct pencil usage is the depth of impression on the page caused by the amount of pressure used. Children should always be given soft lead pencils. Then, if the strokes are too light or too dark or if the paper has holes in it, the child is using either too little or too much pressure. Pressure should be even, or the child will become a slow writer.

Basic Strokes

A fourth skill needed prior to instruction in handwriting is the ability to form basic strokes smoothly, in the appropriate direction, and with clean intersections. Observe a child's drawings. Circles and straight lines occur naturally in children's drawings. Are the circles round and closed? Do the straight lines intersect properly in such cases as body parts attached to bodies, kites to strings, etc.? Until these strokes occur naturally in such drawings as wagons, cars and trucks, houses, people, flowers, etc., the child is

not ready for formal handwriting instruction.

Activities in addition to drawing and painting that give children opportunities to use basic strokes include stirring, sand play, water play, and finger painting. It is important that children not be taught how to make basic strokes in their artwork, but rather that these strokes evolve through time and experience, enhancing creativity as well as indicating readiness for handwriting. Basic strokes can then be "taught" as a part of the handwriting curriculum. Wright and Allen (1975) recommend practice in basic strokes before formal writing begins, so correct sequence of strokes within letters and letter formation can be taught from the start. Teachers should supervise initial writing attempts to discourage the development of bad habits (Enstrom 1965).

The transition from drawing to handwriting is a slow one involving basic strokes in both artistic and written form. A number of principles can be used to identify children who are ready for handwriting.

- Recurring principle—the child repeats patterns (or letters or words) over and over.
- Directional principle—the child goes from left to right and then return sweeps to begin again at the left.
- Generating principle—the child realizes that letter elements can recur in variable patterns.
- Inventory principle—the child lists all of the letters (or words or symbols) he or she knows.
- Contrastive principle—the child perceives likenesses and differences among letter elements, concepts, letters, and words. (Clay 1975)

Not only is it important to observe as a child demonstrates each principle, but abundant drawing and writing experiences should be provided to support the child's acquisition of these skills.

Lamme

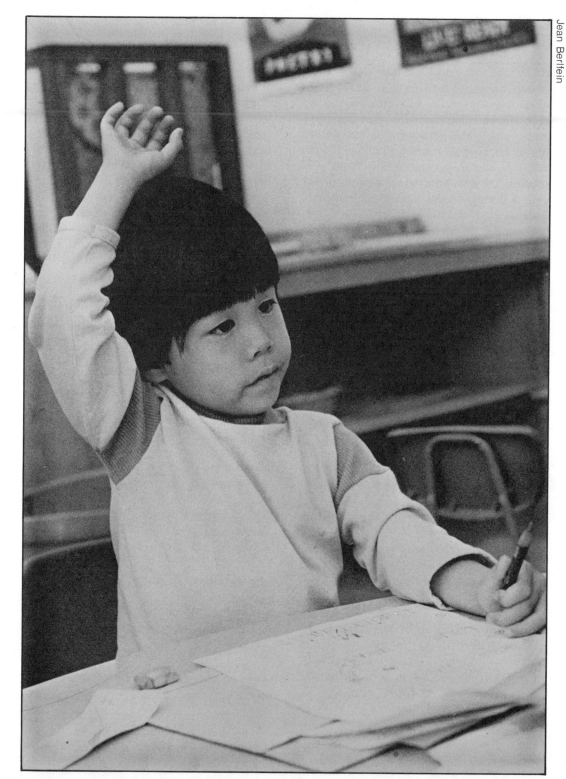

Jean Berlfein

What changes would you make in this learning situation to promote the child's writing development?

Letter Perception

Sometimes handwriting is viewed solely as a physical activity demanding small muscle coordination with little visual perception. In a longitudinal study of children's handwriting development emphasizing the perceptual-motor nature of handwriting, Furner (1969a, 1969b, 1970) demonstrated that attention to perception in a handwriting program develops better writers than a conventional program.

Furner's program suggests that young children need to be able to recognize form, notice likenesses and differences, infer movement necessary to the production of form, and give accurate verbal descriptions of things they see. Children should observe the finished product (letter or word) as well as the formational act (adult writing the letter or word as a model). Left-handers need left-handed models (Foerster 1975). Self-correction of initial attempts at handwriting can also aid in the development of letter perception (Furner 1969a, 1969b).

Knowing the alphabet is not a prerequuisite skill to handwriting. However, the ability to recognize alphabet letters (not necessarily in alphabetical order) is necessary for children who wish to write words and need help in spelling. Early childhood literature is replete with suggestions for helping children learn alphabet letters, so we will not elaborate on those ideas here. In the early stages of handwriting instruction, it is helpful if alphabet letters are kept in meaningful units (e.g., words).

Some letters are easier for children to write than others (Lewis and Lewis 1964). In order from easiest to most difficult, Lewis and Lewis (1964) list: l,o,L,O,H,D, i,v,I,X,E,P,F,V,c,x,T,h,w,J,f,C,N,A,W,K, z,t,B,Q,s,n,Z,r,e,b,S,M,u,Y,d,R,G,a,U,k, m,j,y,p,g, and q. Initially, it is helpful to teach words containing the letters that are formed more easily by young children. Teaching young children to write abstract letters, not associated with words they

know, is beyond the developmental levels of most beginning writers.

It is best to use a standard form of manuscript printing initially to teach children to write alphabet letters. The importance of adult modeling of proper letter formation cannot be overemphasized. Have children use unlined paper at first. Children are ready for lines when their writing has achieved a consistent height on a paper without lines. Children write no better on special wide-lined paper than they do on regular adult paper with narrow spaces for writing (Halpin and Halpin 1976).

Reversals occur frequently in the initial stages of handwriting. They usually disappear as children mature. Teachers can however, help solve reversal problems by (a) helping the child see the differences in direction and (b) giving the child practice dealing correctly with the symbols that cause him or her difficulty (Reilly 1972). Children need to perceive visually the way letters are formed; so the more children see the teacher write (on paper just as the child will write), the better. Some letters cause reversal problems with nearly all children—b and d, s, and upper case N; these need to be taught carefully with special attention to the correct beginning point, correct direction of motion, and correct sequence of multipart letters (Enstrom and Enstrom 1969).

Orientation to Printed Language

A final prehandwriting skill involves a set of skills that parallel reading readiness skills:

- How to attend and orient to printed language.
- How to organize one's exploratory investigation of printed forms.
- How to tell left from right.
- How to visually analyze letters and words. (Clay 1975)

Children can have all of the mechanical skills to perform handwriting tasks, but unless they see the "whole"—what printed language stands for and how it is used to communicate—they will not likely have the motivation to develop good handwriting skills. Just as in reading, we must be careful to avoid subdividing handwriting instruction into minute subskills without at the same time providing lots of examples of the complete end product concurrently.

Herein lies the importance of incorporating numerous language experience activities into the early childhood curriculum. Children need to make lots of books, greeting cards, pictures with labels, charts, maps, letters to mail, signs, etc., where adults do the writing for them. Likewise, they need to "read" lots of favorite songs, stories, and rhymes from charts and class books that have been written in their presence. Each child can have a mailbox or cubby to encourage written communication even before learning to write formally. *Handwriting readiness* ought not to occur in isolation but rather *should be an integral part of the oral and written language program.*

Conclusion

It is important that the six skill areas (small muscle development, eye-hand coordination, holding a writing tool, basic strokes, letter perception, and orientation to printed language) be included but not rushed in an early childhood curriculum. A planned, sequential, curriculum such as the one outlined in this article is necessary prior to formal handwriting instruction. Because children enter school with a wide repertoire of skills and abilities, early childhood teachers need to be able to assess individual differences and provide both prehandwriting activities for children who are not yet ready for formal handwriting instruction and careful beginning instruction for children who are ready.

Because some children learn to write at home and many others receive at least some instruction from parents, the handwriting curriculum should involve parents (Hall, Moretz, and Statom 1976). Teachers can help parents understand why young children should not be pushed into handwriting before they have acquired these prehandwriting skills. Ideas for helping their children with these skills can be valuable as they understand the importance of providing their children with many free writing and drawing opportunities. Because many parents do teach their children how to write, they will appreciate knowing how and when to get them off to a good start. The parent component of the early childhood handwriting curriculum is at least as important as (and may be more important than) the school curriculum.

References

Askov, E. N., and Greff, E. N. "Handwriting: Copying vs. Tracing as the Most Effective Type of Practice." *Journal of Educational Research* 69 (1975): 96-98.

Barbe, W. B., and Lucas, V. H. "Instruction in Handwriting: A New Look." *Childhood Education* 50 (1974): 207-209.

Clay, M. M. *What Did I Write?* Aukland, New Zealand: Heinemann· Educational Books, 1975.

Enstrom, E. A. "Handwriting: Let's Begin in Kindergarten." *Catholic Educator* 36 (1965): 40-41.

Enstrom, E. A. "The Left-Handed Child" *Today's Education* 58 (1969): 43-44.

Enstrom, E. A., and Enstrom, D. C. "In Print Handwriting: Preventing and Solving Reversal Problems." *Elementary English* 46 (1969): 759-764.

Foerster, L. M. "Sinistral Power! Help for Left-Handed Children." *Elementary English* 52 (1975): 213-215.

Foerster, L. M. "Teacher—Don't Let Your First Graders Trace!" *Elementary English* 49 (1972): 431-433.

Furner, B. A. "An Analysis of the Effectiveness of a Program of Instruction Emphasizing the Perceptual-Motor Nature of Learning Handwriting." *Elementary English* 47 (1970): 61-69.

Furner, B. A. "The Perceptual-Motor Nature of Learning in Handwriting." *Elementary English* 46 (1969a): 886-894.

Furner, B. A. "Recommended Instructional Procedures in a Method Emphasizing the Perceptual-Motor of Learning in Handwriting." *Elementary English* 46 (1969b): 1021-1030.

Hall, M.; Moretz, S. A.; and Statom, J. "Writing before Grade One—A Study of Early Writers." *Language Arts* 53 (1976): 582-585.

Halpin, G., and Halpin, G. "Special Paper for Beginning Handwriting: An Unjustified Practice?" *Journal of Educational Research* 69 (1976): 267-269.

Hirsch, E., and Niedermeyer, F. C. "The Effects of Tracing Prompts and Discrimination Training on Kindergarten Handwriting Performance." *Journal of Educational Researach* 67 (1973): 81-86.

Krzesni, J. S. "Effect of Different Writing Tools and Paper on Performance of the Third Grader." *Elementary English* 48 (1971): 821-824.

Lewis, E. R., and Lewis, H. P. "Which Manuscript Letters Are Hard for First Graders?" *Elementary English* 41 (1964): 855-858.

Reilly, V. "Reversals in Writing: Some Suggestions for Teachers." *Teaching Exceptional Children* 4 (1972): 145-147.

Wright, J. P., and Allen, E. G. "Ready to Write!" *Elementary School Journal* 75 (1975): 430-435.

4

Exploring the world

What is more fragile than a snowflake, or softer than a bunny's fur? Helping children integrate what they see, hear, feel, and are is an essential component of every activity. While science and math are the more visible aspects of any curriculum, other areas show us ways of understanding ourselves and others that are equally valuable.

Most children are curious—sometimes to our exasperation. Yet we also know that their inquisitiveness reflects their desire to learn. Bradbard and Endsley help us understand why children are curious, and recommend ways we can influence and direct children's curiosity constructively.

The pluralistic nature of the world makes it imperative that children begin to learn about the diversity of our human experience as well as our commonalities. Guidelines for meaningful multicultural perspectives in the curriculum are offered by Ramsey.

Another approach to helping children better understand the world we live in is through direct experiences with the environment. Children's perceptions about what they find may be different from an adult's, but Smith helps teachers select science activities that are appropriate.

Learning how their own bodies work is a topic of continuing fascination for children as they grow. How do snacks, posters, and art projects reflect our attitudes about nutrition? Practical suggestions for incorporating sound nutrition principles throughout the curriculum are provided by Herr and Morse. Teacher's attitudes about sexuality are also communicated subtly to children. Koblinsky, Atkinson, and Davis recommend ways in which children and adults can be more comfortable with this sensitive topic.

Physics for young children? You probably teach it every day! Dropping clothespins in bottles, blowing bubbles, building with blocks—such simple activities, with appropriate teacher intervention, can lead to a myriad of learnings identified by Kamii and Lee-Katz.

Marilyn R. Bradbard and Richard C. Endsley

How Can Teachers Develop Young Children's Curiosity?
What Current Research Says to Teachers

Young children spend many of their waking hours investigating, manipulating, inspecting, and asking questions about objects and events—behaviors demonstrating curiosity. Theorists have speculated that these examples of curiosity provide the foundations for more complex behaviors, such as reasoning, problem solving, and social competence, which begin in infancy and continue to develop in later years. Since the early 1960s, an increasing amount of research has been conducted and reviewed on children's curiosity (Berlyne 1960; Hutt 1970; Nunnally and Lemond 1973). With few exceptions (Day and Berlyne 1971), these reviews have not attempted to integrate theory and research information on children's curiosity for use by child development practitioners. This article reviews curiosity research and, most importantly, suggests what teachers can do to foster its development in children.

What Is Curiosity?

After describing the attributes of the curious child, we will briefly review some theories that attempt to explain both why

Which of these children is most curious? How can you be sure?

Photo by Mary K. Gallagher

children are curious and the significance of curiosity for other aspects of development.

What Is a Curious Child?

Most people would agree that a curious child (Berlyne 1960; Maw and Maw 1961):

1. *Reacts positively to new, strange, incongruous, or mysterious elements in the environment by focusing attention on them, moving toward them, manipulating them, and/or seeking information about them.* For example, a child who spots a frog hopping across the playground might react first by following the frog, then picking it up and examining it, and finally asking the teacher questions about it.
2. *Persists in examining and exploring stimuli in order to know more about them.* For example, the young child mentioned above might continue to question the teacher about frogs and perhaps other animals until the child

Marilyn R. Bradbard, Ph.D., is Assistant Professor, Department of Family and Child Development, Auburn University, Auburn, Alabama.

Richard C. Endsley, Ph.D., is Associate Professor, Department of Child and Family Development, University of Georgia, Athens, Georgia.

understands them better. Further, if she has the skills, the child might read about frogs until she has obtained enough information to satisfy her curiosity.

Why Are Children Curious?

Theories of curiosity attempt to describe, explain, and predict why children are curious. The theories presented here are *not* necessarily competing explanations of why children are curious. However, they do differ in their primary emphases and the ages of children with which they deal. Teachers may want to borrow ideas from several theoretical orientations to understand the curiosity behavior of their children.

Trait theories. A simple explanation of why children are curious assumes that they possess a curiosity trait which is a relatively stable personality disposition. No attempt is made to explain the origin or nature of that behavior; instead, trait theorists concentrate on linking the curiosity "trait" to other personality traits or use curiosity to explain and predict other behaviors such as creativity or self-concept (Maw and Maw 1970a,b).

Perceptual theories. Another group of theorists (Berlyne 1960) hypothesized that curiosity is influenced by the attributes of objects, people, and/or places in children's immediate environment that they perceive as new, surprising, incongruous, or complex. Children explore stimuli containing these properties to relieve perceptual conflict. For example, the first author's nine-year-old daughter found a model of a centaur, the mythical animal with a man's head and a horse's body. She examined it for several minutes and finally asked several questions about it. The explanation she received apparently did not satisfy her because when she returned home, she attempted to obtain more information about it in the encyclopedia.

Mastery motivational theories. These theories consider curiosity to be one of several ways children can master their environment (White 1959). Exploration is viewed as the core of early childhood experience. Given a safe environment with many things to explore, children will express their curiosity in many ways because they derive pleasure from the mastery, learning, and feelings of competence which result from their explorations.

Learning theories. This perspective stresses the role of learning on curiosity development and the importance of socialization agents in shaping children's curiosity behavior through modeling and providing external incentives such as praise and answers to questions (Berlyne 1960; Bijou 1976).

Cognitive theories. Other theorists concentrate on the use of reason to solve problems by emphasizing the more sophisticated problem-solving strategies acquired by older children (Berlyne 1970). For example, when younger children play the "Twenty Questions" game, they generally guess randomly at the right answer, while older children ask questions that progressively and systematically narrow down the range of possibilities.

Ethological theories. Ethologists study an organism's biological adaptiveness to its natural environment and view exploration as biologically adaptive behavior learned for survival. The genetic bias of the species leads infants, in time, to venture away from their mothers, thereby encouraging the acquisition of knowledge needed for survival (Rheingold and Eckerman 1970).

Implications. Each of these theoretical orientations assumes that curiosity is important for the overall development of the young child. The theories view curiosity as a prerequisite to learning, reasoning, problem solving, and/or functioning as a competent, self-sufficient human being. Teachers should facilitate curiosity by making classrooms interesting places to spend the day and by providing many opportunities for children to explore and inquire about the aspects of their world.

Are There Individual Differences in Children's Expressions of Curiosity?

Just as children vary physically and intellectually, they also vary in the amount of curiosity they display. For example, a number of studies show considerable variability among ten-month-old infants both in their exploratory behavior and in their reactions to novel stimuli (Corter, Rheingold, and Eckerman 1972; Eckerman and Rheingold 1974). In addition, studies of preschool children's question-asking behaviors indicate that some children rarely ask questions about novel objects presented them while others ask questions almost continuously (Endsley and Clarey 1975).

Some theorists have hypothesized that same-aged children often differ considerably in the ways they express their curiosity, particularly as they approach the elementary school years and develop more sophisticated information-seeking and problem-solving strategies (Henderson and Moore 1979; Nunnally and Lemond 1973). Children who frequently ask questions have more overt information-seeking styles while other children have a more internalized, covert style of obtaining information and try to work out solutions to games and problems on their own, or seek information from books (Day and Berlyne 1971).

Teachers often have difficulty determining how curious children are, and researchers have not developed techniques to help teachers interpret individual differences. It is difficult to tell whether children who ask many questions are doing so to satisfy their curiosity or simply to maintain a dependency-like contact with us. The more internalized children are often so quiet and unobtrusive that it is difficult to tell whether they are involved in obtaining information or engaged in other processes such as daydreaming.

Further, although the results are inconsistent, investigators have suggested that there may be sex differences in the ways that same-aged children express their curiosity. A few studies have shown that preschool boys are generally less reluctant to leave their mothers and explore objects and toys than are preschool girls (Maccoby and Jacklin 1974). However, it has been suggested that the nature of the objects that boys and girls prefer to explore might account for this difference. There is evidence that girls prefer to explore toys with faces or objects that are more social while boys prefer to explore novel fixtures and nonsocial toys and objects (Maccoby and Jacklin 1974).

Sex differences among same-aged elementary school children's exploratory behavior might also result from restrictions that adults impose on exploration. For instance, one investigator (Coie 1974) found that boys explored more than girls when permission to explore was not explicitly given by an adult; whereas boys and girls explored equally when permission to explore was made explicit by the adult.

Implications

In summary, among same-aged children, some are like Curious George, the rascal monkey who always gets into trouble in the process of satisfying his curiosity. These children are always touching, asking questions, and exploring places and things—sometimes to the teacher's dismay. Other children satisfy their curiosity more quietly by independently examining objects or obtaining information from available resources. Still other children appear not to exhibit any curiosity, perhaps because they have been punished for past exploratory behavior.

This variability among same-aged children may be linked to genetic differences and/or the ways in which children have learned to relate to other people or situations. Teachers who are aware of these individual differences can more skillfully provide experiences to enhance the curiosity development of each child. For example, we might make a wider variety of activities and materials available for children to explore. Boys and girls whose curiosity is best satisfied by manipulating concrete objects can be provided with an interesting variety of these objects, perhaps followed by a question and answer session concerning these objects. Children whose curiosity is best satisfied by obtaining information independently through books and other resources can be provided with these resources and allowed to work alone. Teachers might also make it clear to children that curiosity behaviors, within limits, are valued and sanctioned in the classroom.

What Are The Correlates of Curiosity?

What Is the Relationship Between Curiosity and Intelligence?

Adults often assume that children who are more curious are also more intelligent, perhaps because curious children are often more motivated to achieve and are more alert, attentive, and interested in the things that are going on around them. However, with the exception of one study comparing normal and mentally retarded preschool children (Richman, Kahle, and Rutland 1972), the findings for normal children ranging from first through fifth grade consistently show little or no relationship between curiosity and intelligence test scores (Coie 1974; Day 1968). Consequently, we should not be too quick to assume that more curious children are also more intelligent children (and vice versa).

What Is the Relationship Between Curiosity and Play?

Almost every existing review article on curiosity and/or play begins with an apology for not being able objectively to define and distinguish these two concepts (Weisler and McCall 1976). The existence of several types of play—imaginative play, games, dramatic play—some of which may be more related to exploratory behaviors than are others—complicates the distinction. Some theorists (Berlyne 1960; Hutt 1970; Nunnally and Lemond 1973) have hypothesized that curiosity is distinct from play in several ways:

1. The function of curiosity is seen as seeking specific information in a stimulus-rich environment; whereas the function of play is seen as seeking diversion or stimulation in a familiar environment.

2. Curiosity is viewed as following a predictable sequence (looking, approaching, touching, inquiring); whereas play is viewed as following an unpredictable sequence.

3. Play is said to follow curiosity in temporal order. That is, when children encounter something new and interesting they explore first (look, approach, touch, inquire). Then as the stimulus becomes familiar, they play with it.

These distinctions between curiosity and play are basically theoretical and with few exceptions have not been tested empirically. We should be aware that when children play with objects they may not necessarily be exploring or seeking information about those objects (and vice versa).

What is the Relationship Between Curiosity and Creativity?

Creativity, the ability to find new solutions to a problem or new modes of artistic expression, is valued highly by most teachers. Creative children have the ability to recognize a good problem and tackle it in appropriate but novel ways. Further, they must have the motivation and persistence to tackle and complete problems having novel, complex, and ambiguous elements (Torrance 1971). A few studies

Bradbard and Endsley

show that highly curious elementary school children also score high on creativity tests (Maw and Maw 1970a). Curiosity is often thought of as a prerequisite condition for creativity; however, there is no research evidence to support this claim. If we attempt to nurture either curiosity or creativity in any given situation, we will probably contribute to the development of both.

What Is the Relationship Between Curiosity and Authoritarianism?

Recall that curious children are interested in new, complex, ambiguous, and incongruous objects, people, and places. In contrast, authoritarian children are said to be prejudiced toward people who are different from themselves, intolerant of ambiguity, inflexible in their thinking, and resistant to new information (Adorno et al. 1950). Although there is only indirect evidence that authoritarian children exhibit low levels of curiosity (Maw and Maw 1970a), it would appear that these two attributes are negatively related.

Teachers who are aware of this relationship will be sensitized to the possibility that some children will be more resistant to novel and discrepant objects, information, situations, or people than will others. Further, we will be better equipped to plan programs and activities that help these children gradually become more open to novelty, more flexible in their thinking, and more creative in their approaches to obtaining information and problem solving.

What Is the Relationship Between Curiosity and Anxiety?

The findings consistently show that highly anxious children exhibit less exploratory behavior and interest in their environment than others. This relationship has been found among both preschool and elementary school children (McReynolds, Acker, and Pietila 1961; Mendel 1965). This relationship should be fairly obvious to teachers who intuitively know that children who are fearful, unhappy, or insecure will not venture out and explore their environment until they are made to feel more comfortable with their surroundings.

Perhaps we can help make highly anxious children feel more secure and more curious by making classroom environments as nonthreatening as possible. For example, highly anxious children may initially prefer to engage in simple and familiar tasks in which they can easily succeed. Teachers may need to gradually increase the complexity and novelty of tasks as children begin to feel more successful.

What Is the Relationship Between Curiosity and Self-Concept?

Mastery motivational theorists (White 1959) have hypothesized that as children explore, they learn that they have some control over their environment and correspondingly begin to develop more positive self-concepts. Consistent with this hypothesis, investigators working with both preschool and elementary school children have shown that children who exhibit the most curiosity also have the most positive self-concepts (Maw and Maw 1970b; Minuchin 1971).

Perhaps children who have low self-concepts do not exhibit much curiosity because they expect failure and avoid situations where failure might occur. Conversely, children may fail to explore their environment and gain those experiences that will help them develop better self-concepts because they lack information-seeking skills (Maw and Maw 1970b; Minuchin 1971). Still a third explanation might be that those outside conditions that create low curiosity also create low self-concepts. Teachers should be thinking of ways to increase children's overall curiosity and self-concepts, since it is likely that children who are low on either of these behaviors will also have problems in meeting the demands of school (Maw and Maw 1970b).

Implications

Curiosity is obviously related to many other important aspects of development. Highly curious children are not necessarily more intelligent (as measured by tests), but they are more creative, flexible, and secure about and interested in their environment, and have a better self-image. These attributes are also generally associated with a broader concept of social and intellectual competence in children (White 1959). To the extent that teachers guide children's curiosity behavior, they may also contribute to many of the correlates of curiosity.

How Is Curiosity Influenced by Variations in Situations and Settings?

Some theorists view curiosity as an enduring personality trait which remains relatively stable in children in all or most situations. Considerable evidence, however, suggests that curiosity varies from situation to situation.

How Do Long-Term Maternal Absence and Environmental Deprivation Affect Curiosity?

Depriving humans of appropriate early maternal (or mother surrogate) and sensory experiences has a deleterious effect on general development, especially curiosity behavior. Observational studies of children who spent their first years in orphanages have shown that these children often develop unusual behavior patterns beginning with continual crying and followed by apathy and detachment (Provence and Lipton 1962). This "social retardation" is generally attributed to the almost complete sensory deprivation in the institutional environment. Infants are placed in cribs where they stay most of the day, with few opportunities to explore or play with toys and people.

One recent study specifically examined the curiosity behavior of infants between the ages of 8 and 13 months old, reared fulltime in residential institutions. Their curiosity was compared to the curiosity of children reared at home (Collard 1971). Institutional babies looked at, touched, mouthed, and showed less variety in the ways that they used a set of test toys than did both lower- and middle-class home-reared babies.

How Does Short-Term Maternal Absence and Stranger-Presence Affect Curiosity?

Any teacher of young children who has been through the experience of the first week of school knows how short-term maternal absence affects young children. Some children leave their mothers easily while others cling to their security blankets and cry if they are left before they are ready.

Well-controlled laboratory studies show that the absence of the mother is associated with response decrements in exploratory behavior among one- to five-year-old children and that these responses abate when the mother returns (Cox and Campbell 1963; Gershaw and Schwartz 1971; Gumusgerdan 1977). These researchers reported that as children get older, similar but less intense effects are found. Based on these findings, it seems that skilled teachers who help children make the transition from home to school will soon have children who express their curiosity more freely than they otherwise would.

Teachers are generally aware that not only the school situation in which children are separated from their mothers, but the "strange" adults in that situation affect children's willingness to explore. Several laboratory studies of children ranging from one- to five-year-olds suggest that children manipulate toys more when their

Bradbard and Endsley

mothers are present than when strangers are present (Ainsworth and Bell 1970). Thus, it seems likely that as strangers become more familiar, children will begin to feel more comfortable exploring their environment.

How Is Curiosity Influenced by Different Educational Programs?

Montessori preschool programs view the young child as naturally curious and eager to learn (Miller and Dyer 1975). Other programs, however, (DARCEE, Bereiter-Engelmann, and traditional), assume that some young children have various motivational deficits, such as lack of curiosity or persistence, that must be remedied by the preschool situation before learning can proceed smoothly (Miller and Dyer 1975).

Recently one group of investigators (Miller and Dyer 1975) examined the exploratory and question-asking behavior of children enrolled in Montessori, DARCEE, Bereiter-Engelmann, and traditional preschool programs, using a novel puzzle-like object called the "curiosity box." It was found that from prekindergarten through second grade, the greatest gains in curiosity development were made among children in Montessori and DARCEE programs, both of which stress carefully sequenced tasks, manipulation of objects, and highly academic content, but which differ in more ways than they are alike. However, overall gains in curiosity were also found among children in Bereiter-Engelmann and traditional programs. Thus, it appears more likely that a stimulating, well-planned preschool experience, coupled with sensitive interactions with teachers and peers, rather than the specific program philosophy, contributes to curiosity development in young children.

How Is Curiosity Influenced by Group Size?

Teachers often express an interest in knowing more about what the optimal group size is for inducing children to explore and ask questions about instructional materials. In one interesting study (Rabinowitz et al. 1975), the children were exposed to a colorful structure of a clown driving a train engine. The clown contained several hidden switches that when activated would make a novel sound or cause the clown's nose to light up. Pairs of children more frequently explored and found the hidden switches than did individual children. Further, there is now some research to show that as nursery school and kindergarten group size increases from 2 to 24, the number of questions generated by the group decreases

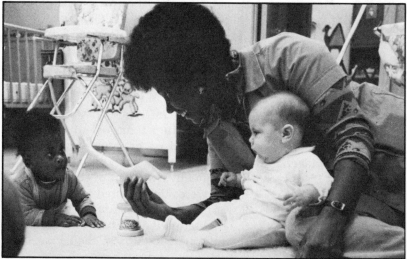

Teachers who are aware of individual differences can more skillfully provide experiences that will enhance the curiosity development of each child.

Florita Botts

Young Children's Curiosity

(Endsley and Gupta 1978; Torrance 1970b). Among nursery school and first grade children, the most questions are asked when the child is in a one-to-one relationship with an adult (Endsley and Gupta 1978; Stallings 1975). To elicit the most questions among three- to seven-year-old children, a smaller group is best.

How Is Curiosity Influenced by the Opportunity to Manipulate Objects?

Teachers have long been convinced that providing children with three-dimensional objects to manipulate will enhance their interest and curiosity about those objects. Children do ask more questions about three-dimensional objects that they are allowed to touch compared to those that they are not allowed to touch (Endsley 1979; Torrance 1970a) or two-dimensional photographs of those objects (Endsley 1979). Thus, question-asking among preschool and kindergarten children can be maximized by providing them with manipulatable objects.

How Does Novelty Affect Curiosity?

Studies that have considered the effect of toy or object novelty on children's curiosity consistently show that children explore more when provided with novel objects (Hutt 1970; Nunnally and Lemond 1973). In one study children became familiar with certain toys and then were offered a selection from sets containing different proportions of novel and familiar toys. Children clearly preferred the set containing 100 percent novelty (Mendel 1965). Findings from another study showed that when nursery school children became familiar with one or two toys, they would subsequently show a preference for one novel toy, even if it were damaged, over the two familiar toys (Harris 1965).

Teachers should be looking for ways to add novel elements to their classrooms to keep children optimally alert and attentive. Alternation of toys and routines, changes in bulletin boards and the arrangement of furniture and equipment, and the introduction of new activities are all relatively simple ways to bring novelty to the classroom. However, remember that too much novelty may make children overly active or frightened.

Implications

Children's curiosity can be optimized by providing a proper balance between novelty and familiarity. Children prefer familiar people and situations and express their wariness when they are placed in unfamiliar settings with "strangers." Yet, children also prefer novel objects and opportunities to seek sensory stimulation from the environment. Thus, teachers must be skillful at achieving the appropriate balance between novelty and familiarity to facilitate children's curiosity development.

How Can Adults Influence Children's Curiosity?

How is Adult Attentiveness, Sensitivity, and Support Related to Curiosity?

The findings consistently show that adult attentiveness, sensitivity, and support are positively related to the exploratory behavior of infants, preschool, and elementary school children. One group of studies shows that high maternal attentiveness is related to increased exploratory behavior among infants, preschoolers, and elementary school children (Endsley et al. 1979; Rubenstein 1967; and Saxe and Stollack 1971). In one of these studies (Rubenstein 1967), mothers were placed in high-, medium-, or low-attentiveness groups based on previous interview and observational data taken in the home. Subsequently, two tests of exploratory behavior were administered to their infants. It was found that the group of infants with the high-attentive mothers exceeded both the other two groups in their visual and tactual exploration of novel objects.

Bradbard and Endsley

In a second group of studies (Ainsworth 1971), mother-infant pairs were observed interacting to determine how sensitive mothers were to their infants' needs. It was found that the most sensitive mothers had the most secure and independent babies. Relatively long periods of holding the infant fostered exploration, rather than "spoiling" the babies. Finally, nursery school children exposed to a friendly, approving adult were found to be more likely to display curiosity behavior and began to explore more quickly than were children exposed to an aloof, critical adult (Moore and Bulbulian 1976). Clearly, adults can be instrumental in fostering curiosity in young children by being attentive, responsive, and supportive of their needs to explore.

How Does Reinforcement Influence Curiosity?

Teachers frequently offer incentives such as grades or stars to children who successfully engage in activities valued by the teacher. With few exceptions (Zimmerman and Pike 1972), the research literature provides little evidence that these extrinsic rewards can alone increase children's curiosity behavior which is often rewarding in itself. Permitting curiosity may be all that is required.

However, a few studies do provide support for the reinforcing effect of providing informative answers to children's questions. Endsley and Clarey (1975) found more than a 60 percent increase in the frequency of questions in sessions in which children received informative answers to their questions as compared to sessions where no information was given. Further, elementary school children remember more information from answers provided to their *own* questions than from overhearing the answers provided to a classmate's questions (Ross and Killey 1977). It was concluded that children are more attentive and receptive to information that stems from their own curiosity and that this information is more easily

stored and later retrieved from their own cognitive structure because they generated it in the first place (Ross and Killey 1977)

The implications from these studies are extremely important for teachers. First, we can encourage and maintain questioning by providing children with informative answers. Second, teachers who generally evaluate their children's learning by asking all the questions themselves might need to provide more opportunities for children to do the questioning. Third, and perhaps most importantly, children need to be provided with more individual opportunities to ask their own questions and receive their own answers (Ross and Killey 1977).

How Does Modeling Influence Children's Curiosity?

Children learn by modeling or imitating the behaviors of respected peers and adults. Preschool children will display more tactual manipulation of objects (Johns and Endsley 1977), and elementary school children will ask more questions (Zimmerman and Pike 1972) when they first observe a model displaying these behaviors. Modeling has been used as a method to teach children to ask more efficient questions and to engage in more efficient problem-solving strategies (Zimmerman and Rosenthal 1974). If we value curiosity, we should also show children how to be curious by being curious ourselves.

Implications

Adults can be instrumental in fostering and maintaining children's curiosity by being attentive, sensitive, and supportive of children's needs to explore, by answering children's questions informatively, and by displaying the positive characteristics of curious people. Further, most people would agree that if children explore objects and ask questions for the intrinsic value they obtain from these activities, other external modes of reinforcement may be unnecessary for most children. However, there are some special cases when curiosity will not be exhibited unless the teacher can initially gain the child's interest and attention. For example, some studies of severely mentally retarded children who exhibit little interest in their surroundings have shown that these children can be trained to attend to a teacher and ask questions about objects through the use of token rewards (Twardosz and Baer 1973). Certainly, there are other special cases of children, such as hyperactive children, whose curiosity behavior would be facilitated by positively reinforcing information-seeking behaviors.

Conclusions

Research consistently points to the gaps in our knowledge and the need for more extensive programs of research. We know little about the generalizability of the existing curiosity research. Most of the research that exists on children's curiosity has been conducted in the laboratory rather than in the home or school. Therefore, we cannot assume that children who are curious in the laboratory will also be curious in their natural environment.

It may be overly simplistic for teachers and researchers to label children's curiosity behavior based on "one shot" observations of behavior because it is more likely that a typical child will ask questions in some situations, touch and manipulate objects in other situations, and express little or no curiosity in still other situations. In future research it may be more useful to examine different modes, patterns, and/or styles of information-seeking that individual children develop in specific situations rather than viewing curiosity as a stable personality trait.

Most researchers have examined only one specific class of curiosity behavior rather than comparing several curiosity behaviors in a given situation (Henderson and Moore 1979). As a result, we have little information on the patterning of information-seeking behaviors and the relationship of these styles to other aspects of children's cognition such as thinking and memory.

The studies reported in this article should pave the way for further research on the development of curiosity in young children. Fortunately, many researchers are interested in formulating research questions that have relevance for classroom practice, and we anticipate that the next decade of curiosity research will be even more relevant for the practitioner. ▽

References

Adorno, T. W.; Frenkel-Brunswik, E.; Levinson, D. J.; and Sanford, R. N. *The Authoritarian Personality.* New York: Harper & Row, 1950.

Ainsworth, M. D. S. "Developmental Changes in Some Attachment Behaviors in the First Year of Life." Symposium presented at the meeting of the Society for Research in Child Development, Minneapolis, April 1971.

Ainsworth, M. D. S., and Bell, S. M. "Attachment, Exploration, and Separation: Illustrated by the Behavior of One-Year-Olds in a Strange Situation." *Child Development* 41 (1970): 49-67.

Berlyne, D. E. "Children's Reasoning and Thinking." In *Carmichael's Manual of Child Psychology* (Vol. 1), ed. P. Mussen. New York: Wiley, 1970.

Berlyne, D. E. *Conflict, Arousal, and Curiosity.* New York: McGraw-Hill, 1960.

Bijou, S. W. "Exploratory Behavior, Curiosity, and Play." In *Child Development: The Basic Stages of Early Childhood,* ed. S. W. Bijou. Englewood Cliffs, N.J.: Prentice-Hall, 1976.

Coie, J. "An Evaluation of the Cross-Situational Stability of Children's Curiosity." *Journal of Personality* 42 (1974): 93-116.

Collard R. R. "Exploratory and Play Behavior of Infants Reared in an Institution and in Lower- and Middle-Class Homes." *Child Development* 42 (1971): 1001-1015.

Corter, C. M.; Rheingold, H. L.; and Eckerman,

C. O. "Toys Delay the Infant's Following His Mother." *Developmental Psychology* 6 (1972): 138-145.

Cox, F. M., and Campbell, D. "Young Children in a New Situation with and without Their Mothers. *Child Development* 39 (1968): 123-131.

Day, H. I. "Role of Specific Curiosity in School Achievement." *Journal of Educational Psychology* 59 (1968): 37-43.

Day, H. I., and Berlyne, D. E. "Intrinsic Motivation." In *Psychology and Educational Practice,* ed. G. S. Lesser. Glenview, Ill.: Scott, Foresman, 1971.

Eckerman, C. O., and Rheingold, H. L. "Infants' Exploratory Responses to Toys and People. *Developmental Psychology* 10 (1974): 255-259.

Endsley, R. C. "Tactual Access, Stimulus Dimensionality, and Peer Presence as Determinants of Young Children's Identification and Transformational Questions," Unpublished manuscript, 1979.

Endsley, R. C., and Clarey, S. "Answering Young Children's Questions as a Determinant of Their Subsequent Question-Asking Behavior." *Developmental Psychology* 11 (1975): 863.

Endsley, R. C., and Gupta, S. "Group Size as a Determinant of Preschool Children's Frequency of Question Asking." *Journal of Genetic Psychology* 132 (1978) 317-318.

Endsley, R. C.; Hutcherson, M. A.; Garner, A. P.; and Martin, M. J. "Interrelationships among Selected Maternal Behaviors, Authoritarianism, and Preschool Children's Verbal and Nonverbal Curiosity." *Child Development,* 50 (1979): 331-339.

Gershaw, N. J., and Schwartz, J. C. "The Effects of a Familiar Toy and Mother's Presence on Exploratory and Attachment Behavior in Young Children." *Child Development* 42 (1971): 1662-1666.

Gumusgerdan, T. "Young Children's Exploration and Questioning of Toys While Alone, with Strangers, and with Their Mothers." Master's thesis, University of Georgia, 1977.

Harris, L. "The Effect of Relative Toy Novelty on Children's Choice Behavior." *Journal of Experimental Child Psychology* 2 (1965): 297-305.

Henderson, B. and Moore, S. G. "Measuring Exploratory Behavior in Young Children." *Developmental Psychology* 15, no. 2 (1979): 113-119.

Hutt, C. "Specific and Diversive Exploration." In *Advances in Child Development and Behavior* (Vol. 5), eds. H. W. Reese and L. P. Lipsett. New York: Academic Press, 1970.

Johns, C., and Endsley, R. C. "The Effects of Maternal Model on Young Children's Tactual Curiosity." *Journal of Genetic Psychology* 131 (1977): 21-28.

Maccoby, E. E., and Jacklin, C. N. *The Psychology of Sex Differences.* Stanford, Calif.: Stanford University Press, 1974.

Maw, W. M., and Maw, E. W. "Establishing Criterion Groups for Evaluating Measures of Curiosity." *Journal of Experimental Education* 29 (1961): 299-306.

Maw, W. M., and Maw, E. W. "Nature of Creativity in High and Low Curiosity Boys." *Developmental Psychology* 2 (1970a): 325-329.

Maw, W. M., and Maw, E. W. "Self Concept of High and Low Curiosity Boys." *Child Development* 41 (1970b): 123-129.

McReynolds, P.; Acker, M.; and Pietila, C. "Relation of Object Curiosity to Psychological Adjustment." *Child Development* 32 (1961): 393-400.

Mendel, G. "Children's Preferences for Differing Degrees of Novelty." *Child Development* 36 (1965): 453-466.

Miller, L. B., and Dyer, J. L. "Four Preschool Programs: Their Dimensions and Effects." *Monograph of the Society for Research in Child Development* 40 (1975): serial #162.

Minuchin, P. "Correlates of Curiosity and Exploratory Behavior in Preschool Disadvantaged Children." *Child Development* 42 (1971): 936-950.

Moore, S. G., and Bulbulian, K. N. "The Effect of Contrasting Styles of Adult-Child Interaction on Children's Curiosity." *Developmental Psychology* 12 (1976): 171-172.

Nunnally, J. C., and Lemond, L. C. "Exploratory Behavior and Human Development." In *Advances in Child Development and Behavior* (Vol. 8), ed. H. W. Reese. New York: Academic Press, 1973.

Provence, S., and Lipton, R. C. *Infants in Institutions.* New York: International Universities Press, 1962.

Rabinowitz, F. M.; Moely, B. E.; Finkel, N.; and McClinton, S. "The Effect of Toy Novelty and Social Interactions on the Exploratory Behavior of Preschool Children." *Child Development* 46 (1975): 286-289.

Rheingold, H. L., and Eckerman, C. O. "The Infant Separates Himself from His Mother." *Science* 168 (1970): 78-83.

Richman, C. L.; Kahle, D.; and Rutland, S. "Curiosity Behavior in Normal and Mentally Retarded Children." *Psychonomic Science* 29 (1972): 212.

Ross, H. S., and Killey, J. C. "The Effect of Questioning on Retention." *Child Development* 48 (1977): 312-314.

Rubenstein, J. "Maternal Attentiveness and Subsequent Exploratory Behavior in Infants." *Child Development* 38 (1967): 1089-1100.

Saxe, R. M., and Stollack, G. E. "Curiosity and the Parent-Child Relationship." *Child Development* 42 (1971): 372-384.

Stallings, J. "Implementation and Child Effects of Teaching Practices in Follow-Through Classrooms." *Monograph of the Society for Research in Child Development* 40 (1975): serial #163.

Torrance, E. P. "Creativity in the Educational Process." In *Psychology and Educational Practice,* ed. G. S. Lesser. Glenview, Ill.: Scott, Foresman, 1971.

Torrance, E. P. "Freedom to Manipulate Objects and Question-Asking Performance of Six-Year-Olds." *Young Children* 26, no. 2 (December 1970): 93-97.

Torrance, E. P. "Group Size and Question Performance of Preprimary Children." *Journal of Psychology* 74 (1970b) 71-75.

Twardosz, S., and Baer, D. M. "Training Two Severely Retarded Adolescents to Ask Questions." *Journal of Applied Behavior Analysis* 6 (1973): 655-662.

Weisler, A., and McCall, R. B. "Exploration and Play—Resumé and Redirection." *American Psychologist* 31 (1976): 492-510.

White, R. W. "Motivation Reconsidered: The Concept of Competence." *Psychological Review* 66 (1959): 297-333.

Zimmerman, B. J., and Pike, E. C. "Effects of Modeling and Reinforcement on the Acquisition and Generalization of Question-asking Behavior." *Child Development* 45 (1972): 892-907.

Zimmerman, B. J., and Rosenthal, T. L. "Observational Learning of Rule-Governed Behavior by Children." *Psychological Bulletin* 81 (1974): 29-42.

Patricia G. Ramsey

Multicultural Education in Early Childhood

"How can we teach children about other cultures when they don't even know what their own ethnic heritages are?" "I have real problems finding materials that don't stereotype cultural or ethnic groups." Questions and comments such as these are frequently voiced by early childhood teachers in response to advocates of multicultural education. Theoreticians and practitioners can point to ample evidence that young children cannot grasp the concept of different countries nor the relationships and correspondences among different cultural groups within a country. In his study of children's views of their homeland, Piaget (1951) found that children before the age of six could not relate the concept of town, state, and country. Many teachers have reported that their children enjoyed the variety of activities involved in United Nations Week programs but were unable to understand the categories of different countries and cultures. Finding information about ethnic groups in this country that is simple enough for children to understand and yet not superficial and stereotypical is another challenge to teachers who integrate multicultural education into the curriculum for young children.

At the same time, there is evidence that children's attitudes toward their own race and toward other racial groups start to form in the preschool years (Goodman 1964; Porter 1971). Infants recognize differences in social objects (Thurman and Lewis 1979) and negative stereotypes appear to be readily absorbed by young children. We once had an Algonquin woman visit our school. Several three-year-olds began to cry and shriek with fright as soon as the visitor mentioned that she was an Indian. Similar accounts of children's stereotyped misconceptions are frequently described by teachers (Califf 1977; Ramsey 1979). During the early years, children are forming their initial social patterns and preferences and their basic approaches to learning about the physical and social worlds. Thus, the difficulties of designing effective multicultural education for young children appear to be considerable; however, there is compelling evidence that in order to influence children's basic racial and cultural attitudes, we must start with the very young.

Challenging some misconceptions

How can we resolve this apparent contradiction? First, there are several prevalent misconceptions about the nature of multicultural education and the rationale for it that need to be challenged. One prevailing idea is that multicultural education should focus on information about other countries and cultures. Plans for implementing multicultural education are often reminiscent of the geography or history

Patricia G. Ramsey, Ed.D., is Assistant Professor, Early Childhood Education, Wheelock College, Boston.

The design and implementation of multicultural education rests with the attitudes, skills, and knowledge of the teacher.

lessons that we learned as children. There is an emphasis on names of countries, their capitals, flags, exports, typical artifacts, and famous people. Efforts to have International Week or to cover a country a week often fall into the trap of teaching children facts for which they have no context. We frequently stress information that is meaningful to adults but not necessarily to children. Moreover, the emphasis on exotic differences often accentuates the "we" and "they" polarity. Thus, in many respects, this type of curriculum may actually work against the goal of under-

Ramsey

standing the shared experiences of all people.

A second misconception is the notion that multicultural education is only relevant in classrooms with students who are members of the cultural and racial groups to be studied. When I suggested the topic of multicultural education for a workshop I was to give, the teachers quickly said that because they did not have any Blacks or members of other minority groups in their classrooms, such a workshop would be irrelevant. These responses reflected a limited view of the effects and responsibilities of intergroup relationships. The fact that teachers and children in this country feel disassociated from issues related to race and culture underscores the importance of multicultural education for children of all cultural groups.

From an early age children who grow up in culturally mixed settings or as members of minority groups are exposed to the idea that our society is comprised of many groups. Through television, books, and school they have been exposed to the life styles and expectations of the Anglo-American middle class. From their own experiences they may also be aware of the existence and effects of discrimination. Many American children however, can grow to adulthood unaware of and insensitive to the experiences of other cultural groups. The extent of this isolation is illustrated by the following incident. Recently, in Boston, a Black, high school football player was shot during a game in a White community. In a subsequent discussion in a class of student teachers, the people working in the inner city talked about the questions and reactions expressed by their young students. In contrast, the students teaching in the suburbs a few miles away reported that neither the teachers nor the children mentioned the incident.

In order to increase the potential for positive relationships among groups of people, all children need to expand their realm of awareness and concern beyond their immediate experience. Since education in this country traditionally has been dominated by the Anglo-American point of view, one important task of multicultural education is to try to balance this lopsided learning by helping children look into and beyond their relatively insulated environments.

A third misconception, that there should be a unified set of goals and curriculum for multicultural education, contradicts the underlying purpose of multicultural education to provide relevant and meaningful education to children from all cultural backgrounds. Many books and activity kits designed for multicultural education describe curriculum with no mention of the cultural backgrounds and attitudes of the children in the class. In order to design effective multicultural education, teachers need to learn about the racial, cultural, and socio-economic background of children in their care, what experiences they have had with people from other groups, and their attitudes toward their own and other groups. In order to respond to these variations, the goals and the curriculum will differ considerably from classroom to classroom.

For instance, in a classroom of children from diverse backgrounds, the primary goal might be to help the children understand the extent of their similarities and the nature of some of their differences. Learning how to communicate if there is not a shared language might also be a major focus of the classroom. However, for a group of White middle-class children who have grown up in a relatively monocultural environment, the emphasis would be in seeing the diversity that exists among the group members and grasping the idea that there are many other cultures and ways of life. For children from low-status groups, one initial goal would be to foster their respect and appreciation for their own culture. Children of high-status groups often need to become more realistic about the relative value of their own culture. The social and political climate of the school and community should also be taken into account. The state of intergroup relationships and the prevalence of negative or positive perceptions of the groups influence the children's attitudes. While published multicultural materials can be used as resources for information and, in some cases, activities, each education program should be designed to fit the backgrounds, awareness levels, and attitudes of the particular group of children in each class.

Finally, the misconception that multicultural education is a set of activities added on to the existing curriculum needs to be reexamined. Multicultural education embodies a perspective rather than a curriculum. Just as teachers constantly assess and address children's social skills, emotional states, and cognitive abilities, so should teachers consider children's cultural identities and attitudes. This type of learning can occur every minute of the day. Effective teachers are ingenious at incorporating language skills, problem-solving abilities, and social experience into all activities. Likewise, teachers can seize opportunities to foster the children's awareness of their immediate and broader social world. A child's comment about a picture of an unfamiliarly clothed person, the arrival of a child who does not speak English, a conflict between two children, the advent of a holiday season, and a visiting grandparent are a few of the many moments that can become opportunities to introduce and reinforce the idea that people share many of the same feelings and needs yet express them in many different ways. In addition to incidental teaching moments, all aspects of the planned curriculum can incorporate a multicultural perspective. Decisions about materials, program structure, the role of parents, and the selection of curriculum topics all reflect attitudes toward cultures.

The role of the teacher

The design and implementation of multicultural education rests, in large part, with the attitudes, skills, and knowledge of the teacher. One initial step is for teachers to become aware of their own cultural backgrounds, their relationships with the larger society, and their attitudes toward other people. This process requires a great deal of honesty and is often painful. However, it is important that we all recognize our biases and ignorance. It is tempting to deny our prejudices and to claim that we find all children equally appealing. Many teachers, in their efforts to minimize differences, maintain that children are all alike. While such comments emerge from genuine intentions to be fair and impartial in their perceptions and their relationships with children, they also reflect a naiveté about the power and effects of social attitudes and conditions. As teachers we need to accept the fact that we, like our young charges, have inevitably been influenced by the stereotypes and the one-sided view of society that prevail in the schools and the media.

I spent several weeks observing in an elementary school noted for its humanistic, child-centered approach to learning. The teachers had met the challenges of mainstreaming special needs children with commitment, sensitivity, and imagination. However, in our conversations, there were frequent disparaging allusions to the "foreign student element." Clearly frustrated by the extra work that these recent immigrants required, the teachers tended to dwell on the things that the children "didn't even know." Differences in life style and language were interpreted as ignorance. Neither the school nor the individual teachers attempted to learn about the diverse cultures of the children or to incorporate that richness into the classrooms. These kinds of attitudes obscure our own biases and restrict our realm of knowledge. Thus, it is important that we dispel the illusion that we are totally without prejudice and recognize that there are many valid ways of life beyond our immediate experience. Humility and a

Ramsey

The ability to see and appreciate others' perspectives is an important skill for understanding and relating to different cultural groups.

genuine desire to know more about other people are absolute prerequisites for designing and implementing multicultural education. From this perspective, we can genuinely learn about the children's cultural backgrounds and attitudes and start to form effective and reciprocal collaborations with parents and people in the community. This knowledge can then provide the base to design ways of promoting cultural identity and positive attitudes toward various cultural and ethnic groups. Once a multicultural perspective has been incorporated into our view of children and educational goals, many ways of implementing it in our classrooms become obvious.

Guidelines for integrating a multicultural perspective

The possibilities for a multicultural program suggested here are by no means exhaustive. However, it is hoped that these concrete ideas will enable teachers to see more clearly how appropriate forms of multicultural education can be woven into their programs.

Enhance self-concept and cultural identity

The development of a positive self-concept is a major goal of early childhood programs. Usually the curriculum related

Multicultural Education

to this goal consists of activities to enhance awareness and appreciation of each child's feelings and competencies. Stories, art projects, and discussions about families, homes, likes and dislikes, and other related topics are frequent. Each child's cultural, ethnic, and racial identity can easily be incorporated into these activities. Activities can focus on how all the children's lives are similar and yet different. This enhances identification with one's own culture as well as awareness of other cultures. For minority children, this theme is ideal for stressing the value of their culture and for neutralizing the impact of negative stereotypes.

In classrooms that are monocultural, the differences among the children may be limited to family size, personal experiences, and physical appearance, but still the idea that people are both similar and different can be explored. For children who have had little or no experience with people from other cultural backgrounds, the notion that people who look different from them have similar needs can be woven into discussions about families and feelings. Photographs in *The Family of Man* (Steichen 1955) and *This Is My Father and Me* (Raynor 1973) help convey the concept that all people have common needs, feelings, and relationships even though they may look, dress, and speak in many different ways. The goal here is not to teach about particular cultures or countries but to incorporate into the children's own framework images and experiences that support the development of cultural identity and the awareness of diversity.

For children, kindergarten age and younger, these activities should be very concrete. Having the children bring in photographs of their families and themselves as babies will provide very immediate ways to talk about the children, their growth, their similarities, and differences. Visiting parents and siblings can also make the children aware that everyone has a family; yet each one is unique. Activities in the role-play area can further stimulate discussion of variations among the children's families.

For primary-age children, these concepts can be incorporated into early language arts activities. Children can write and share stories about their own backgrounds and family. Books that appropriately reflect the different backgrounds of the children in the class should be available. Bringing in family trees and stories can make the idea of background more real. Trips to neighborhoods, museums, and community organizations may also enhance children's awareness of the cultural groups in their class and community. For second and third graders, maps, globes, and simple histories might also be introduced within the context of knowing more about themselves and their classmates.

Develop social skills and responsibility

The ability to recognize that another person has a point of view, state of mind, and feelings that are distinct from one's own is an important area of development. Through maturation and social experience children learn how to identify, predict, and respond to others' points of view. Clearly, the ability to see and appreciate others' perspectives are important skills for understanding and relating to different cultural groups. While these skills are emerging in very young children, they develop quickly as children progress to kindergarten and the primary grades. Flavell et al. (1968) found that children often do not choose to use their abilities to see what others are experiencing. He suggested that there are some ways that we can motivate children to practice and expand these skills. The first one is making provisions for frequent social interaction. Second, we can consistently call the children's attention to the existence of other points of view. Third, children should be encouraged to communicate so that others can understand them. Finally, the presence of younger children may make the reality of others' needs and points of view more concrete. Consideration of these factors would influence both the physical and social structure of the classroom.

Young children spend a great deal of time exploring social relationships. Initially, they watch each other, then play beside, and gradually make attempts to play together with varying degrees of success. Rivalries, inseparable pairs, exclusive "gangs," bullies, and transient friendships all emerge, change, and end in rapidly shifting events. Classroom equipment and activities can be set up to provide many opportunities for cooperative activities, where children have to coordinate their actions to achieve a common goal. Equipment such as seesaws, pulleys, and hoists that require two people, large blocks, double slides, and horizontal tire swings, all facilitate social play. A stimulating and attractive role-play corner invites many group interactions. Almost all activities in the art, construction, and science areas can be adapted to incorporate a cooperative dimension. In creative movement, children can be asked to synchronize their motions in many ways that increase awareness of each other.

Classroom chores such as cleaning up, moving furniture, transporting materials, preparing snack, collecting litter, and emptying the wading pool can all provide increased opportunity for social interaction, communication, and the experience of other (often conflicting) points of view. Conflicts over materials are excellent opportunities to help children express their own feelings and listen to those of their opponents. In helping to resolve these disputes, teachers can guide the children toward cooperation. All too often, we settle conflicts by simply giving the children another object so they can each have one or by telling them to play separately. By emphasizing cooperation rather than individual achievements in our plans and guidance, we can foster the development of social awareness and communication skills.

When children enter the primary grades, teachers tend to focus on children's academic skills. During lunch, recess, and after school children work out their social hierarchies, rivalries, friendships, and cooperative ventures. In many respects, children at this age have gained enough control, awareness of others, and communication skills to manage without a lot of adult supervision. However, there are many classrooms where scapegoating, excluding, bullying, and rivalry go unchecked. Moreover, little time and attention are paid to helping children further develop their skills in cooperating and communicating. Classroom projects such as plays, murals, sculptures, newspapers, and construction projects can provide opportunities to expand social contacts and skills as well as to practically apply academic skills. At recess and gym, cooperative games can be introduced to balance the societal emphasis on competition (Orlick 1978). Certainly in classrooms where there are tensions among racial and cultural groups, it is crucial that teachers take an active role in establishing a positive social climate and helping children explore and resolve their differences.

The inclusion of younger and/or special needs children in classrooms may provide opportunities for children to be aware of others' needs and to learn when it is appropriate to offer help. In age-stratified groups, children usually receive attention, help, care, and teaching from adults and rarely are in situations where they can contribute to the knowledge or welfare of others. Not only is this awareness and concern for others basic to the goals of multicultural education, it is also relevant to recently emerging concerns about the self-centeredness of the me generation. While the presence of special needs and younger children may make the idea of social awareness and responsibility more concrete, these expectations can be incorporated into any classroom. Young children can be encouraged to help each other get dressed to go outside, pick up spilled crayons, carry the trikes onto the porch, etc. For primary age children, this involvement might be extended to raising money or contributing work for community people who need help. These activities are vehicles for fostering cooperation, social responsibility, and awareness of other people. It is important, however, that the children do not view the recipients of their efforts as "less good" or the "needy poor," but rather as people who, like themselves, sometimes need assistance.

Children's orientation to the social world, which begins with their earliest friendships, must be considered as part of any efforts to integrate multicultural education into the curriculum. Efforts to expand children's awareness of others, their capacity to communicate, their willingness and ability to cooperate, and their sense of social responsibility should be emphasized throughout their lives.

Broaden the cultural base of the curriculum

In addition to considering the children's self-concept, cultural identity, and their basic social orientation, teachers also need to broaden the cultural awareness of their students. Here the goal is not to teach children *about* other groups or countries but rather to help children become accustomed to the idea that there are many life-styles, languages, and points of view. Two factors appear to influence children's concepts of other groups (Lambert and Klineberg 1967). One is their perception of their own group. If their view is unrealistically superlative, then it creates an attitude of superiority toward others. Second, if children learn about other groups only in terms of contrasts, then they see them as being more different than groups about which they know nothing. Thus, it is important that teachers present a realistic

view of the children's own group and stress the similarities among all people. Furthermore, children are more likely to integrate new information when they see it in relation to their previous knowledge (Forman and Kuschner 1977).

In a culturally diverse classroom, children can experience this relationship in a concrete way. "When Jorge talks to his mother, I can't understand him; when he talks to me, I can. When we play with cars, he calls them 'carros' so I call them 'carros' too." In these situations, teachers can incorporate a wide cultural content in the curriculum by including experiences and materials that reflect the children's cultural groups. While the teachers need to establish the basic framework for such a curriculum, the children, parents, and community can provide many resources.

In a monocultural group, these concepts are more difficult to convey. The fact that there are many different ways that people look, eat, work, cook, speak, etc., has to be more consciously introduced into the classroom. By concretely experiencing many different ways of doing things it is hoped that children will become more acclimated and receptive to variations among people. Children may develop more flexible expectations of human behavior, which, in turn, will enable them to approach contacts with less familiar people with a more respectful and open-minded attitude.

In early childhood classrooms, there are many opportunities to introduce variations in clothing, cooking, work, music, etc., into the classroom in very concrete ways. For instance, young children can be encouraged to try many ways of carrying objects using their backs, hips, heads, and in a variety of containers. These activities can be encouraged by having pictures that show people carrying objects in many different ways. The message would not be "The people in India carry containers of water on their heads," nor would it be "We do it *this* way, they do it *that* way."

Instead, the idea that "All people carry things in many different ways and you can try some of them" would be emphasized. This same principle and format can be applied to include a variety of clothing, tools, and utensils in the role-playing corner. Singing and dancing from many different cultures are lively ways of conveying this concept. Other languages and nonverbal forms of communication can be introduced in the language arts program with songs, dramatics, books, and pictures. Foods, cooking, and eating are popular vehicles for incorporating unfamiliar experiences in a comprehensible context. Holidays provide high-interest occasions for incorporating cultural experiences into the classroom. There are many similar celebrations across cultures. Seasonal festivals (planting, harvesting, the celebrations of light at the winter solstice, the arrival of the new year) and commemorations of independence and other historical events occur in virtually every culture. Observances of familiar holidays can be greatly enriched by incorporating many cultural expressions of similar themes (Flemming, Hamilton, and Hicks 1977; Ramsey 1979).

In primary classrooms, many similar activities can be introduced in greater depth. Cooking activities, celebrations of holidays, and learning new languages can stimulate a great deal of interest and involvement in all areas of the curriculum. For these older children, teachers may want to make more information available about various groups, but it is important not to get involved in trying to convey information that is not meaningful to the children. When the children seem ready, teachers can start helping them to see the correspondences between their own lives and activities and those of others. When attempting to draw comparisons, it is important to avoid the we/they dichotomy or any suggestion that the unfamiliar forms are inferior. One important factor in reducing ethnocentrism is to see our own behaviors and responses as simply one way of doing things, not the only nor the best way.

Young children can experience in many concrete and meaningful ways the rich variety of human experience. Far from contradicting the goals and practice of early childhood education, this inclusion will enrich and expand them.

Study a particular group

Studying the cultures represented in any group of children is an important contribution to their cultural identity and understanding of their classmates. If there are children in the group who have recently immigrated to this country, then studying their homeland may be a way of easing the newcomers' entry into the classroom. This approach makes the adjustment and learning process a mutual and reciprocal one instead of being the sole responsibility of the recent arrival. Teachers might also want to focus on a particular culture or country if the children express a great deal of interest and/or many misconceptions about that goup of people. In this country, this phenomena often occurs about Native American peoples. Teachers have tried and reported some success in their efforts to reduce negative stereotypes and to promote authentic understanding and appreciation of Native Americans (Council on Interracial Books for Children 1977).

When developing a focus on a particular group of people, it is important that the *people*, not the stereotypes or exotic differences, are studied. The fact that they are individuals who share many of the feelings and needs that children have experienced can be conveyed with photographs, stories, and if possible, actual contact with people from that group. Whenever children learn about a life style that differs from their own, they need to be given a context in which to understand why that particular system was developed. They need to understand all human behavior as

Children may develop more flexible expectations of human behavior, which, in turn, will enable them to approach contacts with less familiar people with a more respectful and open-minded attitude.

reasonable responses to the environment, not simply as isolated actions. Also, the distinctions between the contemporary life styles and historical ones need to be drawn clearly, so that children do not confuse different cultures with different historical periods. For example, they need to understand not just that "The Sioux people lived in tepees," but that "The Sioux people *used* to live in tepees because they needed to have homes that they could move easily as they followed the herds of buffalo. *Now* some of the people live in houses on reservations and others live in cities and suburbs." It is important that we do not convey a romanticized post card image of other people. Some sense of the political and social realities should be incorporated into the curriculum. For instance, it would be a misrepresentation to study Cambodia without some discussion of the present plight of the people there. As mentioned previously, the depth and complexity of the information will obviously depend largely on the age and experience of the children involved. However, efforts to simplify information should not impair its authenticity.

The activities that are developed as part of this curriculum should be concrete and comprehensible to the children. As described earlier, much of this information can be incorporated into materials and experiences that are already familiar. For preschoolers, this immediacy is particularly important. For primary age children, information should be offered only as long as they appear to understand it. Because of the complexity of many of the concepts involved, teachers should carefully monitor the children's responses to insure that they are forming authentic and differentiated perceptions of the people being studied.

Conclusion

Multicultural education can be incorporated effectively into every aspect of early childhood programs. While multicultural education may seem to be most immediately relevant to classes with minority children, it is even more important that all children in this country understand the culturally pluralistic nature of our society. Teachers need to be conscious of their own views and the limits of their knowledge in order to learn about the backgrounds and attitudes of the children in their classes. Using this information, they can design appropriate goals and curricula.

The concept of shared human experience and cultural diversity can be woven into all aspects of the curriculum. The emphasis on social and emotional development can be expanded to incorporate the enhancement of children's cultural identity and their awareness, concern, and respect for other people. Through a variety of materials and activities, young children can become accustomed to the idea that there are many ways of doing things. For primary school children, there should be a continued emphasis on the development of self-concepts, cultural identities, and social skills. As these children start to express curiosity about the world and gain skills to seek information, they should have access to materials that will foster their awareness of the diversity of human experience as well as its common themes.

Despite the complexity of its issues and content, multicultural education is far from incompatible with early childhood education. In fact, by incorporating one with the other, we can enrich and expand the lives of the children with whom we work.

References

Califf, J. "What One Teacher Has Done." In *Unlearning "Indian" Stereotypes*. New York: Council on Interracial Books for Children, 1977.

Council on Interracial Books for Children. *Unlearning "Indian" Stereotypes*. New York: Council on Interracial Books for Children, 1977.

Flavell, J. H.; Botkin, P. T.; Fry, C. L.; Wright, J. W.; and Jarvis, P. E. *The Development of Role Taking and Communication Skills in Children*. New York: Wiley, 1968.

Flemming, B. M.; Hamilton, D. S.; and Hicks, J. D. *Resources for Creative Teaching in Early Childhood Education*. New York: Harcourt, Brace & Jovanovich, 1977.

Forman, G., and Kuschner, D. *The Child's Construction of Knowledge*. Monterey, Calif. Brooks/Cole, 1977.

Goodman, M. E. *Race Awareness in Young Children*. New York: Collier, 1964.

Lambert, W. E., and Klineberg, O. *Children's Views of Foreign Peoples*. New York: Appleton-Century Crofts, 1967.

Orlick, T. *The Cooperative Sports and Games Book*. New York: Pantheon, 1978.

Piaget, J. "The Development in Children of the Idea of the Homeland and of Relations with Other Countries." *International Social Science Journal* (Autumn 1951): 561-578.

Porter, J. D. R. *Black Child, White Child: The Development of Racial Attitudes*. Cambridge, Mass.: Harvard University Press, 1971.

Ramsey, P. G. "Beyond Turkeys and 'Ten Little Indians': Alternative Approaches to Thanksgiving." *Young Children* 34, no. 6 (September 1979): 28-32, 49-52.

Raynor, D. *This Is My Father and Me*. Chicago: Whitman, 1973.

Steichen, E. *The Family of Man*. New York: Simon & Schuster, 1955.

Thurman, S. K., and Lewis, M. "Children's Responses to Differences: Some Possible Implications for Mainstreaming." *Exceptional Children* 45, no. 6 (March 1979): 468-470.

Suggested resource books

Cole, A.; Haas, C.; Hellen, E.; and Weinberger, B. *Children Are Children Are Children*. Boston: Little, Brown, 1978.

Gold, M. J.; Grant, C. A.; and Rivlin, H. N. *In Praise of Diversity: A Resource Book for Multicultural Education*. Washington, D.C.: Association of Teacher Educators, 1977.

Schmidt, V., and McNeill, E. *Cultural Awareness: A Resource Bibliography*. Washington, D.C.: National Association for the Education of Young Children, 1978.

Shepard, M., and Shepard, R. *Vegetable Soup Activities*. New York: Citation, 1975.

Robert F. Smith

Early Childhood Science Education

A Piagetian Perspective

How can we properly teach children unless we know how they think, how their concepts of time, space, number, and cause and effect develop?

Five-year-old Melanie was examining the objects in the water table. She seemed intrigued that some objects stayed on top of the water while others fell to the bottom. Her teacher asked her what was happening to the objects. Melanie enthusiastically responded, "The ping-pong ball is resting on top of the water but the golf ball fell to the bottom." When the teacher asked Melanie why she thought the ping-pong ball stayed on top, Melanie said, "Because it's small!" Her response to the question about why the golf ball fell to the bottom was the same, "Because it's small." Melanie was convinced that her explanation was accurate, yet her response seemed illogical to her teacher because she used the same reason—the object's size—to account for two different phenomena.

It is difficult for adults to think as the young child thinks—to see reality from the eyes of a three-, five-, or seven-year-old child. We cannot go back in time and remember our first thoughts when asked to predict which objects would sink and which would float. When did we first realize that from the tiny bean seed we planted in April emerged the lovely green plant we observed growing in May? Can anyone recollect when she or he understood that the number three stood for a quantity greater than the number two but less than the number four?

The thinking of the adult is far more sophisticated, logical, and flexible than the thinking of the young child. How can we properly teach children unless we know how they think, how their concepts of time, space, number, and cause and effect develop? Our knowledge of how children think and view reality provides us with an appropriate framework from which a science curriculum for young children can emerge.

Preoperational thought

Piaget has provided us with one of the best descriptions of how children think and characteristics of their thinking at different stages of their development. The preoperational stage particularly interests early childhood educators because it encompasses a range from two or two-and-a-half to about seven years of age. Children at this stage have not yet developed the ability to think logically or abstractly; reasoning is unsystematic and does not lead to the generalization or formation of logical concepts. Why is this so?

1. Preoperational children's thinking is bound by perception. Children can focus on only one attribute of an object at a time, usually the most predominant feature such as size, shape, or color. Although *centering* prevents children from observing other properties of an object simultaneously, it nevertheless enables children to acquire knowledge about the object. This physical knowledge is a prerequisite for the development of logical thought.

2. Preoperational children can focus on only the beginning or end state of a transformation, not on the transformation itself. Children can confirm that two balls of clay are equivalent in amount. However, when one ball of the clay is transformed into the shape of a sausage, children can no longer establish that equivalence. The sausage-shaped piece usually is perceived as longer, and therefore children generally conclude that it has more clay. Preoperational children's thinking is not *reversible*.

3. Preoperational children are unable to conserve and thus are not able to recognize the invariance of a number of objects when their spatial arrangement is transformed. Young children also cannot compensate for changes in dimensions. When an equal amount of water is poured from a tall narrow glass into a short wide glass, preoperational children do not recognize that a change in length is compensated for by a change in width. The ability to *conserve* marks the gradual transition from thinking that is perceptually oriented, largely intuitive, and irreversible, to thinking that is logical, flexible, and reversible. Research has shown that these changes in thinking appear between the ages of five and eight.

4. Another characteristic of preoperational thought is egocentrism. Children view the world from their own perspective. This egocentrism can lead to misinterpretations of natural phenomena. Chittenden (1970) cites an example used by Piaget of the young child who claims that the sun moves when he moves, "when one walks, it follows. When one turns 'round it turns 'round too (p. 11)." Egocentrism makes it difficult for children to imagine how an object or scene might look when viewed from positions other than their own.

Preoperational children's inability to think logically does not mean they are deficit thinkers. On the contrary, these children are exploring, manipulating, questioning, comparing, contrasting, labeling, and forming mental images. These activities lay the foundation for the development of children's ability to think logically.

The preoperational child's view of reality

Because science education involves a study of natural phenomena, early childhood teachers planning a science curriculum need to understand how preoperational children interpret such phenomena.

For young children, anything that moves is alive—a car, a cloud, branches on a tree. Things that do not move are not alive. Laurendeau and Pinard (1962) presented children with a list of familiar objects and asked them to group the objects into categories of living and nonliving things. The children's conclusions supported Piaget's earlier findings that children under nine or ten years of age experience some difficulty in correctly identifying whether objects are alive.

The operational-stage concept of identity encompasses an understanding of the invariant in any conservation process. In the case of organisms, preoperational children do not understand that as the or-

Robert F. Smith, Ph.D., is Coordinator, Division of Early Childhood Education, School of Education, Brooklyn College, Brooklyn, New York.

R. Smith

ganism grows and changes over time, it still remains basically the same. Examples of changing organisms include the transformation of a seed into a plant which produces fruit containing new seeds and the metamorphosis of a caterpillar into a butterfly or a mealworm into a beetle.

Gilbert and Voyat (in Howe and Johnson 1975) tested children's understanding of the concept of identity by showing them a series of photographs of plants at various stages of growth. The children in their study had little difficulty recognizing two adjacent photographs as the same plant, but they did find it hard to believe that an early photograph pictured the same plant as shown in a later photograph in the same series.

Piaget's studies of young children's understanding of cause and effect relationships identified three basic characteristics that dominate the child's explanation of causality (Good 1977). Piaget labeled the first characteristic *animism*. Things such as the sun, moon, trees, and air act the way they do because they want to; they have a consciousness and thus can act voluntarily. Good (1977) records an interview with six-year-old Tom who, when asked "Where does the sun go at night?", responded, "It goes to sleep. And then the moon wakes up and *it* shines! (p. 8)"

Piaget used the term *artificialism* to describe "the belief that everything has been built by man or by a divine being who fabricates things in human fashion (Piaget 1968, p. 27)." When asked, "Where did the wind come from in the first place?" Tom answered, "Well, you see, God gave men air so they could breathe, and he wanted to help them out a little more. Like, you know sailboats? Well, the air moves them. The air pushes, and God helped us out so we could ride sailboats (Good 1977, pp. 8-9)."

Lastly, Piaget used the term *magic* to refer to thinking in which cause and effect in special relations are not connected or to refer to causal explanations which are unrelated logically. The child's explanation

that makes people the cause of natural phenomena fits under this category.

Thus, until approximately the age of

Concepts of natural phenomena must be developed through manipulation of items within the child's immediate environment.

seven or eight, children explain causality in terms of animism, artificialism, magic, or various combinations of each. Gradually, however, they progress toward a more objective explanation of cause and effect relationships.

Implications for early childhood science education

Because preoperational children learn by acting on objects, concepts of natural phenomena must be developed through manipulation of items within children's immediate environment and observation of children's reactions under varying circumstances. Abstract concepts outside the realm of immediate experience should not be included in an early childhood science curriculum.

Because children cannot observe these concepts, and thus find them incomprehensible, Kamii and DeVries (1978) reject the following topics as inappropriate for young children:

> *Electricity* . . . Dry cell batteries can be used to ring bells and to light bulbs. Children can learn to complete the circuit to make it work. Show the children the electric element on the hot plate or electric frying pan used for cooking projects. They can learn such words as battery, circuit, outlets, plugs, bulbs, and switches. (Hildebrand 1971, pp. 157-158)

> *Matter and energy* . . . Some machines burn fuel; some use electricity. [(Leeper, et al. 1974, p. 306) Quoted in Kamii and DeVries, p. 11.]

Good (1977) identified the following concepts related to a unit on weather in first-grade science textbooks as inappropriate for the cognitive abilities of typical six-year-old children:

> Water is always evaporating . . .

> The cycle of evaporation and condensation is a result of a heat exchange . . .

> The weather cycle is related to the water cycle. (p. 161)

He also found, particularly in first-grade teachers' guides, the following inappropriate concepts taught under the broad topic of earth, moon, and sun system:

> Day and night are caused by the rotation of the earth . . .

> Planets, including the earth, revolve around the sun . . .

> The sizes of the planets vary as do their relative distances from the sun. (p. 162)

Such concepts demand a thorough understanding of perspective, relative position, and motion. Preoperational children are incapable of such abstractions.

Young children's inability to think logically precludes teaching that attempts to prove principles through appeals to logic. For example, one cannot teach the preoperational child that whereas all birds are animals, not all animals are birds. Nor can one teach this same child that as long as nothing is added or taken away, a given quantity of water will remain the same regardless of the size or shape of the container it is in. Also, because preoperational children cannot consider several variables simultaneously, Elkind (1972) feels that—

> . . . instruction in controlled experimentation probably should not be introduced until adolescence when young people can deal with multiple simultaneous variations. The child must be able to cope with holding some factors constant while others are systematically varied. (p. 10)

Clearly, science instruction in the early childhood years should take into account how children learn. Decisions about appropriate content and experiences should be based upon the immediate needs and developing abilities of each child in the classroom.

An early childhood science curriculum

Although young children might be limited conceptually, there are no limits, unless adults set them, to children's curiosity, imagination, zest for learning, and interest in the many things about them. Experiences in science (Neuman 1972) not only satisfy children's curiosity and interest, but also are the best vehicle for helping children make that important transition from thinking that is perception-bound, egocentric, and illogical to thinking that is flexible, logical, reversible, and capable of conserving.

Science for young children is finding out about the world in which they live. "Exploration of the environment is certainly involved—the examination of what is there. . . . There may be experimenting, there may be measuring, but much of the work will be finding out" (Schools Council 1972b, p. 5). Young children find out

R. Smith

through hands-on experiences with objects and events in the immediate environment.

Why is such experience so important for the developing child? According to Piaget, experiences build upon each other. Children must actively relate something new in their experience to experiences previously encountered, assimilated, and stored as mental structures or understandings. Otherwise there is little chance children will understand a new experience.

For example, Jaime wants an apple, but the fruit basket is on top of the kitchen cabinet, which he cannot reach. How does Jaime accommodate himself to this problem? He has had previous experiences of climbing—stairs, the ladder on his outdoor gym. He has also seen his parents climbing ladders to paint the kitchen ceiling. Jaime has assimilated these experiences into his understanding of climbing. Yet there are no stairs or ladders available in the kitchen. What does Jaime do? He adapts to this new situation by looking for something he can use to climb upon to reach the fruit basket. He may use a kitchen chair or stool. This process of finding a balance between something previously understood and current experience is called equilibration. It is one of the most important factors affecting cognitive development.

Thus, the role of experience in the early years cannot be overemphasized. For example, sinking and floating activities with a variety of objects provides the young child with a conceptual framework upon which to draw while attempting to understand bouyancy problems presented in later grades. Early planting experiences lay the necessary foundation for relating meaningfully to later instruction in the

In direct experiences with the environment, children can observe, predict, classify, and communicate.

Ann-Marie Mott

parts of plants and their functions, how seeds germinate, and how leaves produce food (photosynthesis). Children who have limited experience with natural phenomena in their early years in school will undoubtedly have difficulty understanding new but related phenomena in later grades.

Children can be encouraged to use basic process skills in direct experiences with the environment. Four such processes are observing, predicting, classifying, and communicating. These skills enable children to make sense out of varied, challenging, and interesting experiences.

Observation is the most important skill to be developed in young children as they experience reality (Elkind 1972). Neuman (1972) points out that "observing is the fundamental building block for all of the other processes and thus must be stressed in every way possible throughout *all* of the various activities carried out in sciencing (p. 218)." Observation is much more than a superficial examination of an object accompanied by a one- or two-word description. Observation means a total involvement by children, using all senses, in finding out about an object, its properties, and how it reacts under varying circumstances. To do this, children must act upon the object.

For example, in learning about the properties of water, children do not just taste water. They feel water; they listen to water dripping, splashing, gurgling; and they see how water reacts under various circumstances: Water takes the shape of its container; water flows through some materials and not through others; and water dissolves some substances but not others.

Young children must be encouraged to observe how objects are alike and different. By making comparisons among seeds, leaves, shells, rocks, and various other items found in their immediate environment, children look, touch, taste, smell, and listen. Piaget calls knowledge that comes from the object itself *physical knowledge*, and it is the foundation upon

which intelligence develops (Kamii and DeVries 1978). Children enjoy *predicting* what will happen. Making predictions helps children accommodate their thinking to new experiences. Will a ping-pong ball float or sink? Young children, bound by their perceptions, might say the ball will sink because it is big. The size of the object dominates their thinking. Yet, when the ball is placed in water, it floats! How do children explain this confusing phenomenon? Through further exploring, asking questions, and discovering, children are soon able to accommodate their thinking about floating and sinking so that not only size but also shape and weight begin to emerge as indicators of whether an object will sink or float.

During explorations of science-related phenomena, children should use another important process skill: *classifying* (grouping or sorting objects according to some common property). Even though preoperational children can only group objects on a perceptual level, such an ability precedes higher-level classification skills. Children acquire logico-mathematical knowledge as they group objects according to their own classification schemes. Logico-mathematical knowledge results from children's own actions on objects and fosters the development of logical thought. Children may combine, take apart, and arrange objects in some kind of order. The properties of each object are not as important as the relationships constructed between and among the objects. Numerous opportunities for classifying objects present themselves in an early childhood science curriculum: classifying sounds (higher-lower, louder-softer, pleasant-unpleasant); classifying animals (tame-wild, furry-nonfurry); and classifying leaves according to color, shape, size, and number of veins. The children, however, must decide upon their own classification schemes; otherwise they are not constructing the relationships themselves.

Any quality early childhood education program provides children with numer-

148

ous opportunities for *communicating*—
with each other, with their teacher, or
with some other adults. This fourth process is important not only for language
development, but also for general intellectual development. Piaget has remarked
that "experience is always necessary for
intellectual development (1964, p. 31),"
but such experience should include not
only physical activity but social interactions as well. Because preoperational children are egocentric, increased opportunities to interact with classmates, share
viewpoints, and listen to others will help
children realize there are viewpoints other
than their own. Such understandings will
help children in their transition from
egocentrism to operational thought.

Conclusion

An early childhood science program
should be child-centered and activity-
oriented; it should provide children with a
varied environment to explore at their
own pace and according to their individual cognitive abilities. In their active
explorations, children should be encouraged to observe carefully, note similarities
and differences, make predictions, test out
their predictions, ask questions, and
interact with one another and with the
teacher. They should be constantly encouraged to think and talk about what
they are doing and seeing. Children will
not only be learning science; they will also
be engaging in experiences that develop
logical and systematic thinking.

Ideas abound for early childhood teachers to use in implementing an exciting
science program in their classrooms
(Hill 1977; Holt 1977; Moffitt 1974;
McGavak and LaSalle 1969; Schools
Council 1972a). Resourceful teachers have
much at their disposal to make science education a rich and rewarding experience
for young children.

Elaine Wickens

*What factors would determine whether this is
an appropriate science activity for these young
children?*

References

Chittenden, E. A. "Piaget and Elementary Sci-
ence." *Science and Children* 8, no. 4 (De-
cember 1970): 9-15.
Elkind, D. "Piaget and Science Education."
Science and Children 10, no. 3 (November
1972): 9-12.
Good, R. G. *How Children Learn Science: Con-
ceptual Development and Implications for
Teaching.* New York: Macmillan, 1977.
Hildebrand, V. *Introduction to Early Childhood
Education.* New York: Macmillan, 1971.
Hill, D. M. *Mud, Sand, and Water.* Washington,
D.C.: National Association for the Education
of Young Children, 1977.
Holt, B-G. *Science with Young Children.*
Washington, D.C.: National Association for
the Education of Young Children, 1977.
Howe, A., and Johnson, J. "Intellectual Devel-

opment and Elementary Science: Some Implications from Piagetian Research." *Science and Children* 13, no. 2 (October 1975): 30-31.

Kamii, C., and DeVries, R. *Physical Knowledge in Preschool Education: Implications of Piaget's Theory*. Englewood Cliffs, N.J.: Prentice-Hall, 1978.

Laurendeau, M., and Pinard, A. *Causal Thinking in the Child*. New York: International Universities Press, 1962.

McGavak, J., and LaSalle, D. P. *Guppies, Bubbles and Vibrating Objects*. New York: John Day Co., 1969.

Moffitt, M. W. "Children Learn About Science Through Block Building." In *The Block Book*, ed. E. S. Hirsch, pp. 25-32. Washington, D.C.: National Association for the Education of Young Children, 1974.

Neuman, D. "Sciencing for Young Children." *Young Children* 27, no. 4 (April 1972): 215-226.

Piaget, J. "Cognitive Development in Children: The Piaget Papers." In *Piaget Rediscovered: A Report of the Conference on Cognitive Studies and Curriculum Development*, eds. R. E. Ripple and V. N. Rockcastle, pp. 6-48. Ithaca, N.Y.: Cornell University School of Education, March 1964.

Piaget, J. *Six Psychological Studies*. New York: Random House, 1968. Berkeley, Calif.: Regents of the University of California, 1973.

Schools Council. *Early Experiences, Science Five Through Thirteen*. London: Macdonald Educational, 1972a.

Schools Council. *With Objectives in Mind. Science Five Through Thirteen*. London: Macdonald Educational, 1972b.

R. Smith

Judith Herr and Winifred Morse

Food for Thought: Nutrition Education for Young Children

What nutrition information are you teaching—intentionally or unintentionally? If children are going to eat a well-balanced diet and make wise food choices independently, what you do every day in your classroom will make a difference!

Early childhood educators, perhaps more than any other single group, are aware of and sensitive to the importance of good nutrition for young children, promoting good nutrition and nutrition education in the classroom.

However, nutrition education generally has not been emphasized in the curriculum. It has been mentioned as a small part of the health component of the curriculum (Brophy, Good, and Nedler 1975; Margolin 1976). Discussion has been confined to a description of the Head Start model (Morrison 1976), or has centered on meals and specific food activities rather than on making nutrition education an integral part of all curriculum areas (Seefeldt 1974). When emphasis has been placed on food and nutrition, suggested classroom experiences have often incorporated such limited activities as making Jell-O and sugar cookies (Hildebrand 1976). As a result, nutrition education efforts have been inconsistent from program to program, and sporadic in many centers. This article will encourage the incorporation of nutrition education in the preschool by offering a conceptual framework for nutrition education, increasing awareness of current classroom practices, and providing suggestions for nutrition activities within the major curriculum areas.

Why is nutrition education critical?

Adequate nutrition for children during the early years is essential for good health and for proper growth and development. Investigations in developmental nutrition focus on the possible connections between adequate nutrition and a preschool child's behavior, and the ability to learn (Winick 1976). Other research in the area of nutrition and disease suggests that life-long good health and nutrition habits may result in healthier adult years and perhaps a lower incidence of chronic diseases (Ahrnes and Connor 1979).

Three events have led to the increasing incorporation of nutrition education concepts into early childhood curricula. Since 1965, services for Head Start children have been designed with the recognition that proper nutrition is critical for both good health and for enhancing a child's ability to learn. Emphasis in the program is not

Judith Herr, Ed.D, is Director of the Child and Family Study Center at the University of Wisconsin-Stout, in Menomonie, Wisconsin.

Winifred Morse, M.S., is an instructor in the School of Nursing at the University of Wisconsin-Eau Claire.

only on the type and quality of the food served, but also on setting a conducive meal time environment, incorporating cultural food patterns, and including food and nutrition concepts in all phases of the learning environment (U.S. Department of Health, Education and Welfare 1975).

The second stimulus for early nutrition education was the enactment of P.L. 95-166, the Nutrition Education and Training Act in 1977. This law, under the direction of the U.S. Department of Agriculture, provides funds to states on the basis of the number of children enrolled in day care centers and schools. These funds are used (1) to instruct students with regard to the nutritional value of foods and the relationship to health, (2) to train school food service personnel in the principles and practices of food service management, (3) to instruct teachers in sound principles of nutrition education, and (4) to develop and use classroom nutrition materials and curricula (Wisconsin Department of Public Instruction 1979).

The third stimulus has been the development of early childhood nutrition curriculum guides (Marbach, Plass, and O'Connell 1978; Randall, Olson, and Morris 1979; National Dairy Council 1979) to help teachers incorporate nutrition education activities in the classroom. Each of these guides emphasizes the importance of integrating nutrition education into all curriculum areas, providing activity-oriented lessons, and combining efforts of

Michael Schulman

Positive early food experiences and a familiarity with a wide variety of foods lead to an increased acceptance of more foods by young children.

Herr and Morse

classroom teachers and food service workers for maximum learning. In addition to these program guides, there are many posters, games, stories, puzzles, and movies of varying quality available for classroom use.

Parents and teachers can be assured that evidence exists that their efforts through these and other programs are indeed effective. Positive early food experiences and a familiarity with a wide variety of foods lead to an increased acceptance of more foods by young children (Lamb 1969). Children do learn to accept foods that were previously rejected (Harrill, Smith, and Gangever 1972; Ireton and Guthrie 1972), and children can be encouraged to try new foods (Karsch 1977; Witherall 1978). Finally, efforts at parent education can lead to better nutritional practices in the home (Anselmo 1975; Phillips, Bass, and Yetley 1978). However, while results can be positive, the process is slow, continuous, and measured by small, positive changes in eating behavior.

What concepts do children understand?

The nutrition education framework most frequently used in recent years has focused on the seven concepts developed at the White House Conference on Food, Nutrition and Health (1969). Those concepts are outlined in Table 1.

These concepts are precise, accurate, and intimidating! Consequently, we have used them as a basis for developing ten food and nutrition education concepts that are appropriate for young children (see Table 2). These ten concepts are by no means exhaustive of all appropriate nutrition concepts for young children. Each teacher, depending on the community and the background and needs of the children's families, will emphasize some and minimize other concepts. Additional concepts may be developed to meet particular

needs and problems.

Concepts 1 through 4 stress food awareness and identification and indicate various ways in which foods can be identified and classified. Food identification is the critical introductory step needed to increase children's familiarity with and their acceptance of different foods. We often assume that all children are familiar with celery, pancakes, or broccoli. Frequently, adults are surprised when children reject a food that they have not previously known about, yet we teach children *not* to put strange things in their mouths! Surely the first step in food acceptance is familiarity with a new food.

The use of ten food categories (concept number 7) needs to be explained. Nutritionists, early childhood educators, and parents tend to use the Basic Four Food Groups to teach nutrition because it is such an easy tool to use and because of the availability of teaching material based on it. While most children may learn to categorize particular foods into one of the four food groups, maximum learning may not take place when this technique is used. The use of the Basic Four ignores some basic child development precepts (Spitzer 1977). The Basic Four Food Groups requires too many generalizations for a young child to be able to combine dissimilar foods into a single group as it categorizes food according to nutrients—hence eggs and meats are classified together because both are good sources of iron and protein. Yet children often fail to see any similarity between eggs and meats. The ten food categories suggested here are easily understood by most young children. If necessary, additional categories can be used for very young children. For example, the meats may have to be further categorized as red meats, fish, and poultry for two- and three-year-old children.

The remainder of the concepts deal with food for health and food choices. These ideas provide the basis for many classroom activities that help children to learn about why they eat.

Table 1. Seven basic nutrition concepts.

1. Nutrition is the process by which food and other substances become you. The food we eat enables us to live, to grow, to keep healthy and well, and to get energy for work and play.

2. Food is made up of certain chemical substances that work together and interact with body chemicals to serve the needs of the body.

  a. Each nutrient has specific uses in the body.

  b. For the healthful individual the nutrients needed by the body are usually available through food.

  c. Many kinds and combinations of food can lead to a well-balanced diet.

  d. No natural food, by itself, has all the nutrients needed for full growth and health.

3. The way food is handled influences the amount of nutrients in the food, its safety, appearance, taste, and cost; handling means everything that happens to food while it is being grown, processed, stored and prepared for eating.

4. All persons, throughout life, have need for about the same nutrients, but in varying amounts.

  a. The amounts needed are influenced by age, sex, size, activity, specific conditions of growth, and state of health, altered somewhat by environmental stress.

  b. Suggestions for kinds and needed amounts of nutrients are made by scientists who continuously revise the suggestions in the light of the findings of new research.

  c. A daily food guide is helpful in translating the technical information into terms of everyday foods suitable for individuals and families.

5. Food use relates to the cultural, social, economic, and psychological aspects of living as well as to the physiological.

  a. Food is culturally defined.

  b. Food selection is an individual act but it is usually influenced by social and cultural sanctions.

  c. Food can be chosen so as to fulfill physiological needs and at the same time satisfy social, cultural, and psychological wants.

  d. Attitudes toward food are a culmination of many experiences, past and present.

6. The nutrients, singly and in combinations of chemical substances simulating natural foods, are available in the market; these may vary widely in usefulness, safety of use, and economy.

7. Foods play an important role in the physical and psychological health of a society or a nation just as they do for the individual and the family.

  a. The maintenance of good nutrition for the larger units of society involves many matters of public concern.

  b. Nutrition knowledge and social consciousness enable citizens to participate in the adoption of public policy affecting the nutrition of people around the world.

(White House Conference on Food, Nutrition and Health. Final Report. p. 151)

Table 2. Food and nutrition concepts for young children.

1. There is a wide variety of food.

2. Plants and animals are sources of food.

3. Foods vary in color, flavor, texture, smell, size, shape, and sound.

4. A food may be prepared and eaten in many different ways—raw, cooked, dried, frozen, or canned.

5. Good foods are important to health, growth, and energy.

6. Nutrition is how our bodies use the foods we eat for health, growth, and energy.

7. Food may be classified according to the following categories:

a. milk	f. vegetables
b. meat	g. breads
c. dried peas and beans	h. pastas
d. eggs	i. cereals, grains, and seeds
e. fruits	j. nuts

8. A good diet includes a wide variety of foods from each of the food categories.

cont. on p. 155

Herr and Morse

Table 2. cont. from p. 154

9. There are many factors that influence eating:
   a. attractiveness of food
   b. method of preparation
   c. cleanliness/manners
   d. environment/atmosphere
   e. celebrations

10. We choose the foods we eat for many reasons:
   a. availability and cost
   b. family and individual habits
   c. aesthetics
   d. social and cultural customs
   e. mass media influence

Where is a good nutrition curriculum provided?

Teachers and parents who are interested in instituting a sound nutrition education curriculum or in improving the quality of their existing nutrition education efforts need to take a look at the classroom and lunchroom. What nutrition information is already being taught—intentionally or unintentionally? Negative nutrition messages often are conveyed by the environment; the negative message may be the only message the children are receiving, or it may be contradicting a positive nutrition message the teacher is trying to communicate. Consider some of these examples.

1. Children are told that breakfast is important for their health and well-being, and is the most important meal of the day. Ironically, many parents or centers do not offer breakfast to their children.

2. Vegetables and fruits are stressed for good health while sugar is condemned. These messages are then contradicted by a classroom cooking experience such as making ice cream or candy.

3. The importance of the meal as a pleasant social experience, during which time children learn social skills and manners, is emphasized, as is the economic value of food and its scarcity for many. However, these messages are all contradicted when followed by an art experience such as pudding painting, macaroni collages, popcorn stringing, or vegetable printing.

4. Adults emphasize the excitement and importance of holidays by providing sweet foods, candy, cookies, and cake. These foods will become associated with happy and special times in the minds of children. For example, birthday parties too often feature ice cream and cake rather than less sugary but equally delicious alternatives, such as individual pizzas or fresh fruit.

5. What types of materials decorate the classroom or child's room? Do candles on a cake or oranges on a tree indicate the birthdays of individual children? Is the growth chart an ice cream cone or a carrot? Does the bulletin board show Cookie Monster eating cookies or elephants eating peanuts? What is the nutrition message of food puzzles, grocery store items, and mobiles?

6. Storybooks, fingerplays, and songs are important methods for teaching in most curriculum areas. What is their nutritional message? Do children in the stories eat vegetables and drink milk, or are they eating potato chips and soft drinks? Do the children in the stories want to grow up to own candy stores or vegetable markets?

Adults need to learn to recognize the numerous indirect ways that nutrition concepts are being taught. Once you see how nutrition messages are conveyed, it is easy to deliberately send out positive nutrition messages on a daily basis.

How does nutrition fit into the curriculum?

The Nutrition Education and Training Act is written to encourage teachers to integrate nutrition information into the cur-

We need to learn to recognize the numerous indirect ways that nutrition concepts are being taught, so we can deliberately send out positive nutrition messages on a daily basis.

riculum. A wide variety of activities can be used to teach the ten food and nutrition concepts, making it easy to integrate nutrition information into any of the traditional early childhood curriculum areas. A few activities are suggested using apples.

Sensory development. Food can be identified and made familiar to children if they use each of the senses. Apples can be examined visually and named. Textures can be explored by comparing raw and cooked apples. Sound made by the seeds rattling in small containers can be compared. Of course, different varieties of apples will have different smells, flavors, and textures. Tasting parties are a natural when using senses to explore various qualities of foods! They encourage a child to try new foods because small amounts of food are tasted in a festive atmosphere. Yogurt dips, sharp cheese, or peanut butter can add to the nutritional value and interest of apples. (To avoid choking, apples for children under the age of three must be peeled.)

Language arts. Varieties of apples can be

Herr and Morse

identified, described, and compared. Fingerplays and stories can be used. Experience charts and stories can be dictated or written by the children. Word/picture recipe cards for making such things as apple sauces and breads encourage development of early reading skills as the children learn that pictures and symbols represent words for actions and objects. Bulletin boards can be used to highlight how apples grow or their many uses.

Math. Children can count, weigh, measure, and divide apples into sections. Remember to use metric weights and measures! Apples can be compared, sorted into sets, and seriated according to such characteristics as size, color, and shape. They can be used in estimation activities, such as predicting the number of apples a bowl will hold. As children follow recipes and cook foods that contain the apples they will learn concepts of whole and part, full and empty, more and fewer.

Science. Apple seeds can be planted and grown. The peel, core, stem, and meat of the apple can be explored with magnifying glasses and microscopes by older children. Nutritional values of apples can be compared to other foods. Cooking experiences can demonstrate how form and consistency change as apples are processed.

Dramatic play. The dramatic play corner or classroom grocery store can contain several varieties of raw apples, apples in different forms such as applesauce, and apples in different foods such as salads. Having scales, bags, cartons, and other implements available for use in this area can help reinforce math and science concepts. Chef's hats and aprons can be used to introduce the need for sanitation and to provide further opportunities for dramatic play. These activities lend themselves to discussion of careers associated with nutrition and the food industry. Classroom demonstrations by cooks and bakers or field trips to farms, grocery stores, packing plants, and restaurants could bring an

exciting way of reinforcing these ideas. Children can learn about how other cultures cook and eat apples.

Art. With inedible portions (apple seeds, stems, and occasionally peels) the children can make prints, collages, or ornaments. Seeds and stems can be combined with clay for sculpture activities. The tree leaves and uneaten peels can be used as unique paint brushes in art projects.

Music. Seeds can be used to make shakers. Songs about apples can be used or familiar tunes can be reworded to include the apples being studied. As music is played, children can imitate the movement of apple trees in a breeze or the falling of ripe apples.

Fine and gross motor development. Fingers or tongs can be used to pick up and sort the apples and parts of apples. Games and races using apples can be developed. (Bobbing for apples, however, is not a healthy practice.) Apple tosses using felt replicas can be used as a variation of bean bag tosses. Children enjoy slicing, peeling, and preparing apples in various ways. Always select safe utensils for the children—even plastic knives can cut apples.

Social studies. Field trips to orchards, neighborhood trees, and markets help children to learn about the sources of apples and about the various ways that apples can be processed. Different cultures can be studied as children learn ways that apples are used in the foods of other countries. Parents or community members from various cultures can demonstrate how apples are used in their native foods. As children cook and eat apple products, they learn basic social skills of cooperation, sharing, taking turns, and table manners.

Positive nutrition messages should always be emphasized so that children develop healthy attitudes about food and nutrition. Avoid the negative approach of "Don't eat that, it's bad for you." Such messages are not only unsuccessful, but also cause children to lose interest in nutrition education (Blackburn 1970).

An excellent way to introduce nutrition in the classroom is to provide frequent food preparation activities in the classroom (Galen 1977; Kositsky 1977). Cooking can be as simple as peeling an orange for a snack, or as complicated as baking yeast breads and preparing culturally authentic meals. Cooking is an excellent means for teaching nutrition and many other concepts because the children are directly involved in the activities. Not only is this the best learning method for young children, but it also encourages them to try new foods if they have observed and assisted in the food preparation. The goal of nutrition education should be that children *eat* a well-balanced diet that contains a wide variety of foods, and that children learn to make wise food choices independently.

Many nutrition education materials and cookbooks are available for use with young children (Ferreira 1969; Harms 1976; Johnson 1976; Wanamaker, Hearn, and Richarz 1979; Goodwin and Pollen 1980). Teachers will want to first select books that emphasize nutritious foods that children like to prepare and eat. Beyond this single basic criterion, these books often provide nutrition information for parents and teachers, curriculum ideas, and ways to modify the classroom environment for cooking activities. Cookbooks that emphasize the awareness of different cultures and of American ethnic groups are particularly meaningful.

Summary

Children can learn nutrition concepts while they are developing the central concepts in all other major curriculum areas. This comprehensive approach can lead to the development of skills and attitudes children need to select a good diet (American Dietetic Association Position Paper 1973; Ulrich 1979).

Bibliography

Ahrnes, E. H., Jr., and Connor, W. E. "Symposium Report of the Task Force on the Evidence Relating Dietary Factors to the Nation's Health." *American Journal of Clinical Nutrition* 32 (1979): 2621–2748.

American Dietetic Association. "Position Paper on the Scope and Thrust of Nutrition Education." *Journal of the American Dietetic Association* 62 (1973): 429–430.

Anselmo, S. "Nutritional Partnership Between Day Care Center and Home." *Journal of Nutrition Education* 7 (1975): 116.

Blackburn, M. L. "Who Turns the Child 'Off' to Nutrition?" *Journal of Nutrition Education* 2 (Fall 1970): 45–47.

Brophy, J. E.; Good, T. L.; and Nedler, S. E. *Teaching in the Preschool.* New York: Harper & Row, 1975.

Ferreira, N. J. *The Mother-Child Cook Book.* Menlo Park, Calif.: Pacific Coast Publishers, 1969.

Ferreira, N. J. "Teachers' Guide to Educational Cooking in the Nursery School: An Everyday Affair." *Young Children* 29, no. 1 (November 1973): 23–32.

Galen, H. "Cooking in the Curricula." *Young Children* 32, no. 2 (January 1977): 59–68.

Goodwin, M. T., and Pollen, G. *Creative Food Experiences for Children,* rev. ed. 1980. Center for Science in the Public Interest, 1755 S St., N.W., Washington, DC 20009.

Harms, T., and Veitch, B. *Cook and Learn: Pictorial Single Portion Recipes—A Child's Cook Book.* 1976. 656 Terra California Dr. #3, Walnut Creek, CA 94595.

Harrill, I.; Smith, C.; and Gangever, J. A. "Food Acceptance and Nutrition Intake of Preschool Children." *Journal of Nutrition Education* 4 (Summer 1972): 103–106.

Hildebrand, V. *Introduction to Early Childhood Education,* 2nd ed. New York: Macmillan, 1976.

Ireton, C. L., and Guthrie, H. A. "Modification of Vegetable-Eating Behavior in Preschool Children." *Journal of Nutrition Education* 4 (Summer 1972): 100–103.

Johnson, G., and Povey, G. *Metric Shake and Witches' Cakes.* New York: Scholastic, 1976.

Karsch, B. B. "Nutrition Education in Day Care." *Journal of Home Economics* 69 (September 1977): 14–17.

Kositsky, V. "What in the World Is Cooking in Class Today?" *Young Children* 33, no. 1 (November 1977): 23–31.

Lamb, M. W. "Food Acceptance, A Challenge to Nutrition Education—A Review." *Journal of Nutrition Education* 1 (Fall 1969): 20–22.

Marbach, E.; Plass, M.; and O'Connell, L. *Nutrition in a Changing World, A Curriculum for Preschool, Nursery-Kindergarten.* Washington, D.C.: Nutrition Foundation, 1978.

Margolin, E. *Young Children—Their Curriculum and Learning Processes.* New York: Macmillan, 1976.

Morrison, G. S. *Early Childhood Education Today.* Columbus, Ohio: Merrill, 1976.

National Dairy Council. *Food . . . Early Choices.* Rosemont, Illinois, 1979.

Phillips, D. E.; Bass, M. A.; and Yetley, E. "Use of Foods and Nutrition Knowledge by Mothers of Preschool Children." *Journal of Nutrition Education* 10 (April/June 1978): 73–75.

Randall, J.; Olson, C.; and Morris, L. *Early Childhood Nutrition Program.* Ithaca, N.Y.: Cornell University, 1979.

Seefeldt, C. *A Curriculum for Child Care Centers.* Columbus, Ohio: Merrill, 1974.

Spitzer, D. R. *Concept Formation and Learning in Early Childhood.* Columbus, Ohio: Merrill, 1977.

Ulrich, H. D. "Towards a National Nutrition Education Policy." *Journal of Nutrition Education* 11 (April/June 1979): 60.

U.S. Department of Health, Education and Welfare. *Handbook for Local Head Start Nutrition Specialists.* Washington, D.C.: U.S. Government Printing Office, 1975.

Wanamaker, N.; Hearn, K.; and Richarz, S. *More Than Graham Crackers: Nutrition Education and Food Preparation with Young Children.* Washington, D.C.: National Association for the Education of Young Children, 1979.

White House Conference on Food, Nutrition and Health, 1969. Final Report. Washington, D.C.: U.S. Government Printing Office, 1970.

Winick, M. *Malnutrition and Brain Development.* London: Oxford University Press, 1976.

Wisconsin Department of Public Instruction. *State Plan Nutrition Education and Training Program.* FY 1980 funding. Food and Nutrition Service Section, Wisconsin Department of Public Instruction, July, 1979.

Witherall, J. "From Pretzels and Potato Chips to Liver and Lettuce: A Case History." *Day Care and Early Education* 5 (Summer 1978): 15.

Sally Koblinsky, Jean Atkinson, and Shari Davis

Sex Education with Young Children

Michael (age 3) is watching Katherine (age 3) undress for swimming. As she begins to pull up her bathing suit, he stoops down to stare at her genital area. Student teacher Mary approaches the children with a frown on her face. Taking Michael by the hand, she states, "That's not nice. Go over and play with the boys."

The previous incident, recorded in Oregon State University's Child Development Laboratory, illustrates the anxiety and discomfort many teachers and parents experience in responding to children's sexual curiosity. Although early childhood is considered to be an important period in the formation of sexual attitudes (Gagnon 1965; Woody 1973), most adults have little background knowledge for dealing with children's sexual feelings and behaviors. A review of early childhood education texts reveals that the topic of sex education is generally omitted or limited to a discussion of plant reproduction.

Many teachers and parents want to learn more about children's emerging sexuality.

Sally Koblinsky, Ph.D., is Associate Professor, Family Studies and Consumer Sciences, San Diego State University, San Diego, California.

Jean Atkinson, M.S., is Doctoral student in Human Development and Family Studies, The Pennsylvania State University, University Park, Pennsylvania.

Shari Davis, Ph.D., recently graduated from the Department of Human Development and Family Studies, Oregon State University, Corvallis, Oregon.

Their daily experiences with children have increased their awareness of how much sexual learning occurs in the early years. Between the ages of two and six, children become aware of genital differences between the sexes; express curiosity about reproduction and birth; develop childhood romances; and engage in various types of sex play. Although many of us associate the topic of sex education with adolescence, young children ask more sex-related questions than do children in any other age group (Hattendorf 1932; Strain 1948).

Because young children are curious about human sexuality, more extensive teacher training is clearly needed in this area. Although parents remain the primary sex educators of their children, teachers may facilitate the child's sexual learning and supply guidance for anxious mothers and fathers. We have been exploring ways in which teachers and parents may complement one another's efforts in providing responsible sex education. The Oregon State University Early Childhood Sex Education Project was initiated in the spring of 1978. We asked 150 parents of three- to five-year-old children in our Child Development Laboratory and

160   Koblinsky, Atkinson, and Davis

community day care centers to complete questionnaires dealing with their attitudes toward sex education and responses to children's sexual behaviors. Meetings were held with parents to discuss early sex education and to explore parental expectations concerning the teacher's role in this process.

In response to the concerns of both parents and teachers, we have attempted to develop guidelines for sex education with young children. These guidelines are based upon our research (Koblinsky, Atkinson, and Davis 1979) and that of others, as well as the wisdom of fellow early childhood educators.

Guidelines for teaching

Genital differences

By the age of three, most children can distinguish between males and females (Gesell and Ilg 1949; Kreitler and Kreitler 1965). Although early distinctions are generally based on clothing and hairstyles, children soon become inquisitive about genital differences between the sexes. Such curiosity may be revealed in questions like "Why is Megan different?" or "Why don't I have a thing like Philip?" Adults

who straightforwardly respond to those questions may provide a foundation for healthy and open communication about sexuality.

Use correct vocabulary. Children need correct terms for labeling their genitals, just as they need correct terms for other body parts (Calderone 1966; Gordon 1974). Such terms not only help them to learn about human anatomy, but also give them a vocabulary with which to ask questions.

Slang or nicknames such as pee pee or wiener are generally inappropriate for genitalia. Not only will children have to relearn new terms, but they may also suffer embarrassment when they use family words in the presence of their peers.

Adults frequently wonder about what terms to use in explaining genital differences. Our research indicates that adults are more likely to provide children with labels for the male genitals than the female (Koblinsky, Atkinson, and Davis 1979). This finding probably reflects the greater visibility of the male organs. Moreover, adults may have difficulty deciding which female organs (vulva, vagina, clitoris, labia, uterus) should be introduced to children. While young children may be confused by too many different labels, they need to know that both males and

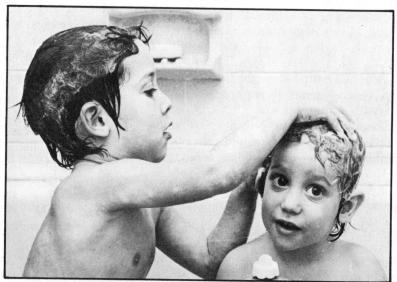

While young children may be confused by too many different labels, they do need to know that both males and females possess unique and equally valuable genitalia.

Ellen Levine Ebert

females possess unique and equally valuable genitalia. Therefore, one response to questions about body differences might be to say "Girls and boys are made differently. Girls have a vagina and boys have a penis."

Provide natural opportunities for children to observe each other. One natural place for children to learn about body differences is in the bathroom. Some early childhood programs have shared bathroom facilities so that girls and boys can use them together. This provides an especially good opportunity for a teacher in the bathroom area to clear up misinformation and model an accepting attitude about body differences. The following anecdote from our preschool illustrates this point:

> The teacher is helping David to use the toilet. Sara comments, "He gots a penis just like my brother." The teacher replies, "That's right. David and your brother have penises because they are boys." Sara replies, "Yup! And I got a bagina." "That's right," responds the teacher, "you have a vagina."

Children's curiosity about genital differences may also lead them to question why boys and girls usually urinate differently. Here again, one might stress the differences in male and female anatomy. An adult could respond, "A boy stands up because he urinates through his penis. But a girl's urine comes out from an opening near her vagina. It doesn't stick out like a penis, so she sits down." Child-size toilets make it possible for boys to stand up, because some are not yet tall enough to reach adult facilities.

Regardless of how casual and open a teacher's attitude, there will always be children who have received strict modesty training at home. Teachers need to respect the needs of these children and their parents. Placing a portable screen or divider in the bathroom may help the modest child to feel more comfortable.

Use classroom resources when discussing body differences. Brenner's book, *Bodies*

(1973, see Bibliography) provides an excellent introduction to the subject for preschool and elementary children. Black and white photographs depict clothed and unclothed children using their bodies to eat, sleep, defecate, bathe, and read. Another good book, *What Is A Girl? What Is A Boy?* (Waxman 1975, see Bibliography) uses both photographs and drawings to illustrate biological sex differences from infancy through adulthood. Magazine pictures and other photographs of nude children may also be posted on walls as conversation sparkers.

Another excellent stimulus for discussing body differences is anatomically correct dolls or puzzles (Constructive Playthings, Childcraft, Horsman). While such dolls may initially create a stir, children soon seem to enjoy differentiating between the girl and boy babies.

Reproduction and birth

In addition to learning about body differences, children often display curiosity about reproduction. Children begin the questioning process at about the age of three with "Where do babies come from?" This question is typically followed by "How does it get there?" or "How does it get out?" (Selzer 1974). Observations of pregnant women often stimulate curiosity about the origin of babies (Koblinsky, Atkinson, and Davis 1979). Children who are about to experience a birth in their own family are particularly likely to question teachers about reproduction.

Begin by finding out how much the child knows. Because young children will have encountered different information, it is important to determine how much they know. Therefore, a good rule to follow when answering questions is to ask a question. Throw the question back to the child by asking, "Well, where do *you* think babies come from?" or "How do *you* think it got there?"

Children often come up with remarkable and totally erroneous responses even

162

though they have received accurate information. In our program, a child whose mother worked for Planned Parenthood gave the following explanation:

> The baby grows and grows inside the mommy until she gets so big that the baby just about pops out! Then the mommy goes to the hospital to have the baby pop out. And if *you* go to the hospital, you'll have a baby too!

Although her mother had explained the birth process in great detail, Debbie's understanding was influenced by her level of cognitive development. Debbie, like other young children, is in Piaget's stage of preoperational thought and thus interprets information in terms of her own past experiences (Piaget 1929; Bernstein 1978). Just as balloons expand until they pop, babies will grow so big that they pop out of the mother. Debbie also uses transductive reasons to connect unrelated events. She reasons that anyone who goes to the hospital will return with a new baby.

Because children's ideas are influenced by their cognitive maturity, teachers should avoid laughing at fanciful explanations. Teachers should look for ways of correcting mistaken concepts, rather than telling children they are wrong. For example, a teacher overhearing Debbie's explanation might respond, "That's an interesting way of putting it, Debbie. You're right. . . . The baby does come out of the mother. Do you know where the baby comes out?" If the child is unable to answer, the teacher might describe the birth process or suggest that they look through a book on birth together. This approach enables the teacher to acknowledge the child's correct information as well as clear up any misinformation.

Give accurate information about reproduction. Our research indicates that adults explain the origin of babies in different ways, but the most common response is that they come from the mommy's tummy (Koblinsky, Atkinson, and Davis 1979). Some adults also explain that the baby began as a small seed. Few adults mention

the uterus or union of sperm and ovum, and even fewer deal with the topic of sexual intercourse.

A major problem with these more common adult responses is that they are inaccurate. Babies do not grow in tummies, and they do not sprout from seeds! Children deserve a more accurate explanation of reproduction. Good responses are simple and contain correct terminology. These points are illustrated in the following suggested exchanges between a child and an adult:

Child: Where do babies come from?

Adult: Babies come from a place inside the mother called the uterus. That's where they grow until they're ready to be born.

Child: How does the baby get out?

Adult: There's an opening between the mother's legs called the vagina. When the baby's ready, the opening stretches enough to let the baby come out.

Child: How does the baby get in there?

Adult: The mother has a tiny ovum inside her uterus. The father has a tiny sperm. When the sperm and the ovum come together, the baby starts growing.

Child: How does the daddy get the sperm in the mommy?

Adult: The father and mother lie very close together and put the father's penis inside the mother's vagina. The sperm come out through the father's penis.

Child: Why can't a man have a baby?

Adult: They aren't meant to. A man's body doesn't have a uterus where babies grow. The man's part is to help make the baby and to help care for it after it's born.

As teachers discuss reproduction and birth, they should remember that these processes are not easily understood the first time around. They must be prepared to answer children's questions again and again and to present the information in a variety of contexts. With an open exchange of information, children will

Children deserve an accurate explanation of reproduction.

gradually bring their understanding of these events closer to reality.

Use books to explain reproduction and birth. Sex education books (see Bibliography) are especially helpful because they include pictures illustrating concepts that teachers cannot demonstrate. It is important to leave these books out on the shelf, right alongside children's other favorites, so that children may look at them again and again. Easy availability reinforces the notion that sexual curiosity is natural and healthy.

Avoid using plants and animals as substitutes for discussing human reproduction. Young children are greatly interested in reproduction and are intrigued by all new babies. Therefore, teachers are encouraged to plan experiences that familiarize children with the principles of reproduction in plants, fish, rodents, and other animals (Holt 1977). However, there is some risk in attempting to use other species to convey an understanding of human reproduction and birth. Children may have considerable difficulty generalizing from plants and animals to human beings or vice versa. The following exchange illustrates the confusion that can be created by using analogies from the animal kingdom:

Adult: How would the lady get a baby to grow inside her?
Child: Um, get a duck. Cause one day I saw a book about them, and

Koblinsky, Atkinson, and Davis

. . . they just get a duck or a goose and they get a little more growned . . . and then they turn into a baby. (Bernstein and Cowan 1975, p. 87)

It is likely that this child had been read the popular book, *How Babies Are Made* (Andry and Schepp 1968). Although this book provides accurate information, it reviews reproduction in flowers, chickens, and dogs before it discusses humans. Because children are used to hearing stories in the once-upon-a-time to happily-everafter sequence, it is easy to understand why children might reason that humans were once ducks or flowers.

Individualize discussions about reproduction. It may be best to use a less formal instructional approach than might be used for concepts like colors or community helpers because young children vary widely in their knowledge of sexuality. When a teacher explains reproduction and birth, children will need an opportunity to ask questions. In one-to-one encounters or small groups, fewer of their questions are likely to go unanswered. Parents' concerns can also be responded to more easily when talking with individual children.

Masturbation

Masturbation is now widely accepted as natural and healthy for both children and adults (Arnstein 1976; Selzer 1974). Children will touch or rub their genitals because this behavior is pleasurable or soothing. Experienced teachers know that young children may absentmindedly fondle their genitals when they are tired, bored, or listening to a story. Children may also clutch their genitals when they are tense or nervous. Although some teachers may feel uncomfortable, adults will handle these situations most effectively if they adopt a relaxed approach to masturbation.

Ignore masturbation in most classroom situations. A teacher will probably notice that the child's behavior usually does not bother anyone else in the classroom.

Avoid negative responses. Adults should refrain from scolding or punishing children for engaging in masturbation. Responses like frowning or pulling the child's hands away from the genitals may communicate that these organs are bad or dirty. Criticisms or threats can lead children to develop unhealthy feelings of anxiety and guilt which can persist throughout life.

It is probably most difficult to refrain from scolding children when they are using masturbation as an attention-getting device. When a child masturbates to bring on laughter from others, you may say firmly and matter-of-factly, "Please put your penis back in your pants. That's where it belongs unless you're going to the bathroom."

Stress that there is a better time and place for masturbation. At times this behavior may interfere with other activities and may be bothersome to the entire class. A teacher might then take the child aside and explain, "I know that feels good, but other people don't like to see you play with your penis/vulva. You can do that when you're by yourself." This response acknowledges the pleasurable aspects of masturbation but also conveys the inappropriateness of its public display. However, teachers will need to be especially aware of any cultural prohibitions specific to their group of children.

Consult the child's parents if masturbation becomes compulsive. Compulsive masturbation, like compulsive scratching or nail biting, may be a symptom of deeper emotional problems. Should a teacher encounter a child who masturbates compulsively, we advise the teacher to discuss such behavior with the child's parents. The discussion may clarify factors contributing to the behavior and may inform teachers about the way masturbation is handled at home. Compulsive masturbation may be a reaction to family stress and may suggest that the child needs more time and attention from others. Parents and teachers can work together to help the child overcome anxiety and find other means of satisfaction.

Sex play

Like masturbation, sex play is an extension of childhood curiosity about body differences and functions (Pomeroy 1976). Children engaged in sex play typically examine one another's bodies and may attempt to place objects into genital openings. Sex play often occurs within the context of children's games, such as doctor or house. Teachers may discover these games in a quiet corner of the classroom or outdoor play area.

Acknowledge children's curiosity. Teachers' responses to children engaged in sex play will vary according to assessments of each situation. It may be sufficient to acknowledge the children's behavior and redirect their interest. A teacher might respond, "Oh, you were just looking to see how boys and girls are different. That's the way we are made. Now, how about a game of hide and seek?" In some cases, sex play may appear to be motivated by unanswered questions about body differences. A teacher may then suggest that children join her in the story corner to review appropriate books on the human body.

Explain potential consequences. If children's play involves inserting objects into each other's genital openings, it is important to discuss the potentially dangerous consequences of this behavior. After acknowledging children's natural curiosity, a teacher may explain that this practice could hurt another child. Use a familiar example, like putting pencils in someone's ears, to suggest the harmful effects of placing objects in body openings.

Discuss consideration for others. If children repeatedly engage in sex play, despite efforts to distract them or satisfy their curiosity, teachers may wish to bring up the issue of consideration for others. A teacher might respond, "I know you're curious about each other's bodies, but it bothers people to see you playing like that. I'd prefer that you didn't do it here." In asking children to stop this behavior out of respect for others, avoid trying to instill a sense of guilt. Severe scolding or hysterical outbursts may have long-term negative effects on later sexual adjustment.

Obscene words

Almost all adults have encountered children using such bathroom language as "This juice looks like pee" or "You're a poop face!" While such statements are generally accepted as normal experimentation with language, teachers may experience real discomfort when children begin using the more offensive four-letter words. Adults often fear that use of obscene language will become rampant among children. Consequently, many teachers express concern about the proper method of handling obscenities in the classroom.

Ignore obscene language whenever possible. Because children are likely to experiment with any new words they hear, it is best to let a spate of obscene language run its course. Extreme teacher reaction will probably increase children's interest in using these words rather than reduce it. Some children may be scolded for using these words at home, and repeating them at school may help children get them out of their systems.

Explain the word's meaning when it is appropriate. Because children often parrot an offensive word without any idea of its meaning, teachers may question children about what a specific word really means to them. Should their responses indicate a lack of understanding, teachers may define the word and use it matter-of-factly.

Koblinsky, Atkinson, and Davis

The following anecdote from our pre-school illustrates how this strategy may diffuse the potency of a four-letter word for the child:

> John screams that Billy is a "shithead." The teacher asks John, "Do you know what shit means?" John shakes his head. The teacher explains, "Shit is another word for bowel movement. Is that the word you wanted to use!" "No!" John exclaims, "I didn't want to say that!"

Stress the offensive nature of obscene language if it persists. When children's repeated use of obscene language disturbs classroom activities, teachers may need to take firmer measures. Children should be told that obscene words offend many people, and that the times and places for their use are limited. The teacher might respond, "Most poeple don't like to hear words like that. I don't want you to use them here at school."

General recommendations

Involve parents. It is extremely important to consider the specific backgrounds and concerns of parents because they remain the primary sex educators of their children. Early childhood educators must recognize that their own beliefs and values about sex education may not be shared by many parents. In some communities, sex education is a volatile issue. Consequently, efforts must be made to open discussions in which both parents and teachers can air views about the best ways of responding to children's sexual curiosity.

Teachers who represent their general philosophies of education at an initial get-acquainted parent meeting may allocate a portion of the program to discussing sex education. Parents should be encouraged to share their own ideas about handling sexual behaviors and should feel free

Because parents remain the primary sex educators of their children, it is extremely important to consider their backgrounds and concerns.

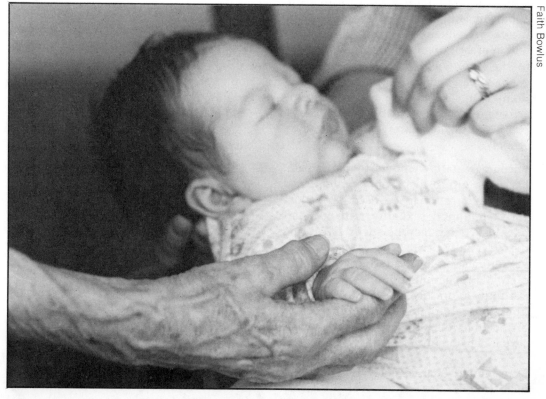

Faith Bowlus

to question the rationale behind any program policies. Placing an emphasis on an *exchange* of information will facilitate the development of mutual strategies for educating young children about sexuality.

Many parents seek extra help from teachers in communicating to their children about sexual issues. Therefore, we suggest planning at least one parent meeting to deal exclusively with the topic of sex education. Such meetings can be used to present information on normal psychosexual development and to address parental anxieties about specific behaviors. Meetings should be planned for a time when both mothers and fathers may conveniently attend. Teachers who feel uncomfortable directing a session on this topic may wish to solicit the services of speakers from a family planning agency or other community service organizations.

Parent involvement may play a crucial role in linking the young child's family experiences with those encountered in the school environment. Moreover, parents who establish family communication about human sexuality in the early years increase the likelihood that their children will approach them with sexual questions in the future. Finally, parents who develop an early concern for educating children about sexuality are likely to become active proponents of quality sex education programs in elementary and secondary schools.

Encourage staff members to participate. Lectures, group discussions, films, and other resources may be used to explore early childhood sexuality with all staff members. Time may be spent examining the ways in which teachers transmit sexual information and values to young children. Staff meetings provide an ideal opportunity to practice answers to children's questions about body differences and birth and to role play responses to specific sexual behaviors.

Examine personal sexual values. We believe that teachers must feel positively about their *own* sexuality before they attempt to discuss this sensitive subject with children. Therefore, discussion groups or values-clarification exercises may be used to explore sexual values and to increase comfort in responding to sexual issues. A relaxed and accepting attitude is just as important as the information provided.

Be a positive role model. Although we have focused on responding to children's overt sexual behaviors, sex education involves more than teaching facts about genital differences and birth. Indeed, sexuality is an integral part of the personality and involves the whole sense of what it is like to be a male or female. Teachers and parents are important role models for young children. Teachers who demonstrate warmth, affection, and support for others provide children with positive models for interpersonal behavior. The affective component of sexuality may also be stressed by reading children stories that describe the love, loyalty, and trust in human relationships.

Evaluate staff efforts. It is important to seek feedback from both teachers and parents about the effectiveness of sex education strategies. Efforts should be made to encourage a free exchange of feelings, attitudes, and personal experiences. Teachers may wish to evaluate their personal effectiveness as sex educators by answering such questions as "What have I learned?" "What have I relearned?" "How do I now feel about responding to various sexual behaviors?" It is wise to plan a specific time for dealing with sex education because the staff may be reluctant to bring up this subject in routine meetings.

Conclusion

Sex education is an important but often unrecognized component of early childhood programs. All children express curiosity about sexuality, and they deserve honest and thoughtful responses. The early childhood educator with a background in sex education may play a vital role in helping children experience the joy and responsibility of their sexuality. ▼

Bibliography of Recommended Sex Education Books for Preschoolers

Suggested age levels are designated with overlapping age ranges as follows: **N**—nursery, up to age 5
K—kindergarten, ages 4-6
P—primary, ages 5-9

The Birth of Sunset's Kittens. Carla Stevens. New York: Young Scott, 1969. NKP

Black and white photographs illustrate the birth of kittens. The text includes correct terminology for body parts and the birth process and subtly relates the birth of kittens to the child's own birth.

Bodies. Barbara Brenner. New York: Dutton, 1973. NK

Beautiful photographs of males and females from all age groups and cultural backgrounds are used to explore the fascinating topic of bodies and what they can do. The text stresses the uniqueness of each child's body.

Did the Sun Shine Before You Were Born? Sol and Judith Gordon. Fayetteville, N.Y.: Ed-U Press, 1974. NKP

With a focus on the family, the book explains male-female genital differences, intercourse, conception, and the birth process with multicultural illustrations and suggestions for parents and teachers.

Girls Are Girls and Boys Are Boys: So What's the Difference? Sol Gordon. Fayetteville, N.Y.: Ed-U Press, 1979. P

The differences between boys and girls are explained in terms of body build and function, rather than play, clothing, or career preferences. Masturbation, menstruation, intercourse, birth, and breast-feeding are discussed. The illustrations are multicultural.

How Babies Are Made. Andrew C. Andry and Steven Schepp. New York: Time-Life, 1968. KP

Simple, eye-catching illustrations enhance a long book that covers sexual differences, intercourse, and the birth process. Children may be confused by the sequential presentation of plant, animal, and human reproduction.

How Was I Born? Lennart Nilsson. New York: Delacorte, 1975. P

A story of conception, prenatal development, and childbirth is told in a sequence of beautiful photographs by the author/photographer. The text is clear and scientifically accurate and may be edited for younger children. The photos depict body differences in the sexes from early childhood to adulthood.

Making Babies. Sara Bonnett Stein. New York: Walker & Co., 1974. NKP

One of the *Open Family* series, the book presents a simple description of pregnancy and birth with vivid photographs of the fetus. There is a separate text for children and adults on each page, with the adult text suggesting strategies for responding to children's sexual curiosity.

What Is a Girl? What Is a Boy? Stephanie Waxman. Culver City, Calif.: Peace Press, 1975. NKP

Black and white photographs depict body differences between the sexes from infancy through adulthood. The book points out that, despite anatomical differences, both boys and girls can have the same names, enjoy the same activities, and feel the same emotions.

Where Did I Come From? Peter Mayle. Secaucus, N.J.: Lyle Stuart, 1973. P
· An amusing text with cartoon-like illustrations explains body differences, sexual arousal, intercourse, conception, fetal development, and the birth process. The text may be too long for some children.

Where Do Babies Come From? Margaret Sheffield. New York: Knopf, 1972. NKP
A beautifully and sensitively illustrated book that discusses intercourse and fetal development and depicts natural childbirth and genital differences in infancy, childhood, and adulthood.

The books listed in this bibliography are available from the publisher or at your local bookstore.

Sources for anatomically correct dolls and dressing-undressing puzzles:

Constructive Playthings
P.O. Box 5445
Kansas City, MO 64131

Childcraft Education Corp.
20 Kilmer Road
Edison, NJ 08817

Horsman Dolls, Inc.
200 Fifth Avenue
New York, NY 10010·

References

Arnstein, H. "How Sex Attitudes Develop." *Day Care and Early Education* 3, no. 5 (May-June 1976): 11-14.

Bernstein, A. *The Flight of the Stork.* New York: Dell, 1978.

Bernstein, A., and Cowan, P. "Children's Concepts of How People Get Babies." *Child Development* 46 (1975): 77-91.

Calderone, M. S. "Sex Education and the Very Young Child." *The PTA Magazine* 61, no. 2 (October 1966): 16-18.

Gagnon, J. "Sexuality and Sexual Learning in the Child." *Psychiatry* 28 (1965): 212-228.

Gesell, A., and Ilg, F. L. *Child Development.* New York: Harper & Brothers, 1949.

Gordon, S. "Three Short Essays Toward a Sexual Revolution." *The Humanist* 34, no. 2 (March-April 1974): 20-22.

Hattendorf, K. W. "A Study of the Questions of Young Children." *Journal of Social Psychology* 3 (1932): 37-65.

Holt, B-G. *Science with Young Children.* Washington, D.C.: National Association for the Education of Young Children, 1977.

Koblinsky, S.; Atkinson, J.; and Davis, S. "Early Childhood Sex Education Project, 1979." Unpublished research report. Corvallis, Ore.: Oregon State University Family Life Department, 1979.

Kreitler, H., and Kreitler, S. "Children's Concepts of Sexuality and Birth." Child Development 37 (1965): 363-378.

Piaget, J. *The Child's Conception of the World.* New York: Harcourt, Brace, 1929.

Pomeroy, W. B. *Your Child and Sex: A Guide For Parents.* New York: Dell, 1976.

Selzer, J. G. *When Children Ask About Sex.* Boston: Beacon, 1974.

Strain, F. B. *The Normal Sex Interests of Children.* New York: Appleton-Century-Crofts, 1948.

Woody, J. D. "Contemporary Sex Education: Attitudes and Implications for Childrearing." *Journal of School Health* 43 (1973): 241-246.

Constance Kamii and
Lucinda Lee-Katz

Physics in Preschool Education
A Piagetian Approach

Science education for young children has traditionally consisted mainly of observation and description. Examples of this tradition are teaching about magnets and magnifying glasses. Magnets are given to children so that they will find out which objects or materials are attracted to them and which ones are not. Magnifying glasses facilitate observation of objects.

Piaget (1977) contends, however, that young children learn about objects not by observing and describing them but by *acting* on them materially and mentally, and observing the objects' reactions. Magnets and magnifying glasses encourage children to observe and describe objects but not to act on them. This article will emphasize the importance of young children knowing objects through their actions.

A Piagetian preschool program cannot be divided into traditional academic subjects such as science, arithmetic, and language arts, as Piaget states that young children's knowledge develops as an indissociable whole. An article on science education, therefore, would be in contradiction with Piaget's theory, since science cannot be separated from knowledge.

Copyright © Constance Kamii and Lucinda Lee-Katz 1978. This article was written with the support of the Urban Education Research Program and the assistance of K. Gruber of the College of Education, University of Illinois at Chicago Circle.

It is nevertheless possible to examine the foundation of physics in the preschool years, keeping in mind that the activities described in this article are part of a larger educational program described elsewhere (Kamii and DeVries 1977).

Criteria for Evaluating Activities

Activities such as those involving elementary mechanics, or the movement of objects, are suitable for young children. An example of such an activity is the game of bowling in which children arrange plastic bottles and try to knock them down by rolling a ball from a distance. These types of activities are good because they meet two criteria:

1. *Children can produce the phenomenon with their own actions and can vary their actions.* Children learn about objects by acting on them and observing how they react. For example, it is only by dropping a ball and a block that children can find out that one bounces more than the other. Children can also find out how the object's reaction changes as they change their actions. Instead of dropping the ball on the floor, children can throw it hard on the floor. By observing how the ball bounces differently as a function of the variation in their actions, children build more knowledge about the ball.

2. *Children can observe the object's reaction, which is clear and immediate.* Clarity and immediacy of the object's reaction are important because ambiguous and/or slow reactions make it difficult for children to observe the variation in the object's reaction. Bowling meets both these criteria but playing with magnets does not. A nail may move when the child brings a magnet close to it, but this movement is caused by the magnet, not the child. Magnetism is beyond the comprehension of even most adults. When young children are asked why a nail sticks to a magnet, they often say, "because there's glue." Rolling a ball, in contrast, is a phenomenon children can

understand because it is children who produce it with their own actions. If children miss the target by rolling the ball too far to the left or right, they can vary their actions to produce the desired effect. With a magnet, on the other hand, children cannot make a piece of paper stick to a magnet, no matter how much the action is varied. Furthermore, metals react to magnets in ambiguous ways, since metals having exactly the same appearance are not always attracted. Children cannot possibly know by observation that metals have to contain iron, cobalt, or nickel to be attracted by magnets.

The chain of a cuckoo clock reacts immediately to the child's action of pulling the end that does not have any weight. After this immediate reaction, however, the weight reacts very slowly by pulling the chain down. This is another example of an inappropriate activity for early childhood education because the reaction is too slow for children to establish a correspondence between the lengthening of one side and the shortening of the other side of the chain. Correspondences are much easier for children to establish when the object's reaction is immediate such as in bowling.

Physics Activities for Young Children

The following activities involve children's actions on objects that produce movement. Teachers can modify these suggestions or develop similar ones suitable for the children they work with.

Rolling on rollers. Wooden rollers of various diameters and lengths, and boards of various sizes, can be combined by children to take rides on rollers (see photo).

Rolling on rollers.

Photos by Constance Kamii and Rheta DeVries. Drawings by Caroline Taylor.

Jumping. By using a roller and a board, children can make appropriate objects fly in the air by jumping on the other end of the board (Fig. 1).

Figure 1. *Jumping.*

Tilting. A maze with a small ball bearing provides children with opportunities to try to make the ball bearing go into the hole in the middle by tilting the maze in various ways (see photo).

Dropping. Children can try to drop clothespins into plastic bottles (or other containers) having narrow openings.

Blowing. Children can try to blow on a ping-pong ball (or other object) with a straw to direct it toward a goal (see photo). Blowing soap bubbles is another good activity.

Kamii and Lee-Katz

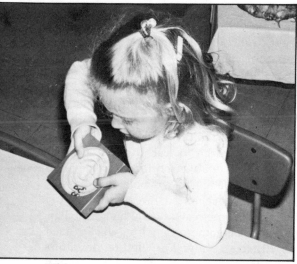

Tilting.

Blowing.

Sucking. Children can have a race transporting various small objects (such as pieces of paper and cloth) from one box to another by using straws and sucking the objects to the bottom of them.

Pulling. The simple action of pulling is too easy, since toddlers play with pull toys as soon as they learn to walk. A better activity for older children is running with streamers (Fig. 2). This activity encourages children to establish a relationship between streamer length and the running speed necessary to produce the desired effect.

Swinging. Children enjoy trying to knock a target down by releasing a pendulum (Fig. 3).

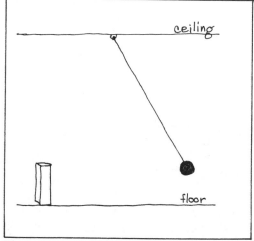

Figure 3. *Swinging.*

Figure 2. *Pulling.*

Constance Kamii, Ph.D., is currently Associate Professor of Education at the University of Illinois at Chicago Circle, Chicago, Illinois, and Chargée de Cours, Faculty of Psychology and Sciences of Education, University of Geneva, Switzerland.

Lucinda Lee-Katz, Ph.D., is Assistant Professor of Early Childhood Education at the University of Illinois at Chicago Circle, Chicago, Illinois. She is a former bilingual/bicultural primary grade teacher and day care center director.

Balancing. A race with one or two books on each child's head is great fun. Making constructions with cans and/or blocks is another example of a good balancing activity. A large sheet of paper with areas marked on it to indicate the shape and size of the foundation blocks can stimulate a great deal of creative construction (Fig. 4).

All these activities involve physics in the sense of "doing" physics rather than "studying" it. It is important for young children to "do" physics because they learn by trying to put the variation in their actions into correspondence with the variation in the objects' reactions.

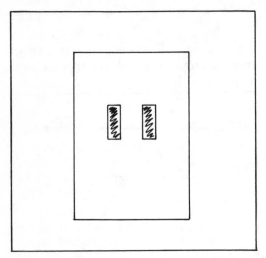

Figure 4. Balancing.

Helping Children Learn Through Construction of Their Own Knowledge

Young children who learn physics through these types of activities are learning by actively constructing their own knowledge. This view of learning is very different from the traditional belief that children learn only when they are instructed by another person. Children who have active minds are alert and curious about objects in their environment and experiment with them spontaneously. Most parents have observed their children

investigating electric switches and outlets, matches, flashlights, bulbs on the Christmas tree, and a variety of other phenomena. Programs for young children must attempt to build on this natural curiosity, since children who have experimented a great deal on their own will have a better foundation for the more formal study of the physical sciences later.

This approach to teaching is good also because it enables children to develop their knowledge as a whole in areas including space and time relationships, logico-arithmetical knowledge, and language. The game of bowling will be used to illustrate how knowledge develops simultaneously in these areas as children interact with the ball and bottles, as well as with each other.

Space and Time

Children may see the ball roll between two bottles arranged in a straight line with lots of space in between. When this happens, they may think about the desirability of having less empty space between the bottles, and rearrange the bottles so that they touch each other in a straight line. When children find out that with this arrangement they can make almost all the bottles fall over simultaneously, they might try to think of a way to knock all of them down. These are examples of the kinds of spatial reasoning children engage in as they act on objects to produce a desired effect. Temporal relationships, too, are involved in this process, as children think about what they did and what happened on the previous attempt, the time before that, and the time before that.

Logico-Arithmetical Knowledge

One aspect of logico-arithmetical knowledge is *classification*. As children look for other objects to try to knock down, they may choose long blocks but not dishes. This reflects that the children are able to classify objects into those that will work

Kamii and Lee-Katz

and those that won't. Another aspect of logic is *seriation*. If the teacher suggests putting sand in each bottle, children may establish a serial correspondence between the amount of sand in the bottle and its stability.

To establish correspondences between the variation in the children's actions (actions of *arranging* the bottles and *rolling* the ball in a variety of ways) and the variation in the objects' reactions (the fact that the ball knocked over none, some, or all of the bottles), children must structure, or establish relationships among, the facts. If a child made the ball go too far to the left on the first trial, too far to the right on the second trial, and too far to the right but less than the time before on the third trial, he or she must be able to recall which action went with which reaction of the object. If the child can establish these correspondences, the chances of success on the fourth trial are much greater than if his or her memory were undifferentiated and unorganized. The child develops logic by putting objects and events into relationships.

Children also make progress in quantification as they play bowling games. At age three, they engage only in gross quantification such as "I knocked down some (or a lot)." At age four to five, children like to count the number of bottles they knocked down. At six to seven years of age, many children like to keep score, first by merely writing down the number hit each time, and later by adding up these numbers to get a total score for each player. Children learn arithmetic in this kind of personally meaningful situation much better than in artificial lessons.

Language and Social Development

The activities discussed here are good also for fostering children's language and social development. Language develops best by being used in personally meaningful communication, rather than in meaningless exercises. When everybody wants to be the first one to start, for example, children are motivated to solve this problem. Terms such as *first, second,* and *third* are more easily learned in such natural situations. The resolution of conflicts is excellent also for enhancing children's social development, as they negotiate a solution that will be acceptable to all concerned.

Importance of Teacher Intervention

The teacher's interactions with children are vital to the success of this approach. A good question may involve the anticipation of the result of an action ["What do you think will happen if (you do X)?"]. In another situation, a teacher may ask what the child might do to produce a desired effect ["What can you do to (produce the desired effect)?"]. We can stimulate children's thinking if these questions are raised sparingly and at the right moment. To know what moment is right, the teacher needs to observe children to guess what each child is thinking. Adults have a tendency to talk too much, thereby preventing children from thinking. For example, adults may be inclined to pose a barrage of questions such as "What did you do differently? . . . Did you knock over a lot or a few? . . . What do you have to do to knock over more? . . . Does it help to stand closer to the bottles?" In a game of bowling, it is often enough to step in at moments of conflict to ask each child for a suggestion and guide the group toward agreeing on one of the ideas suggested.

Piaget's theory serves as a tool for the teacher to invent and analyze activities for children. It also serves as a tool for understanding the child's thinking process. If knowledge is acquired by *con*struction by children rather than by *in*struction from the adult, we must truly meet the children where they are and help in **their** process of construction. Too often, our tendency is to meet children where **we** are. The approach described in this article is not an easy one to practice, but it enables the teacher to be more creative and theoretically precise.

References

Kamii, C., and DeVries, R. "Piaget for Early Education." In *The Preschool in Action,* ed. M. C. Day and R. K. Parker. 2nd ed. Boston: Allyn and Bacon, 1977.

Kamii, C., and DeVries, R. *Physical Knowledge in Preschool Education: Implications of Piaget's Theory.* Englewood Cliffs, N.J.: Prentice-Hall, 1978.

Piaget, J. *Understanding Causality.* New York: Norton, 1974.

Piaget, J. *The Development of Thought: Equilibration of Cognitive Structures.* New York: Viking, 1977.

5

Integrating the arts

Art and music are probably two of the activities most preferred by young children, and these areas too overlap all other parts of the curriculum. Knowing what young children can do, and ways in which we can expand their learning through art and music are basic to our planning for all learning experiences.

Francks reviews the stages through which children generally develop art skills and suggests ways in which teachers can contribute to art as a process rather than a product.

Listening, singing, moving—how can we help children develop an appreciation for and the ability to create music? McDonald and Ramsey make specific suggestions for extending children's learning through sound.

How can your curriculum help children express their creativity?

Olive R. Francks

Scribbles?
Yes, They *Are* Art!

In their early years, young children draw marks on a surface, and the marks become scribbles. With this effort as a visual and written statement to the world these children know, two-year-olds say a great deal about themselves and their perceptions of the world—more than a cursory glance at their artwork would reveal. Adults tend to look upon scribbling with a range of expectations. Some of us expect and make too much of the event, while others belittle it as quite unimportant. A few insights in the art and thought of the young child will provide us with understanding concerning the importance of scribble art in the life and development of young children.

A Cycle of Scribbles

Kellogg (1967), in her studies of children's scribbles, has shown that children universally proceed through the same series of stages in their early art development. The approximate life cycle of scribbling begins at age two, or even earlier, and extends through ages four and five. Kellogg defines four distinguishable stages that are of major importance in understanding the place of scribble art in human development: (1) the *placement stage*, in which the two- or three-year-old

Placement Stage—multiple line crossings with emerging diagram shapes (right hand base area). Age 2 years.

children experiment spontaneously with the basic scribbles on paper or another surface, rather than uncontrolled "writing" in the air; (2) the *shape stage*, in which three- or four-year-old children discover some of their scribbles actually are shapes that may also be referred to as "gestalts;" (3) the *design stage*, when the child combines different shapes and lines into structured designs or diagrams; and (4) the *pictorial stage*, when the scribble art of the four- and five-year-old will generally start to resemble familiar objects according to adult standards.

Placement Stage: Early Scribbling

Two-year-old children at first make chance forms in their scribbling. Later they move on toward more controlled marks and scribbles, until twenty kinds of scribble forms have been discovered. Art at this early stage may be demonstrated by marks the child puts on paper, clay, finger paint, or other surfaces by using a tool. For example, children may use a pencil, paint brush, crayon, or even fingers—on paper, wood, cloth, clay, or any material that is available. These are highly visible

Olive R. Francks, Ed.D., is Assistant Professor, Division of Curriculum and Teaching; Director, Arts in Education Program; and Director, Elementary Preservice Program, Fordham University at Lincoln Center.

acts that can easily be observed and analyzed.

On the other hand, very young children often create in less visible ways—by "painting" in water, or by "drawing" in the air. This fluid type of artwork is important to an understanding of the purpose and meaning of children's artwork as a process of thinking. We have all watched the infant or toddler wave a stick or pencil in the air. This is a preliminary stage to actual scribbling. Young children work spontaneously, trying out their thoughts in concrete fashion through art. The art forms each child creates have meaning to that child, although these forms are often unrecognizable to the adult (Bland 1968).

By the age of two or three, children are adept and earnest scribblers. They are often deeply involved in this enjoyable intensive activity. Children perceive anything and everything in their environment as a canvas for artwork, including their own bodies. At the beach, they may scribble on sand. In the city, children will scribble on concrete, buildings, bathtubs, tile, furniture, or nearby walls. This early, innocent, and free-flowing activity is similar to graffiti, for it is a way by which children affirm themselves to the world.

Children express themselves through scribbling in ways that are self-taught, universal, and fundamental to their total development. Young children's art is a unity of their thinking *and* feeling at a particular stage of their lives. In this sense, scribble art is a visual and a creative presentation of each child's uniqueness as a young being.

The adult must be free of preconceived notions and judgments about art to decipher early scribbles. Many artists and researchers have rediscovered the beauty in childhood scribble art. In speaking of the fresh, new looking forms and designs found in the young child's scribble art, Picasso once remarked that "adults should not teach children to draw, but should learn from them" (Kellogg and O'Dell 1967, p. 22). Contemporary abstract artists, such as Kandinsky, Chagall, and Miro consciously returned to the sources of child art for their own study and inspiration.

Scribbling is similar to the babbling of early speech: a kind of "making" activity for the young child that later acquires symbolic overtones (Gardner 1973). Kellogg and O'Dell (1967) have described scribbles as the building blocks of children's art. There are at least twenty basic scribbles used by young children. They include the use of lines that are vertical, horizontal, diagonal, circular, curved or waving, as well as several fascinating patterns of dots (Kellogg 1970).

Scribbles may also be studied in a variety of patterns of placement. For example, children may draw their scribbles in the left half, right half, or center of the paper. Seventeen scribble placement patterns have been identified by Kellogg (1970) and substantiated by other researchers. These patterns are utilized by children in self-paced, self-initiated practice; each pattern is discovered at a particular stage of development. Once children have discovered and developed specific placement patterns, these become part of their art repertoire, reappearing throughout the years of their artistic development, even into adulthood when they are sometimes referred to as "doodles."

Shape Stage

Soon after the placement stage, three- and four-year-old children begin to experiment with shape (Kellogg 1967). Alert, keen observers will notice the subtle change in style to the shape stage. At first, children will form scribbles with several strokes of the crayon, pencil, or paint brush. The first shapes are implied, rather than overtly drawn, and are usually not contained within a boundary line or an outline. Later, as children continue to discover shape, they also begin to outline the shapes they have drawn. They may then also draw familiar shapes, such as circles, ovals, squares, rectangles, triangles, crosses. Each shape has been self-taught and mastered by the child through endless scribbling exercises. These shapes or forms should not be taught by the adult, but should be left to the child's personal discovery during this stage of artistic development.

Design Stage

The design stage follows the shape stage. At this time, the child will place a shape into a familiar structured form, such as a cross inside a square (fig. 1) or a smaller circle within a large one (fig. 2).

Fig. 1.   *Fig. 2.*

When this occurs, the child has formally entered the design stage (Kellogg 1970). Children learn that shapes can be moved about, juxtaposed, placed near, or far from each other. They may combine two, three, or more simple shapes into a design, such as figures 3 or 4. Children are also capable

Fig. 3.   *Fig. 4.*

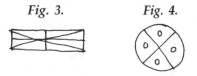

of making aggregates or combinations of other kinds of objects as well, such as geometric blocks or balls of clay. They can see that these objects have color, shape, weight, and tactile qualities and also learn that such objects have names (Droz and Rahmy 1976). By putting a cross in the

Shape Stage—concentric-type circles. Age 3 years, 3 months.   © Rod Salazar Studio

Design Stage—*mandala-type scribbling with a cross in circle. Age 3 years, 5 months.*

square, or smaller circles in a large one, children gain important perceptual and sensory information that will aid them later in forming abstract concepts and ideas.

Pictorial Stage: Toward Realism

The pictorial stage flows directly from the design stage (Kellogg and O'Dell 1967). Usually, between the ages of four and five, children will begin to set down structured designs that are clear enough for the adult to recognize. The pictorial stage represents an important, dramatic breakthrough for the young child. All the scribbles, placement patterns, shapes, and designs are combined as children move toward realism and representational art.

At this stage, however, children are seldom interested in drawing an object or a scene according to adult expectations. They are concerned with "creating esthetically satisfying structures" (Kellogg and O'Dell 1967, p. 20) that bring pleasure. Thus, children will continue to draw according to their own perceptions and visions, bringing them inner joy and satisfaction, an experience in common with other creative artists.

Although there have been numerous research studies on the subject of the scribble art of young children (Lindstrom 1957; Gardner 1973; Ecker 1976), there is still much to be learned about this particular form of art and thought. Young children are far more delighted in describing their pictures of the world than in satisfying the adult's wishes. They have not yet reached the stage of artistic development when "reality" is perceived as the adult perceives it. In drawing a house, for instance,

Francks

the five-year-old is likely to add wiggly lines and loops around the picture. The adult is apt to interpret these decorations as "real" smoke from a "real" chimney. For the young child, these lines and loops may just as likely be wiggling strings or floating tracks as "smoke," and their meaning is more intuitive than reality-bound. When asked what they are drawing, four- or five-year-olds may shrug their shoulders or explain, "How do I know until I have finished?" (Kellogg and O'Dell 1967). The child's world is filled with objects that change shape and form while they are being created. Drawings are molded in much the same way as clay sculpture: over and over, continually re-arranged to fit the meaning of the moment. This is an excellent example of the fluid and spontaneous nature of children's scribbling.

Underlying the child's pictorial efforts is a visual order that develops gradually, until, with the security that comes from having practiced scribbles and outlines, four- to five-year-old children reach the point of synthesis, putting everything they have learned together. Suddenly, or so it seems, they create all sorts of shapes and figures that are familiar to adults. Schaefer-Simmern called this visual synthesis activity a move toward recognizing figure-ground relationships—connections between each shape (figure) and its surroundings (ground). It is similar to the place words have within the context of a sentence, for example. This direction toward understanding figure-ground relationships is an important step in the child's cognitive and artistic growth, since children learn primarily by perceptual and other sensory experiences (Schaefer-Simmern 1973).

The circle or circular figure becomes a starting point for still-to-be-discovered relationships in art. For example, the child may draw lines that radiate out from the center of a circle, looking like the customary sun-with-rays (fig. 5) or perhaps, like

© Anita Lynn Miller

Pictorial Stage—*scribble art starts to resemble objects according to adult standards.*

a modified centipede (fig. 6). In fact, they may be neither!

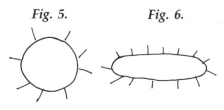

Fig. 5. *Fig. 6.*

This particular type of formative artistic effort—art that is in the process of being created—has its own kind of unified structure. A unified structure like the sunburst or the centipede is an organized visual form that holds together as an entity rather than as a series of isolated lines and shapes. It is truly a work of art in that each part is related to the entire picture or design, as well as to other parts of the structure. Art, when described in this fashion, is the visual means by which children learn to structure their thinking. Some writers refer to this mental activity as *visual conception*, a creative process that continues throughout childhood. As children mature, they increasingly come to terms with their external world. They use and sharpen their powers of observation, bringing back to their artwork greater visual awareness of the world they see.

At the same time as they are expressing themselves creatively, young children also begin to learn about the symbol system of our culture. Scribbling soon takes on symbolic, cultural overtones (Gardner 1973). For example, four-year-old children will begin to pick up clues about writing and reading. Drawing and scribbling have much in common with early attempts at writing letters and words.

> In fact, observations of four- and five-year-olds in a nursery school setting quickly confirm that many children at these ages not only draw spontaneously, they attempt to write as well. . . . They soon can write their own name, then other things, and before long, they begin to read things other children have written. It all evolves very naturally. . . . (Douglass 1978, p. 108)

The Process: Meaning and Message

Many of us tend to look for finished products, rather than enjoyment of the artistic process itself. We have become conditioned to evaluate along a continuum of good-better-best. Whether or not we realize it, our critical judgment is usually directed toward the completed work of art as an end in itself. At best, this is a limited way of enjoying art. There is, however, a world of difference between the artwork and process of children between the ages of two and five, and that of mature, skilled artists.

First, young children's artwork is not created for the express purpose of becoming a work of art in itself. It exists solely for its own sake—as a record of each child's personal exploration of the world. Second, young children cannot detach themselves from their scribbling and drawing in order to look at their work critically. This complex act occurs much later. Third, for young children there is no difference between inner and outer reality because "everything *is* and nothing merely seems" (Lindstrom 1957, p. 10). Their artwork, as all learning activity, acts as a bridge between the two worlds. The skilled, mature artist searches for ways and processes by which to express inner visions in contexts that best convey a particular message. Young children lack the options, skills, insight, and critical stance to evaluate their own scribble art from that of any other. The trained adult artist can transcend self to view critically other artists and works of art and can thereby make informed decisions about his or her own work. This is not true of the very young artist in the nursery school or kindergarten class whose scribble art is part of a spontaneous evolutionary process of development.

The process of childhood scribble art *is* the message that contains meaning for the child. The "making and doing" of art are crucial learning tasks. Through their visual statements in crayon scribbles or red-smeared paintings, children are better able to resolve for themselves some of life's mysteries and thus gain control over what they may have perceived to be overpowering, unmanageable "things" (Lindstrom 1957). Such phenomena are dealt with naturally and with immediacy through the medium of art. These expressions need not be understood by the adult in order to be valid for the child. **The child's art validates itself by its very existence.**

The Role of the Quiet Observer

Because of art's process orientation, it is often wiser for the adult to observe and enjoy the art experience along with the children, rather than interrupt the flow of their thinking by asking questions. Whether or not young children wish to talk about their drawing is of far less significance than the fact that they have chosen to set down their thoughts in a manner they selected, unaided and unhampered. This process is indicative of children's growing ability to organize and order reality according to their own perception of the world (Piaget 1976).

If you must know about the image that children have created, ask them to tell you about it, if they are willing. Knowledgeable adults will restrain themselves from such evaluative remarks as, "That's very good" or "I like Linda's train better because it is a *real* train" or "What is it?" Let children talk or be silent about their work, as they choose.

A nursery school teacher recorded one parent's reaction to her child's work:

> I gave back a water painting today. The water had dried, so basically, what Adam proudly presented to his mother was a wrinkled piece of white paper. She asked him what it was. When she received no answer, she said, "Adam, there's nothing there at all, so let's throw it out and take home one that has a pretty picture on it. Can you make me a pretty picture tomorrow? (Eisenstadt 1974).

Later, the same teacher reflected upon her experience in watching well-intentioned parents question their children about their artwork, compare their effort with another child's, and then try to suggest ways to improve the work. "It has been my experience that, in no way does a young child need help in expressing himself better than the way he chooses to do it for himself" (Eisenstadt 1974, p. 4).

The great variety of scribbles tempts us to help the child along, to speed up the process. We, however, are not there to "teach" scribbling, drawing, or art at this early level of development but, wisely, to let children go about their own discoveries in peace without comparison, correction,

or projecting ourselves into the children's burgeoning art world. Our important role is to encourage young children to facilitate their artistic ventures and to be quiet observers and carers for young children, privileged to share in an act of creation with them.

Yes, They Are Art!

Young children encounter the world by exploring, experimenting, testing, sensing, and generalizing on their own. Children's discoveries in art, as in all their inquiries, help them define this universe and structure their thinking in a visual way. Young children's art is important, not as a finished product but rather for the mediation it provides between their inner and outer worlds. Art acts also as a means of self-affirmation and is, therefore, a very valuable vehicle in the child's total development. From the moment children discover what it looks and feels like to set down their scribble marks, they have once and for all time found art!

We must tread carefully within the realm of art at these early stages, from infancy to ages five or six, so that children may work out their own thoughts and feelings without the constraint of evaluation. We should provide time, space, place, materials for children, and then allow them the dignity of "doing their own thing." We should be patient, learn to wait generously, and be prepared for whatever evolves. Above all, we can be happy for the child creator, even if he or she does not create what we would like to have created for us (Grözinger 1955).

Before our eyes, young children make their own personal, visual, written statement as a map of the mental and emotional strides they have already taken and as proof of their uniquely creative personality. Out of confusion young children establish a degree of visual order, sense, and beauty. It is our responsibility as caring adults to encourage such creation so that it may continue to evolve spontaneously and joyfully throughout life. ⬧

Bibliography

Arnheim, R. *Visual Thinking.* London: Faber and Faber, 1969.

Bland, J. C. *Art of the Young Child.* New York: Museum of Modern Art, 1968.

Douglass, M. "On Reading: The Great American Fetish." In *Reading, the Arts, and the Creation of Meaning,* ed. E. Eisner. Reston, Va.: National Art Education Association, 1978.

Droz, R., and Rahmy, M. *Understanding Piaget.* New York: International Universities Press, 1976.

Ecker, D. "The Critical Act in Aesthetic Inquiry." In *The Arts, Human Development, and Education,* ed. E. Eisner. Berkeley, Calif.: McCutchan Publishing Co., 1976.

Eisenstadt, E. "Young Children's Art." Fordham University, 1974.

Gardner, H. *The Arts and Human Development.* New York: Wiley, 1973.

Grözinger, W. *Scribbling, Drawing, Painting.* New York: Praeger, 1955.

Kellogg, R. *Analyzing Children's Art.* Palo Alto, Calif.: Mayfield Publishing Co., 1970.

Kellogg, R. "Understanding Children's Art." *Psychology Today* 1, no. 1 (May 1967): 16-25.

Kellogg, R., and O'Dell, S. *The Psychology of Children's Art.* Del Mar, Calif.: CRM Associates for Random House, 1967.

Lewis, H. P., ed. *Child Art.* Berkeley, Calif.: Diablo Press, 1973.

Lindstrom, M. *Children's Art.* Berkeley, Calif.: University of California Press, 1957.

Piaget, J. *The Child and Reality.* New York: Penguin Books, 1976.

Schaefer-Simmern, H. "The Mental Foundations of Art Education." In *Child Art,* ed. H. P. Lewis. Berkeley, Calif.: Diablo Press, 1973.

Dorothy T. McDonald
with Jonny H. Ramsey

Awakening the Artist:
Music for Young Children

A visitor to any center for early childhood education in this country would probably hear music of some kind. Children like to sing; they like to play musical instruments; they like to listen to records. Teachers of young children generally include musical activities daily for the pleasure they give, for the release from tension they can often provide, and for aid in developing cognitive skills in many curricular areas. Most teachers, however, find it necessary to proceed by instinct; there is little information about the kinds of musical experiences that are appropriate for the young child, the methods and techniques which might be helpful in planning musical activities, or the criteria which might be applied when choosing musical materials for young children. From study of the research and theory about the musical development of young children, we have formulated the following guidelines for teachers to use in planning for one of children's most meaningful human experiences—responding to and making music.

Learning to Listen

From studies of infant responses to music, a first guideline seems appropriate:

Music should be included daily for infants as well as for older children. The presence of music, whether through recordings or the teacher's singing or playing, can awaken early responses to musical sound and can encourage infants to *learn to listen*.

Noy (1968) described music as an auditory channel of communication and emotional exchange between the infant and the outside world. McDonald (1970) also suggested music's importance in the emotional well-being of children; she wrote about children selecting a familiar song or composition, heard in the home, as a *transition tune*—something of the child's world which helps the child alleviate anxieties and makes acquaintances with the outside world more pleasurable. Michel (1973) reported that children receive and respond to music at a very early age—"at two months [an infant] will lie motionless, with fixed attention to the sound of singing or playing of an instrument" (p. 17). It would appear that musical experiences can and should be purposefully planned even for infants.

A baby seldom is thought of as a singer. Ostwald (1973), however, noted that even infants attempt to vocalize musical intervals at an early age. Described as a period of *vocal contagion*, this stage can begin before the second half of the first year. He cited studies by Mead of cultures where nurses are specifically instructed to encourage infants' vocalizations by mimicking the babies' sounds.

Thus, the presence of music in the first year, when the child is primarily a receiver of music, appears to be an important prerequisite to participation in the music-mak-

Dorothy T. McDonald, Ph.D., is Associate Professor, Music Education, Elementary Education Division, University of Iowa, Iowa City, and a former music teacher in Iowa, Illinois, and North Carolina.

Jonny H. Ramsey, Ph.D., is Coordinator for the Arts in Education Program of Pennsylvania's Intermediate Unit #10.

ing process. *Receiving* evolves to *sound-making* and, subsequently, to *music-making*.

Learning to Sing

As young children become interested in participating in making music, certain questions arise. At what pitch levels can they sing most comfortably? Are there certain melodic patterns which children sing easily? What kinds of musical experiences could help them achieve accuracy and "tunefulness" in singing?

A second guideline, based on studies of young children's singing, is:

Singing should be included in the daily activities of preschool children, but expectations of achievement should be based upon knowledge of the developmental nature of this ability. Songs for classroom use should be chosen with careful consideration of tonality, range, melodic configurations, and vocal developmental stages of the children.

Singing attempts have been reported in children as young as four to six months of age (Michel 1973). From six months to one year, babies try out clearly audible musical intervals, usually within a range of three to five tones (Shuter 1968). Around the age of

Visual, verbal, and motor cues may be effective in helping young children develop concepts of melodic interval and direction.

McDonald and Ramsey

two, before many children will attempt to join in group singing, *chanting*, a form of spontaneous singing, is often heard among children at play. Many children experiment with familiar word patterns by giving them a tune—*language-related chants*—while others like to repeat a melodic pattern, experimenting with tonal sounds (Simons 1964). Often chants do not seem rhythmically related to the physical activity they accompany. The melodic patterns reported by observers appear to be those commonly found in songs of the child's culture (Scheihing 1952). Ascending and descending scale patterns, falling minor thirds, fourths, and fifths seem to be frequently used intervals. One of the most commonly heard melodic patterns in play activities is the familiar *teasing chant*—two falling minor thirds separated by the upper neighbor of the higher tone ("sol-mi-la-sol-mi"). The familiar song "Rain, Rain, Go Away" uses this pattern for the entire song. Perhaps *musical conversations* can be created by teacher and child using this common pattern.

At what pitch levels do young children sing easily? Cooper (1973) has reported that two-year-old children seem to sing most comfortably in a range from D_4 to A_4*—a range of five diatonic tones above middle C. Songs such as "Go Tell Aunt Rhody," the chorus of "Jingle Bells," "Twinkle, Twinkle, Little Star" (six tones), and "This Old Man" (six tones), long favorites with children, can be pitched to fit comfortably in this range; these songs also employ the melodic patterns cited above.

As children grow, their vocal range expands. Simons (1964) reported, in the spontaneous singing of children nine to 31 months of age, a usable range from C_4 to C_5.

---

*Middle C on the piano keyboard is identified as "C_4"; the pitches identified with subscript "4" lie in the octave above middle C. Pitches identified with subscript "3" lie in the octave below middle C; pitches with subscript "5" lie in the octave above third-space C (treble clef).

in twins and A^b_3 to B_4 in singletons. Kirkpatrick (1962) reported that the range used most frequently by five-year-old children extended from G_3 to B^b_4. Over half the children tested had extensive ranges from F_3 to E_5; however, approximately 20 percent had limited ranges from B_3 to $F^\#_4$. From a comparison of these ranges, it seems that even for children who have wide singing ranges, tones in the relatively low range below middle C become usable as soon as, or before, those in a relatively higher range (above A_4 or B_4).

When learning songs (imitative singing), however, the requirements of matching tones and words result in more restricted ranges (Jersild and Bienstock 1935). Drexler (1938) found that the most frequently used range of three- to six-year-old children was from C_4 to $D^\#_5$, but that the lower pitches were sung more easily. Young (1971) and Smith (1963) reported similar findings.

These researchers also reported certain sequential stages in the development of tuneful singing. While great individual differences exist among children, and no age seems significantly related to each stage, teachers may observe the following growth pattern. First, young children attempt to use the range of their speaking voices to reproduce songs. Next, they might exhibit inconsistent melodic direction. Gradually gaining vocal control, they may become accurate directionally, but inaccurate in interval reproduction. The hoped-for final stage is the accurate reproduction of a melody within a given tonality.

Maturation appears to be the most significant factor in range development; Boardman (1967) and Smith (1970) found that first grade children who had received early group training in singing, as well as those who had not, had more difficulty with upper range accuracy than with lower tones.

When choosing songs for beginning group singing, teachers might be advised to include many songs in ranges from approximately B_3 to A_4. Perhaps the concept of tuneful singing—important to all subsequent musical experiences—may be formed more easily in songs of this limited range.

Hermanson (1972) suggested that teachers teach songs using voice rather than piano; in her study, pitch accuracy was best when the children imitated a woman's voice and worst with a piano. One finding of a larger study by Sergeant and Roche (1973) drew attention to the matter of pitching songs in a consistent manner (each time a song is sung, it is sung in the same tonality). In their study, children three or four years of age tended to remember and reproduce songs at the same pitch levels in which the songs were learned.

Studies of techniques for helping children discriminate melodic intervals—a skill important in singing accuracy—provide a third guideline.

Visual, verbal, and motor cues may be effective in helping young children develop concepts of melodic interval and direction.

Yendovitskaya (1971) designed a pitch discrimination training program for three- and four-year-old children in which the subjects were taught to represent melodic intervals with matching arm amplitude; wide intervals were represented with arms far apart, narrow intervals with arms close together. He found that the physical representation was prerequisite for these children's successful identification of paired pitches as same or different. Repina trained children to associate low and high pitches with pictures of large and small animals. Williams (1932) used the piano keyboard as a visual cue in helping young children acquire concepts of melodic direction (tones moving "upstairs" or "downstairs").

In a similar manner, a teacher may provide visual cues, such as moving the hands up and down with the tones of a song or playing the melody on songbells held vertically. The inclusion of songs whose lyrics describe direction ("number songs" might fit in this category) or suggest directional physical movement ("I Put My Arms Up High") can provide experiences with the concept of melodic direction.

Ellen Levine Ebert

One of the first spontaneous rhythmic activities among children is producing a beat.

Learning to Move

To a young child, melody and movement are closely related; studies of children's spontaneous singing have shown that songs often grow out of motor activities. Studies by Greenberg (1972), Romanek (1974), and Belyayeva-Ekzemplyarskaya show that concepts of beat, tempo, and dynamics may develop before those of pitch, melody, harmony, and form. However, most young children need experience with rhythmic movement before they are successful in duplicating or synchronizing movement with music. One of the first spontaneous rhythmic activities among children is producing a *beat* (Shuter 1968). These regular, unaccented pulsations are quite fast in tempo ($\quarternote = 120$ to $\quarternote = 176$) (Scheihing 1952; Simons 1964) and little attempt is made to synchronize them with those of other children. When accents appear, they are often irregular and experimental in nature. At three years of age, the ability to synchronize beat with music for a controlled duration of time begins to develop (Christianson 1938); at age four, interest in dramatizing ideas in music appears; at age five, most children are able to march, clap, and otherwise keep time with music at relatively fast tempi (Jersild and Bienstock 1935).

McDonald and Ramsey

Training does not seem to improve these skills significantly; maturation is the most important factor. Therefore, a fourth guideline for planning rhythmic experiences might be expressed:

Rhythmic activities should start with exploration rather than duplication. Synchronization training is less important then opportunity to explore movement and rhythm.

Fingerplays, action songs, and musical games provide many exploratory experiences with rhythmic expression. Songs such as "This Old Man," "Jim Along Josie," "In and Out the Window," and "Little Rabbit in the Wood" are but a few which can be used to encourage rhythmic expression. Many recent recordings for young children also encourage creative exploratory movement rather than synchronization with a beat or pattern. Hap Palmer's *Creative Movement and Rhythmic Expression* (Educational Activities, Inc.) provides delightful exploratory experiences with rhythmic movement.

Learning to Hear

Music is an aural art, and the development of listening skills is one of the most important objectives of any music program. What kinds of music attract young children? How can teachers encourage attentive listening?

Alford (1971) reported that young children show a greater degree of response to music which is predominantly rhythmic or melodic rather than that which is harmonic or dissonant. McDonald and Schuckert (1968) found that when children were allowed to choose between a jazz selection and a classical selection, jazz was the preferred choice. However, some children showed increased interest in the classical selection over a period of exposure time.

Studies by Fullard (1967), Greer, Dorow, and Hanser (1973), and Allen (1959) revealed very young children's ability to learn to identify orchestral instruments by matching pictures of the instruments with their sound when played. Instruments identified by three-, four-, and five-year-old children included violin, clarinet, cello, flute, viola, French horn, bassoon, oboe, and trumpet. Young children appear to be discriminating in selecting an appropriate timbre, also, when choosing percussive instruments for rhythmic activities (Shuter 1968). Such information suggests a guideline for planning listening experiences:

Music listening experiences may be included as an important part of an early childhood music curriculum. Discrimination tasks, including identification of individual or families of instruments may be appropriate and may increase interest in listening to many different kinds of music.

The Bowmar albums, including *The Young Listener*; records developed for identification of instruments; and selected albums from the Folkways recordings of music from other cultures are valuable sources.

Learning to Learn

A final guideline is formulated from studies in which music was used as an aid to cognitive development in other curriculum areas:

Music and movement may be useful in motivating and helping children to

Dorothy McDonald

Rhythmic activities should start with exploration rather than duplication.

acquire verbal concepts, oral communication, and aural discrimination skills.

Because music is a pleasurable and non-threatening experience for most children, it can sometimes be used to help children with special needs feel comfortable while learning. Seybold (1971), a speech therapist, reported that a remedial program which included singing conversations, and singing games which required primary color identification and provided experiences with verbal concepts such as "up and down," yielded significant posttest gains in language development test scores for normal, but speech-delayed, children. Greenberg (1972) and Pruitt and Steele (1971) developed programs for children in Head Start classrooms, and have cited significant gains, not only in music concept formation, but also in cognitive skills such as right-left discrimination, color identification, counting, and body image.

In similar fashion, a teacher may use familiar, favorite songs to enhance developmental skills. The use of substitute words in many familiar songs can provide reinforcement for skills such as color identification ("Mary Wore a Red Dress," for example).

What can be said can also be sung. A teacher can initiate singing conversations using tonal chants (perhaps the familiar descending minor third, "sol-mi") to encourage children to formulate thoughts into phrases and sentences. Music may help these kinds of experiences become enjoyable and successful games.

Music for the young child should be planned for more than tension release or leisure-time entertainment. Developing sensitivity to one's world—perceptual, cognitive, and emotional—is an important goal for the education of young children. For "if we awaken the artist . . . at a tender age, when [the child] is so receptive to all beauty, then [the child's] later life will be incomparably more fulfilled and enriched" (Michel 1973, p. 19).

References

Alford, D. L. "Emergence and Development of Music Responses in Preschool Twins and Singletons: A Comparative Study." *Journal of Research in Music Education* 19, no. 2 (Summer 1971): 222-227.

Allen, E. B. "A Study of Perception of Instrumental Tone Color by Children of Nursery School Age." Master's thesis, University of Kansas, 1959.

Boardman, E. L. "An Investigation of the Effect of Preschool Training on the Development of Vocal Accuracy in Young Children." *Council for Research in Music Education Bulletin* 11 (Fall 1967): 46-49.

Christianson, H. *Bodily Movement of Young Children in Relation to Rhythm in Music*. New York: Columbia University, 1938.

Cooper, R. M. "Music and the Two-Year-Olds." *Music Journal* 31, no. 1 (January 1973):13.

Drexler, E. N. "A Study of the Development of the Ability to Carry a Melody at the Preschool Level." *Child Development* 9 (March-December 1938): 319-332.

Duerkson, G. L. *Teaching Instrumental Music*. Washington, D.C.: Music Educators National Conference, 1972.

Fullard, W. G., Jr. "Operant Training of Aural Musical Discriminations with Preschool Children." *Journal of Research in Music Education* 15, no. 3 (Fall 1967): 201-209.

Greenberg, M. "A Preliminary Report of the Effectiveness of a Music Curriculum with Preschool Head Start Children." *Council for Research in Music Education Bulletin* 29 (Summer 1972): 13-16.

Greer, R. D.; Dorow, L.; and Hanser, S. "Music Discrimination Training and the Music Selection Behavior of Nursery and Primary Level Children." *Council for Research in Music Education Bulletin* 35 (Winter 1973): 30-43.

Hermanson, L. W. "An Investigation of the Effects of Timbre on Simultaneous Vocal Pitch Acuity of Young Children." *Dissertation Abstracts International* 32, no. 7 (January 1972): 3558-A.

Jersild, A. T., and Bienstock, S. F. "A Study of the Development of Children's Ability to Sing." *Journal of Educational Psychology* 25, no. 7 (October 1934): 481-503.

Jersild, A. T., and Bienstock, S. F. *Development of Rhythm in Young Children*. New York: Columbia University, 1935.

Kirkpatrick, W. C. "Relationships Between the Singing Ability of Prekindergarten Children and Their Home Musical Environment." *Dissertation Abstracts* 23, no. 3 (September 1962): 886.

McDonald, M. "Transitional Tunes and Musical Development." *The Psychoanalytic Study of the Child* 25 (1970): 503-520.

McDonald, R. L., and Schuckert, R. F. "An Attempt to Modify the Musical Preferences of Preschool Children." *Journal of Research in Music Education* 16, no. 1 (Spring 1968): 39-44.

Michel, P. "The Optimum Development of Musical Abilities in the First Years of Life." *Psychology of Music* 1, no. 2 (June 1973): 14-20.

Noy, P. "The Development of Musical Ability." *The Psychoanalytic Study of the Child* 23 (1968): 332-347.

Ostwald, P. F. "Musical Behavior in Early Childhood." *Developmental Medicine and Child Neurology* 15, no. 1 (February 1973): 367-375.

Pruitt, H., and Steele, A. L. "Music by Head Start Teachers for the Educationally Disadvantaged." *American Music Teacher* 20, no. 6 (June-July 1971): 29-30, 37.

Romanek, M. L. "A Self-Instructional Program for Musical Concept Development in Preschool Children." *Journal of Research in Music Education* 22, no. 2 (Summer 1974): 129-135.

Scheihing, G. "A Study of the Spontaneous Rhythmic Activities of Preschool Children." In *Music Therapy 1951*, edited by E. G. Gilliland, pp. 188-189. Lawrence, Kans.: Allen Press, 1952.

Sergeant, D., and Roche, S. "Perceptual Shifts in the Auditory Information Processing of Young Children." *Psychology of Music* 1, no. 2 (June 1973): 39-48.

Seybold, C. D. "The Value and Use of Music Activities in the Treatment of Speech-Delayed Children." *Journal of Music Therapy* 8 (Fall 1971): 102-110.

Shuter, R. *The Psychology of Musical Ability*. London: Methuen and Co., 1968.

Simons, G. M. "Comparisons of Incipient Music Responses among Very Young Twins and Singletons." *Journal of Research in Music Education* 12, no. 3 (Fall 1964): 212-226.

Smith, R. B. "The Effect of Group Vocal Training on the Singing Ability of Nursery School Children." *Journal of Research in Music Education* 11, no. 2 (Fall 1963): 137-141.

Smith, R. B. *Music in the Child's Education*. New York: Ronald Press, 1970.

Williams, H. M. "Techniques of Measurement in the Developmental Psychology of Music." In *Studies in Child Welfare: The Measurement of Musical Development*, edited by G. D. Stoddard, pp. 11-31. Iowa City, Iowa: University of Iowa, 1932.

Yendovitskaya, T. V. "Development of Sensation and Perception." In *The Psychology of Preschool Children*, edited by A. V. Zaporozhets and D. B. Elkonin, translated by J. Shybut and S. Simon, pp. 1-64. Cambridge, Mass.: MIT Press, 1971.

Young, W. T. "An Investigation of the Singing Abilities of Kindergarten and First Grade Children in East Texas." Bethesda, Md.: ERIC Document Reproduction Service, ED 069 431, 1971.

6

Techniques for implementing an effective curriculum

How does the atmosphere in our classroom affect what children learn? This final section focuses on strategies for guiding children as they become more self-disciplined and in control of their lives—a key component of any curriculum.

What are children learning while they wait in line? Are the children in your group learning how to learn? Your ideas may be challenged by Davidson and Stipek's suggestions for channeling children's learning opportunities.

If you find that the puppets in your classroom are merely entertaining, Smith's educational approach for children's active involvement with puppets to generate imaginative solutions can bring about a refreshing change.

How do you handle situations in which a child firmly states "No!" You may be less baffled or infuriated if you implement Haswell, Hock, and Wenar's proven approaches to dealing with

negativism as an indication of the child's growing independence.

Though we tend to avoid difficult issues such as divorce or death, preparing ourselves now to help children and their families will help give us confidence when we are faced with the situation. While the processes of separation and mourning are sensitive issues, Skeen and McKenry, and Furman provide particularly insightful suggestions as we struggle to cope with life's harsh realities.

Curriculum Planning for Young Children ends with a professional development plan that involves administrators, teachers, and children. Making the most of available resources is the key to the S.W.A.P. program described by Stalmack. Her ideas, incorporated with those throughout the book, can be implemented in any curriculum for young children.

Jane Davidson

Wasted Time
The Ignored Dilemma

Providing a meaningful experience for young children is not an easy job. Even in schools and centers where the basic program is exciting and full, there are occasions in which children are waiting or their time is being wasted. Children may be waiting for everyone to finish lunch before they can leave the table. Children may be waiting for a turn on the swing because there are only two swings for 70 children, and both are being used. Or, they may be waiting for a story to be continued because the teacher has stopped reading to quiet a noisy child. Each instance may involve only a short waiting time. However, all too often these small incidents are so numerous they add up to a substantial amount of wasted time per day.

Effects of Wasted Time

Boredom that results from waiting or from not being adequately challenged is one of the main causes of anxiety. There is a toxic quality in waiting. The most comfortable, self-assured children can show signs of anxiety when forced to wait. Children with more tenuous self-control will fall to pieces. As any adult who has taken a beloved friend to the train—then wished they were gone—can tell, waiting causes almost physical discomfort. (Hirsch 1972, p. 4)

Besides promoting boredom, large quantities of wasted time can have serious implications for the children involved.

Wasted time at school can negatively affect children in three ways. First, it may **lower the child's self-esteem.** Teachers of young children consider building self-esteem in each child a prime goal. Self-concept is based on personal success and on respect and admiration from others. Adults who often make children wait for them or the group, or who otherwise waste children's time, convey a basic lack of respect for children, which may well have a detrimental effect on the way children view themselves.

Second, long periods of waiting **encourage children to behave inappropriately.** Few children are able to sit and do nothing. If made to wait at the door until everyone is lined up for lunch, children are likely to find something to do. Often it will be such things as fiddling with a nearby picture until it falls down, pushing another child, going for a preliminary scouting trip down the hall, or some other inappropriate activity. This is not because children wish to misbehave; it is merely their natural desire to keep busy. Constant "misbehavior" at these times brings teacher disapproval, contributing to a child's negative self-esteem, a poor child/teacher relationship, and an uncomfortable classroom atmosphere.

Third, **children need to learn to value and use their time wisely**, both for effective work and for fulfilling relaxation and recreation. A school which does not respect the children's time is not going to encourage them to value it themselves, or help them build skills for structuring its use wisely.

Causes and Practical Solutions

I visited ten day care centers (names of schools and children are fictitious, but the incidents are real) to observe the ways

Jane Davidson, M.S., is a preschool teacher and lecturer at the University of Delaware, Newark.

Davidson

children's time was wasted and to discover what methods were used to enrich time that was often wasted in other centers.

Organizational and Administrative Restraints

Teachers are constantly hampered by inflexible bus schedules, inaccessible playgrounds, uncoordinated staff hours, too many children, cramped bathrooms, and other problems over which teachers have little control. These problems fit into three main categories: (1) those particular to the school that cannot be changed (bus schedule, the time children are picked up by parents, and playground accessibility); (2) those activities common to most early childhood programs which, by their group nature, create a certain amount of waiting (lunch, nap, snack, cleanup, and transition times); and (3) organizational problems arising from the individual classroom schedule and management.

Lunchtime. At both Greenhill and Developmental Learning child care centers, the children's varying schedules created organizational problems for the teachers. At both schools, lunch was served at 11:30, but some of the children came just for the morning and did not leave until 12:00 or 12:30. At Greenhill these children were expected to sit and wait until their mothers came, while their classmates ate. It was a situation bound to encourage misbehavior from the bored, waiting children! The teachers at Developmental Learning, on the other hand, realized this problem and assigned a teacher to read stories and do other quiet activities with departing children until their parents arrived. The teachers at Developmental Learning used the time to help children learn to use waiting time constructively.

Although most programs have group times such as lunch, snack, bathrooming, nap, and transitions in common, Prescott et al. (1972) observed the great differences in lunchtimes between schools. Lunchtime ranged from a formal, rigid eating time with no talking; to a happy, relaxed family-like event in which teachers and children ate and chatted together. This same range in lunchtime atmosphere was apparent at the centers I visited.

Children who are quick eaters may spend only 5 minutes of lunchtime eating and another 25 minutes waiting for everyone else to finish. Lunchtime should be pleasant and filled with conversation, stories, guessing games, or other interesting activities.

At Community Day Care the teachers ate with the children, and all served themselves. There was a busy, happy hum of conversation. The children at the table where I ate discussed the morning's activities, talked about the children who were absent, played rhyming word games, and invited the cook's helper to come read the Spanish phrase he had written on the chalkboard at the back of the room. When the children at the first table were done, they cleared their places and returned to their classroom for quiet activities until naptime. As children from the second table finished, they were free to join the children in the classroom or sit and chat with the hungrier tablemates.

Naptime. Nap is another time which differs considerably between schools in both length and allowable behaviors. At Developmental Learning children were expected to remain quietly on their cots from after lunch, around 12:30, until 3:00. The teachers said that a few children did not sleep, but these children had learned to be quiet. Most adults would find it difficult to lie still for even half an hour, much less for two and a half hours. Imagine how difficult this must be for a child. Naptime should give children a chance to relax, but two and a half hours of enforced, nonsleeping rest is instead likely to bring tension and frustration.

The teachers at Discovery Day Care had an excellent solution for this problem. The children were divided into groups of "sleepers" and "resters." The sleepers went to their cots in the sleeping room right after lunch, around 12:30. For about half an hour they had a story, back rubs, and lullabies until everyone was asleep. The resters had 45 minutes of quiet activities (using such things as playdough, puzzles, interlocking plastic blocks, or crayons). The children were expected to be quiet if they wanted the privilege of being a rester. They then had 15 minutes to look at books on their blankets and a half hour of quiet rest listening to a story record. The resters who fell asleep were allowed to sleep. The resters who were still awake at 2:00 went outside. The sleepers joined the others outdoors as they awakened. This arrangement assured that all the children had some quiet restful activities. It ensured that the children who needed sleep were not disturbed by the restlessness of others.

Transitions. Transition times are difficult for teachers and children.

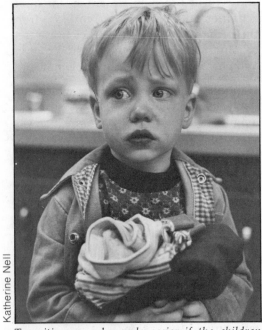

Transitions can be made easier if the children know clearly what will be coming next and if teachers try to make transitions an interesting time in themselves.

A group of children is doing a marvelous job with unit blocks in a free play activity. Then it is time to clean up—the teacher steps to the piano, hits a chord: CLEAN UP TIME. At this time three boys go and kick over the block buildings, three others throw themselves on top of the pile of blocks and make swimming motions with their arms and legs. The teacher looks on in horror. Suddenly her peaceful class is "high" and she does not know how to get them down. Almost certainly, she feels, anything she does now will be useless; she has lost her group.

Children are standing in line waiting to go to the bathroom. This is when somebody kicks, this is when somebody punches, this is when thumbs pop into their mouths and children remember that they miss their mommies. The teacher does not know whom to look at first; she does not know whom to comfort; whom to chide; whom to separate from the group before trouble spreads. This is a very difficult time. (Hirsch 1972, p. 1)

Hirsch also describes a chaotic cleanup time in which the teacher looks around to discover that her two co-teachers are not in the room; one has gone to put on pants for outside time, and the other has gone to make an important call she just remembered. This scene is all too common. Even conscientious teachers find reasons to disappear at transition times because, like the children, they find these times tense and unpleasant.

Hirsch suggests that the problems of transition times are increased by boredom, teachers' disorganization, insistence on conformity (like lining up), and by children's basic dislike of change. Transitions can be made easier if the children know clearly what will be coming next, and if teachers try to make transitions an interesting time in themselves. If children have to bathroom together, why not have bear hunts, guessing games, songs, simple stories, finger plays, or other activities for the children who are waiting for a toilet?

At Exploration Unlimited the teachers played the "people game" while waiting for a late lunch to be served or for slow eaters to finish. The teacher or a child would describe a child in the class and each child would have a turn to guess who was being described. The children learned one way to occupy themselves constructively during waiting times.

Teachers can make moving from place to place easier by having each adult take a few children instead of going in a large, over-excited mob. Why have children line up? Why not, instead, have a novel way of going from classroom to yard? Give each child a direction: "Put a hand on your nose and a hand on your knee and walk to the first door." The children love it and will wait quietly at each stop to see what silly directions you have for the next stop of the trip. Another idea is having the children count how many steps it takes, or how many doors they pass, or see how well they can march to a marching song. Such games help children to see that even regimented times can be made fun. It shows them that with a little imagination, they can control their time and use it to good advantage.

Poor Organization

After snacktime the three-year-old class at Unity Day Care had a time devoted to movement followed by free play. The children spent ten minutes waiting while the teacher found and remembered the game on the record she wanted to use. Another fifteen minutes were spent sitting while the teacher set up free play. Obviously this is extreme, but all teachers are occassionally less organized and prepared than they would like. If children arrive before the next activity is ready, why not let them help with setting up? If group time is approaching and the necessary book or record player has not been located, why not just continue the preceding activity until the preparations are complete?

One teacher at Greenhill had 18 children to care for by herself. She selected activities for free choice time which re-

quired little or no advance preparation. Painting, the one activity which took some time to prepare, was not set out until each child was involved in some other free play activity.

Lack of Equipment, Space, or Teachers

Lack of Equipment. If equipment is sparse, children must wait for the toys they want or spend time hoarding and guarding the few available toys. At three of the centers I visited, the scarcity of equipment in the classrooms was due not to lack of funds, but to the teachers' not making enough of the existing toys available to the children. At Young People's Place and Unity Day Care, the children were limited to certain areas and activities during free choice time. Often they finished all of the scheduled activities early. These children seemed bored and restless, and they did not seem to know what else to do.

If teachers limit the number of available resources, it is important to determine if too many, too few, or the right number of materials is available. The mood of a class can change daily, and teachers should consider adding additional toys and activities if it becomes apparent that the children will not have enough to do.

Exploration Unlimited and Discovery Day Care experienced none of this "I've tried it all" problem. The teachers at both these schools spent time interacting or observing the children as they used the classroom equipment. Special activities were available each day on a staggered basis. Some activities were introduced at the beginning of free play, some in the middle, and some toward the end so the children could always find something new to interest them.

In some cases equipment was not used by the children because needed accessories were not available. Greenhill Day Care had expensive wooden kitchen furniture for the housekeeping area, but no dishes, dress-up clothes, or dolls were

Vivienne della Grotta

If equipment is sparse, children must wait for the toys they want or spend time hoarding and guarding the few available toys.

provided. Neglect of this area led to over-crowding and waiting for the other available equipment. If one area of the classroom is being ignored by children, teachers should consider why. Is the area too crowded? Are accessories needed? Do the accessories there need to be changed to bring variety? Does that area need more teacher support?

Sometimes adults can help children learn to use new toys. At Exploration Unlimited the teachers in one classroom bought a set of unit blocks with many accessories such as small cars, people, and furniture. The first few weeks the children used the blocks often; but after the newness wore off, the blocks were rarely used unless a teacher was there to encourage the builders. When the blocks were a year old, a student teacher planned a series of activities to help the children learn the

rudiments of construction techniques. The children now initiate intricate, extensive block-building projects on their own.

Lack of Space. Lack of space or poorly arranged space can bring tension and frustrations, and may precipitate fights. The children in one class at High Street Day Care were all looking at books, or working puzzles in the library corner during the quiet time before lunch. The area was so small that the children were constantly bumping or kicking their neighbors, stepping on fingers, or interfering with their neighbor's activity. The children could not use this time well because of the constant interruptions caused by the crowded conditions.

Community Day Care's kindergarten is an excellent example of good use of a poor space. If seen empty, the long narrow

Davidson

room would appear unusable; however, the teachers have arranged it into a homey, comfortable classroom. Low shelves and displays divide the room into usable areas and provide good traffic patterns without crowding. The shelves can be moved to allow more room for a special activity when needed. Instead of trying to cram too much into a small space, the teachers regularly change the materials and learning centers. As a result, the children are totally involved, and no time is wasted in the classroom.

Lack of Teachers. A shortage of teachers can cause children to spend time waiting for teacher assistance, can decrease the amount of teacher stimulation in the classroom, and can leave children unprotected from themselves and others.

The children at Unity Day Care were continually waiting for teacher help. A child who wished to finger paint—an activity on the schedule the day I visited—needed a teacher to get the finger paint paper, to put paint on the paper, to put the paper on the drying rack, to get a paper towel, and to unfasten the smock.

To my surprise, the amount of time children waited for teachers was not necessarily dependent on the child/teacher ratio. The three-year-old class at Greenhill had 18 children and only 1 teacher, yet the children rarely needed to wait long for teacher assistance. The activities at this school were simple and self-directing. Many other schools decreased the amount of waiting for teacher assistance by encouraging the children to learn self-help skills, and by placing toys and supplies within the children's reach.

Children are often understimulated when there are not enough teachers. At Greenhill, 6 of the 18 three-year-old children had just enrolled the week I visited. It was Carl's second day. He was dropped off by his mother around 10:00 a.m. He stood and watched until 10:30 when the one teacher in the room came over, patted his head, and asked how he was. Before

Carl had a chance to answer, she was off to help another child. Carl stood and watched for the rest of the morning. His only other interaction was a second quick hello from the teacher. New children often like to observe the classroom events for a few days before feeling comfortable enough to join in, but Carl was not given the teacher support which can often expedite the getting comfortable process.

A shortage of adults can also leave children unprotected from the bullying of their classmates or from their own worst impulses. At Greenhill one three-year-old boy hovered protectively over his pile of blocks. He shouted, "These are mine," as the class bully took them away to enlarge his own building. The other child watched sadly for awhile before he wandered off. The teacher did not see the incident. This type of occurrence was common at Greenhill, Unity, and many of the other understaffed child care centers. When children cannot rely on teachers for protection, they spend time worrying about "territory" and personal safety, leaving little time for the normal play and exploration of childhood. At Community Day Care, one class had 25 children and 2 teachers. The teachers alternated the responsibility for general supervision and facilitation and the role of special activity leader, so that one teacher was always available to give special attention where needed.

Lack of Respect for Children

Unity Day Care had just introduced a new "centers approach" in an attempt to strengthen its educational program. Children were to select from the special activities for the day. The day I visited, teachers were constantly interrupting children's activities to demonstrate the "proper" way to do something or to point out that what the children were doing was not "on the schedule"; therefore, they would have to find something else to do. It was not clear to me, as a visitor, which activities were acceptable, and it also did not appear to be clear to the children. A great deal of the children's time was involved in starting activities and checking to see if a teacher would disapprove. The only activities that were considered acceptable were the ones the teachers started. Unity teachers, in trying to provide more educational activities, unconsciously communicated a lack of respect for the child's natural interests and activities.

Age-Inappropriate Activities

Seven of the centers I visited had some activities that were inappropriate to the child's age level. Frequently the activity was too complex, too structured, involved too many children, or required skills that children of that age would not yet have gained. At Discovery Day Care, all 57 children (from two to five years of age) assembled for a 30-minute group time where songs were sung, and a long story was read. The four- and five-year-olds seemed to find the story interesting but had difficulty controlling themselves in such a large group. The two- and three-year-olds had a difficult time behaving and paying attention to the story.

Community Day Care had a 30-45 minute "sit-down time" every morning. The class was divided into a "low" and a "high" group. Each group of about ten children had a structured group time with the teacher, including discussion of the calendar, the weather, and letter games or some other "learning" activities. A five-minute attention span was typical of the low group of two- to three-year-olds. The remaining 25 minutes of the "sit-down time" were spent trying to get this child or that one to sit down, turn around, pay attention, or stop pushing her or his neighbor.

At both Community and Unity, as well as at many other child care centers, children were bored into misbehaving by

Children can be bored into misbehaving by being expected to participate in activities inappropriate for their age level.

Lynne Bruna

being expected to participate in activities inappropriate for their age level. It is important to evaluate activities in order to modify or eliminate those which are inappropriate. The teachers at Play School found their children lacked the group skills needed to follow long stories when sitting with the whole class of 20. Until children gained these skills, the class was divided into three small groups for stories and group games. Shorter stories would be another possible solution.

Special Occasions

Planned or unplanned special occasions such as trips, birthdays, teacher absence, holidays, rainy days, or lunch being late may be unscheduled, but they are certainly not unexpected. It is important for teachers to have plans ready for these unscheduled emergencies to ensure that, despite minor disruptions, the school is still able to meet the children's needs.

It was raining the days I visited five of the centers. At each school I heard comments on how hard rainy days were because of the loss of outside time. During outside play times, the pressures to be a good group member are relaxed, and the extra space gives the children more room. Outside play allows the child to release pent-up energies and rest from the more structured indoor activities. It is important to consider the nature of outside time when planning substitute activities for rainy days.

Due to rain, Developmental Learning Center replaced an hour of outside time with an hour of large group time for all 40 children (ages 2−5). The director led exercises to activity records, followed by songs, stories, and finger plays. The exercises provided the children with some opportunity for releasing energy, but the group time did not accommodate the children's need for unstructured activities, or for the relaxation of group demands found in outside play.

Children's Place made an effort to offer

better rainy day activities. The teachers in each class took out some climbing equipment for their group. Unfortunately, not enough activities were offered for the number of children involved. The firefighter's gym for the four-year-old children was overcrowded, thereby causing waiting and fighting. No other options were available when children became tired of climbing. Those who had finished climbing occupied their time by bothering and teasing the children who still wanted to climb.

The Community Day Care teachers found an excellent solution for rainy days. They extended the free play time and added some more active options. For example, the two-year-olds could dance to rock and roll music.

Planned special occasions, such as field trips, birthdays, and holidays, are common events in child care centers. Often these occasions are carried out in traditional ways. It was Delbert's birthday the day I visited the High Street Day Care Center. Delbert took more than 15 minutes carefully passing out cupcakes to his 40 classmates. After snacktime, Delbert opened a present from his "friends at High Street." The gift was a small, inexpensive book which the teacher proceeded to read to the class. The pictures were so small that no one beyond the first row could see them. High Street's birthday procedure, a procedure common to many schools, added unnecessary waiting and frustration to this special day. Instead, why not let the teachers or other children help the birthday child pass out the snack? Let the birthday child pick a favorite book to be read to the class.

Holidays, nursery school "graduations," and other ceremonies are often designed more for parents than for children. At Play School the parents insisted on having a formal graduation ceremony with the children dressed in caps and gowns. The children spent 20 minutes getting dressed and waiting for the parents to be seated. Each child walked over to the teacher when her or his name was called to get a sheet of paper. Then they sat down and waited for all the other children to be called. The children seemed scared, bored, nervous, and restless. Meaningless ceremonies such as "graduations" have no place in child-centered programs. If teachers wish to celebrate the end of school, why not have a last day party—a time for children to play one last time with their favorite toys or their best friends, and a time for parents to have a last cup of coffee with the teachers and other parents?

Krown (1974) and her associates found that holidays involved so much teacher preparation that often the children and their program were neglected for the two or three weeks preceding the holiday while teachers prepared. Krown and her fellow teachers decided to simplify holiday celebrations. The preparation began a day or two before the holiday. The celebrations were simple and child-centered.

Conclusion

Although many of these incidents of wasted time were small and seemingly in-significant, they often add up to well over an hour of waiting and boredom for each child during an eight-hour day. It is important for teachers to evaluate their program in terms of how it uses or wastes children's time. Where it is not possible to eliminate waiting, teachers should help children to gain the valuable skills needed for dealing constructively with their own time.

I would like to thank Dr. Sara Van Camp and Dr. Ruth Hamlin for their helpful suggestions and comments.

References

Hirsch, E. S. *Transition Periods: Stumbling Blocks of Education.* New York: Early Childhood Council of New York City, 1972.

Krown, S. *Threes and Fours Go to School.* Englewood Cliffs, N.J.: Prentice-Hall, 1974.

Prescott, E.; Jones, E.; and Kritchevsky, S. *Day Care as a Child-Rearing Environment.* Vol. II. Washington, D.C.: National Association for the Education of Young Children, 1972. Out of print.

Deborah J. Stipek

Work Habits
Begin
in Preschool

So many parents lament their teenager's C average, "If only he would apply himself, I know he is smart enough to be a good student." The parent of a third grader similarly exclaims, "She would learn so much better if she would just pay attention." The assessments made by these parents are, for the most part, correct; with few exceptions, children do have the ability to learn what is expected in school. Yet so many children have difficulty. The poor work habits deplored by parents may, indeed, be a major impairment to efficient learning in school.

Some children's poor work habits are already apparent in early childhood. Teachers influence children's work habits through their interactions with children in play and learning activities, sometimes doing so in subtle and unintended ways. This article reviews evidence on work habits believed to affect learning. Special attention is given to the role of the preschool teacher in helping children develop more positive work habits. *Work habits* pertain here to situations requiring concentrated effort such as when children are working on a cognitive task or an art project. Excluded from this analysis are many activities, such as group games or playing on playground equipment, that may call for altogether different teacher behaviors.

Work habits learned in preschool take on particular significance in light of evidence on social-class differences. One study, for example, found that in a standardized task situation, low-socioeconomic status (SES) four-year-olds were less attentive to the task and more attentive to the experimenter or an observer than were high-SES children (Stipek, Roberts, and Sanborn 1980). Furthermore, according to teachers' reports of behavior in the natural preschool environment, low-SES children gave up more easily, paid less attention to the task, chose easier tasks, and worked less independently. Since most of these behaviors have been shown to be associated with intellectual performance on an IQ test in preschool (Stipek, Roberts, and Sanborn 1980) and in elementary school (Bridgeman and Shipman 1978; Kohn and Rosman 1973; 1974), teachers need to be aware that low-SES children's lower test and school performance may be, in part, a result of less-effective work habits. Teachers may ultimately contribute as much to children's cognitive functioning by helping them develop good work habits as they do by directly teaching them academic skills.

Which work habits contribute to learning?

The children who learn most are those who persist at tasks rather than giving up as soon as the task becomes difficult, who pay attention to the task and select tasks that offer some challenge rather than the easiest available or ones that they could not possibly do, and who work on a task alone without unnecessary requests for help (Bridgeman and Shipman 1978; Kohn and Rosman 1973; 1974).

Deborah J. Stipek, Ph.D., is Assistant Professor, Early Childhood Education and Developmental Studies, Graduate School of Education, University of California at Los Angeles.

Persistence

Consider two children working on puzzles. The puzzles have a few more pieces than most they have put together and require a little more effort and a little more time. More importantly, the challenging task offers an opportunity to learn something new about spatial relationships, colors, and shapes. Christopher works for a few minutes and then declares unabashedly, "This is too hard. I'm going to do a different puzzle," and returns the uncompleted puzzle to the shelf. His efforts end in failure rather than a feeling of self-satisfaction or accomplishment. The other child, Danielle, continues to search for appropriate matches. It takes a while, but Danielle succeeds and after the victory smiles approvingly at the accomplishment and is rewarded with feelings of pride and self-efficacy.

We have all witnessed these extremes in children's persistence on tasks. In a research project one child in a standardized task situation gave up on a puzzle within one minute; another child grabbed a puzzle back from the experimenter after working on it for ten minutes and announced that he was not leaving until he finished. Several researchers have found that the child who gives up easily in one situation is likely to give up easily in another (Hamilton and Gordon 1978; Stipek, Roberts, and Sanborn 1980). As one would expect, these individual differences in persistence are also associated with differences in intellectual performance (Stipek, Roberts, and Sanborn 1980).

Attention

Consider again the children putting puzzles together. Christopher works on the puzzle a few minutes. Soon, his eyes turn from the puzzle to the teacher walking across the room. Easily distracted from the task, he makes slow progress. Danielle focuses her attention on the puzzle, ignoring what is going on in the room. She is clearly the more efficient worker, and may finish two puzzles in the time that Christopher finishes one. Compared to Christopher, Danielle spends more time in problem-solving activities. The difference between these two children's behavior is important because of all of the classroom measures believed to influence school achievement, time-on-task is the most powerful predictor of academic skills (Fisher et al. 1980).

As was found for persistence, individual differences in attention are, to some degree, consistent across tasks and situations. Stipek, Roberts, and Sanborn (1980) found, for example, that children who paid relatively more attention while doing an embedded pictures task in a standardized task situation were rated by preschool teachers as the more attentive to classroom tasks. Furthermore, the attention ratings children received from their teachers were strongly associated with their performance on an IQ test.

Choice of tasks

Researchers in the field of motivation have found repeatedly that individuals who are most motivated to succeed in academic endeavors select tasks that are optimally challenging (Atkinson 1957). Preschool children in many programs are allowed to select their own tasks most of the time. Consequently, their tendency to select tasks that are too easy, too hard, or just right may have important implications for their intellectual development. Some consistency has been found in the difficulty level children choose across different kinds of tasks. Furthermore, a relationship between children's choice of tasks and their cognitive level has been found; children who chose to do relatively easy tasks performed, on the average, less well on an IQ test than children who chose to do a task that would require some effort (Stipek, Roberts, and Sanborn 1980).

Independence

Some young children ask for help before making any effort to solve a problem on their own, often before the teacher has even finished explaining the task. Other children appear to resent help when it is offered, or will at least do the best they can on their own before asking for help.

Consider again the two children working on the puzzles. When it is clear that the puzzle is not an easy one, Christopher may look at the work of other children for clues, or ask for help either explicitly or by gazing beseechingly at the teacher. Christopher thus deprives himself of an experience in problem solving and, perhaps even more important, of pride in completing a task without help. Danielle keeps her eyes on the puzzle and attempts to solve it alone. When successful, she beams with pride. Christopher's more dependent behaviors are particularly common among low-IQ children (Achenbach and Weisz 1975).

What factors account for individual differences in work habits?

The behavioral differences we observe among preschool children are most likely the result of an interaction between the child, adults, and specific situations. Parents respond to their young children differently in part as a function of the child's temperament and other characteristics (Bell 1971). Preschool teachers' interactions with children are also influenced by child characteristics. For example, teachers in one study were most attentive and nurturant to dependent children (Yarrow, Waxler, and Scott 1971). Furthermore, teachers were more attentive to children who reinforced them (i.e., responded with interest, attention, enjoyment, or compliance) for their attention. Perhaps teachers' first step in fostering good work habits is to become conscious of how their own behavior is influenced by the children's behavior.

Peter Waugh

The children who learn most are those who persist at tasks rather than giving up, who pay attention to the task and select tasks that offer some challenge, and who work on a task alone without unnecessary requests for help.

Children's perceptions of their competence and their accompanying expectations for success are also believed to affect their work habits (Harter 1978). Children who expect to succeed are more likely to persist on a difficult task and to try to complete the task without help than are children who believe that failure is inevitable or that they are unable to complete the task without help. Children lacking self-confidence also have good reason to select either the easiest task (thus increasing their chances for success) or the most difficult task (thus decreasing responsibility for failure).

Children's perceptions of the cause of task outcomes (Stipek and Weisz 1981) is another variable related to their task behaviors. Children who see effort as the primary cause of outcomes persist longer at difficult tasks than children who perceive factors over which they have no control, such as ability, as the cause of outcomes (Dweck and Goetz 1978). Preschool teachers who provide appropriate learning activities and communicate their belief that children *can* do most tasks if they try may help children to develop high expectations for themselves and to attribute outcomes to their efforts.

How can preschool teachers foster good work habits?

For many years psychologists and educators believed that the key to children's self-confidence and adaptive behavior in educational environments was a heavy dose of success. Zigler (1971) suggests that the outer-directed or adult-dependent behaviors common among retarded children are the result of too many failure experiences. These same maladaptive behaviors are also found disproportionately among low-SES children (Stipek, Roberts, and Sanborn 1980). More recent evidence suggests that success is not enough to guarantee good work habits. Indeed, in one study, extensive success experiences were totally ineffective in developing self-confidence and positive work habits (Dweck 1975).

Promote independence

If young children need to succeed, should not teachers assist them so that they are spared failure experiences? To some degree, this question deserves an affirmative response, but recent evidence suggests that too much help can be harmful. First, it appears that children experience greater pride when they can attribute their success to their own efforts (Stipek and Weisz 1981). Pride is important because it is believed to motivate further mastery attempts (Harter 1978). If the teacher had a major role in a success, the

positive outcome may not have the same effect on the child's self-confidence or desire for further mastery attempts as it would have if the child had been allowed to complete the task alone. Furthermore, by offering assistance, the teacher gives the child the message that the child's ability to do the task without help is in doubt.

Young children seem to enjoy individual attention from teachers. If they are given this attention whenever they ask for help, whether or not it is needed, they are being reinforced for their dependency behaviors. Individual contact with children can be achieved with more positive consequences by reinforcing children's independent mastery efforts without offering unnecessary assistance.

This, of course, is not to say that teachers should never help children complete tasks or should never respond to children's requests for assistance. A successful comic with cerebral palsy has claimed that the secret to her success and self-confidence was that her mother let her fight her own battles. She described a scene from her childhood in which a group of children were teasing her in the front yard. Her mother simply waved from the window and made no move to rescue her from her tormentors. The mother probably did intervene when her help was really needed, but offered her assistance sparingly, allowing her daughter to develop a sense of self-efficacy. The same strategy may be effective in preschool classrooms.

Specific recommendations for interacting with children around tasks are provided by several studies on teacher-child interactions. Fagot (1973) found that the teachers of preschool children with good work habits tended to be less directive in their interactions with children than teachers of children with poor work habits. Teachers of children with good work habits gave fewer directions, responded to children's questions more, and offered unrequested information less. Farnham-Diggory and Ramsey (1971) found that children whose play was interrupted (assisted) by an adult persisted for less time on a subsequent task than did children who were left alone. The adult interruption appears to have made the task less intrinsically motivating to the child. Finally, Hamilton and Gordon (1978) report that children who persisted in an experimental setting were observed receiving less direction from teachers for their mastery attempts in the preschool classroom than children who gave up quickly.

Taken together, this research suggests that preschool teachers contribute positively to children's work habits by assisting them without being obtrusive or directive. It is often difficult to resist the urge to offer assistance to a child who appears to be having difficulty completing a task. I once observed a cerebral palsy child wrapping a gift for his mother. It was pure agony watching his abortive attempts to get tape from the dispenser to the package, and I had to grip my chair to keep myself from offering assistance. After 20 minutes, that were obviously much more painful for me than for him, he succeeded in taping the package, and despite the tape all over his hands and arms, he beamed with pride in his accomplishment. I sighed with relief for not having denied him that learning experience and pleasure.

A good principle to follow when the urge to help is first recognized is to stop and ask oneself whether help is *really* needed. Is the child in danger by using equipment (e.g., scissors) improperly? Will assistance result in additional learning? Even when help is requested it is a good idea to ask these same questions. In many cases an indirective response is more helpful to the child eventually. Children's requests for help can usually be responded to with a question that may give them clues, but will allow them to solve the problem themselves (see Bailis and Hunter, in press, for good examples of indirective responses).

Allow success to be its own reinforcement

When learning theory dominated the field of psychology, behavior was assumed to be controlled by reinforcement. Translated into educational policy, this meant that children's efforts leading to success should be reinforced. We need only examine practices in most educational settings today to be convinced of the pervasiveness and persistence of this belief; children's efforts are reinforced with stars, special privileges, publicity (putting pictures on the wall), and many other external rewards. Recent research suggests that in some circumstances external reinforcement is unnecessary and may actually undermine positive work habits.

White (1959) argues that most efforts to master a task or a skill are *intrinsically* rewarding. Researchers have found evidence that external reinforcement can actually undermine children's intrinsic motivation. Thus, Lepper, Greene, and Nisbett (1973) found that children who were rewarded for drawing lost their interest in drawing when the reward was withdrawn. Children who were never rewarded for their efforts maintained their interest in drawing. The results of considerable research on the undermining effect of external reinforcement (see Condry 1977) suggest that the negative effect occurs only for tasks that children are likely to do spontaneously. There are some tasks that are so unappealing to children that external reinforcement may be necessary. Most activities in preschools, however, are intrinsically reinforcing.

Use informative praise

Verbal reinforcement usually does not have the same negative effect on intrinsic motivation as tangible reinforcers. However, even verbal reinforcement should not be given gratuitously. Praise given for less-than-optimal performance can give children the message that the person giv-

Teachers who promote independence, provide intrinsically rewarding learning experiences, use praise to extend children's learning, and encourage children's efforts support the development of children's effective work habits.

ing the praise has low perceptions of their ability (Meyer et al. 1979). Furthermore, praise that is not contingent on the child's best efforts can teach the child that success is unrelated to effort. Given too frequently and indiscriminately, praise loses its meaning.

One method of encouraging children's mastery efforts while avoiding the potential negative effects of too much external reinforcement is to focus on the process rather than the product. Rather than tell children that their completed drawing is pretty, the teacher might comment to children working on a drawing about which colors they are using or the way in which parts of the drawing relate to each other. In this way children have the opportunity to learn and are reinforced for their efforts rather than for their products.

Encourage children's efforts

Children who attribute both their successes and their failures to effort tend to show positive work habits. By the time they reach the upper elementary grades, many children believe that success is no longer possible, regardless of their efforts, or they believe that they have no control over success because it is determined by external factors. Children who do not attribute performance outcomes to effort are more likely to exhibit helplessness. Programs designed to change children's attributions to effort have been successful at the elementary school level (Dweck 1975). However, it would be more effective to prevent the development of self-defeating attributions and helpless behavior in the first place. Thus teachers of young chil-

Stipek

dren might emphasize children's efforts whenever it is appropriate. For example, asking children to think of and try a new strategy might be helpful when they say, "I can't." There are two corollaries of this principle. One is that the task should be within the child's range of abilities so that effort can result in success. The second corollary is that less-than-optimal performance should not be overly praised. Children who are praised indiscriminately for everything they do may never develop an understanding of the relationship between effort and performance. These children may be in for a rude shock when they reach elementary school where half-hearted attempts are no longer valued.

Conclusions

Many factors contribute to children's achievement including the way children approach academic tasks. Young children who are developing strategies for approaching tasks and perceptions about their abilities can greatly benefit from adults who can help channel children's efforts and interests most productively. 🔲

References

Achenbach, T., and Weisz, J. "A Longitudinal Study of Relations Between Outerdirectedness and IQ Changes in Preschoolers." *Child Development* 46 (1975): 650–657.

Atkinson, J. "Motivational Determinants of Risk-Taking Behavior." *Psychological Review* 64 (1957): 359–372.

Bailis, P., and Hunter, M. "Are Your Words 'Think Starters' or 'Think Stoppers'?" *Learning Magazine,* in press.

Bell, R. "Stimulus Control of Parent or Caretaker Behavior by Offspring." *Developmental Psychology* 4 (1971) 63–72.

Bridgeman, G., and Shipman, V. "Preschool Measures of Self-Esteem and Achievement Motivation As Predictors of Third-Grade Achievement." *Journal of Educational Psychology* 70 (1978): 17–28.

Condry, J. "Enemies of Exploration: Self-Initiated Versus Other-Initiated Learning."

Journal of Personality and Social Psychology 35 (1977): 459–477.

Dweck, C. "Role of Expectations and Attributions in the Alleviation of Learned Helplessness." *Journal of Personality and Social Psychology* 31 (1975): 674–685.

Dweck, C., and Goetz, T. "Attributions and Learned Helplessness." In *New Directions in Attribution Research. Vol. 2,* ed. J. Harvey, W. Ickes, and R. Kidd. Hillsdale, N.J.: Lawrence Erlbaum Associates, 1978.

Fagot, B. "Influence of Teacher Behavior in the Preschool." *Developmental Psychology* 9 (1973): 198–206.

Farnham-Diggory, S., and Ramsey, B. "Play Persistence: Some Effects of Interruption, Social Reinforcement, and Defective Toys." *Developmental Psychology* 4 (1971): 297–298.

Fisher, C.; Berlinger, D.; Filby, N.; Mariave, R.; Cahen, D.; and Dishaw, M. "Teaching Behaviors, Academic Learning Time, and Student Achievement: An Overview." In *Time to Learn,* ed. C. Denham and A. Lieberman. Washington, D.C.: National Institute of Education, 1980.

Hamilton, V., and Gordon, D. "Teacher-Child Interactions in Preschool and Task Persistence." *American Educational Research Journal* 15 (1978): 459–466.

Harter, S. "Effectance Motivation Reconsidered: Toward a Developmental Model." *Human Development* 21 (1978): 34–64.

Kohn, M., and Rosman, B. "Cognitive Functioning in Five-Year-Old Boys As Related to Social-Emotional and Background-Demographic Variables." *Developmental Psychology* 8 (1973): 277–294.

Kohn, M., and Rosman, B. "Social-Emotional, Cognitive and Demographic Determinants of Poor School Achievement: Implications for a Strategy of Intervention." *Journal of Educational Psychology* 66 (1974): 267–276.

Lepper, M.; Greene, D.; and Nisbett, R. "Undermining Children's Intrinsic Interest with Extrinsic Reward: A Test of the 'Overjustification' Hypothesis." *Journal of Personality and Social Psychology* 28 (1973): 129–137.

Meyer, W.; Bachmann, M.; Biermann, U.; Hempelmann, M.; Ploger, F.; and Spiller, H. "The Informational Value of Evaluative Behavior: Influences of Praise and Blame on Perceptions of Ability." *Journal of Educational Psychology* 71 (1979): 259–268.

Stipek, D.; Roberts, T.; and Sanborn, M. "Mastery Motivation in Four-Year-Olds." Unpublished manuscript, University of California at Los Angeles, 1980.

Stipek, D., and Weisz, J. "Perceived Personal Control and Academic Achievement." *Re-*

view of *Educational Research* 51 (1981): 101–137.

White, R. "Motivation Reconsidered: The Concept of Competence." *Psychological Review* 66 (1959): 297–333.

Yarrow, M.; Waxler, C.; and Scott, P. "Child Effects on Adult Behavior." *Developmental Psychology* 5 (1971): 300–311.

Zigler, E. "The Retarded Child As a Whole Person." In *Advances in Experimental Clinical Psychology*, ed. H. Adams and W. Boardman. New York: Pergamon, 1971.

This article was based primarily on research supported by a grant from the Bureau for the Education of the Handicapped, #300-77-0306. The author is grateful for the assistance of teachers and children at Happyland, John Adams, Ocean Park, and Pilgrim Lutheran Preschools and the UCLA University Elementary School.

Charles A. Smith

Puppetry and Problem-Solving Skills

Puppetry can be an especially effective tool for teachers to use in helping young children learn. Young children are fascinated by puppets and readily accept the apparent magic that is responsible for giving them life. Puppets share with fairy tales that timeless enchantment of "Once upon a time. . . ." Because they belong in the realm of fantasy, puppets encourage children to think both imaginatively and creatively, and can foster children's abilities to solve their problems.

During my years as a preschool teacher, puppets were very important personalities for the four-year-old children in my classes. On one occasion, after I put my puppets on and disappeared behind the stage, I introduced a new puppet character never before seen by the children, a rabbit named Briarbutton. One little girl immediately asked Briarbutton if he liked the new clothes she was wearing. The rabbit responded by saying, "Oh, *April*, I like what you have on!" The puppet show then proceeded. But throughout the presentation, April continuously asked those around her, "How did he know my name?" Now April knew that I was behind the stage, and she also would readily admit that I knew who she was. But for April and the other children at this moment it was as though Briarbutton were truly alive, with a mind and personality all his own. April knew that Briarbutton was not alive in the sense that she and real rabbits are alive. But in the magical world of fantasy, where all the restrictions made by reality are suspended, Briarbutton was most definitely "alive."

Teachers can use puppets to gain entry into the child's world. The joy, enthusiasm, and sense of wonder adults experience there with children does not diminish their educational usefulness. On the contrary, adults who are able to relate to this part of the child's life will actually enhance their teaching effectiveness.

There are many different educational approaches to using puppets. Teachers can simply set puppets out and encourage children to create their own "shows" or act out a familiar story. The adult may become involved by commenting on and clarifying what the children do or briefly joining in the play. But young children very often do not have the skill to coordinate their puppet characters to tell a unique story. This form of puppetry may encourage language development but fail to challenge children to think about resolving problems.

Teachers can also use puppets to make educational presentations to children. With this approach, the children play the role of an audience while the adult manipulates the puppets. The show can be either informal and brief or more elaborate with the addition of sound accompaniment and special props. This approach is limited because children are required to be passive spectators. Observational learning may take place, but the lack of involvement by children often prohibits other valuable forms of learning from occurring.

Charles A. Smith, Ph.D., is an Extension Specialist in Human Development in the Department of Quality of Living Programs at Kansas State University, Manhattan. He is a former director of a preschool laboratory and head teacher of four-year-old children.

Photos by
Karin Wikstrom

A more productive approach combines the above two methods, emphasizing both the involvement of children and the planning and skill of adult teachers. This strategy involves an adult *puppeteer* who presents the dramatization from behind the stage and an adult *facilitator* who sits immediately in front of the stage and promotes interaction between the children and the puppets. The *children* can interact with the puppets by commenting on what is happening and by making suggestions. The *puppets* respond by asking for help, disagreeing/agreeing with the children, and making comments about their suggestions.

The adult facilitator plays a critical role in the interactional strategy of puppetry by clarifying what the puppets are trying to communicate and helping the children put their own ideas into words. The facilitator can also be instrumental in securing the involvement of shy children by demonstrating that involvement with the puppet characters is acceptable. Since the puppeteer most often cannot see the children, the facilitator can help by identifying the names of children who are talking and making certain that unacceptable behavior does not interfere with the activity.

Developing Problem-Solving Skills

Sensitivity to Problems

The interactional approach to using puppets is an especially powerful technique for helping children clarify their values and develop social problem-solving skills. Puppet presentations can nurture a *sensitivity to personal and interpersonal problems* by portraying a particular social difficulty that is relevant to young children. Children are not born with an understanding of social interaction; they must *learn* how to identify and resolve the variety of possible problems which can arise over the course of human relationships.

For example, one of the problems we have been concerned about in our child development center is the type of unfavorable judgment that is often made about the worth of other people because of their appearance. Making judgments about others on this basis is often inaccurate and unfair. To present children with this problem, we introduce Seymour, a very unusual, frightening puppet with a large mouth and wild, red hair. When Seymour appears all the other puppets run away; they think he will hurt them because he looks so scary. Seymour and the facilitator let the children know that he won't hurt them or anyone else. He just wants to be friends; he knows he looks different, but he can't help that. Once this introduction is made, the interaction could result in the following exchange:

Seymour Puppet:	"Oh I wish I had a friend!"
Child:	"Seymour, I'll be your friend!"
Facilitator:	"Yes Seymour, Sarah would like to be your friend. She is not scared of you."
Seymour:	"Thank you Sarah. That helps."
Facilitator:	"Oh, Seymour still feels sad. What's the problem?"
Child(ren):	"Briarbutton and Prissy won't play with Seymour. He wants to be friends with them. He's sad."
Seymour:	"Yes, it helps that you are not afraid of me, but I want to have puppet friends too."

C. Smith

The children, with the facilitator's assistance, become involved with Seymour. His sadness touches them. They believe that what they have to say is important to him. They feel close to him and concerned about the misunderstanding. Through this type of dialogue with Seymour, young children become aware of his problem and, thus, more sensitive to the misunderstandings and injustices that can occur because of improper responses to any individual's appearance.

Alternative-Solution Thinking

Another interpersonal cognitive problem-solving skill (Spivack, Platt, and Shure 1976) is *alternative-solution* thinking. This skill involves the ability to identify a number of possible solutions to a particular interpersonal problem. For example, how many solutions could a child think of if her toy gets taken away by another? Grab it back? Threaten the other person? Ask for it? Tell the teacher? Cry? The ability to generate multiple solutions increases the likelihood of selecting an effective strategy to resolve a problem.

In the puppet show about Seymour the interaction might proceed like this:

Facilitator:	"Can you think of anything Seymour could do to get some puppet friends?"
Child:	"He could tell them that he won't hurt them!"
Facilitator:	"Yes, he could do that. Let's think of some more ideas."
Child:	"We could tell the others he is not scary."
Seymour:	"That's a good idea. You could tell them I won't hurt them."
Child:	"Seymour, you could find some other puppets for friends."
Facilitator:	"That's possible. Maybe other puppets won't run away from you Seymour."

Once the children have identified as many solutions as they can think of, then the adult facilitator could offer other possibilities. At some point the resulting list of solutions must be evaluated. This evaluation should be well-timed because quick decisions, even though they may be correct, may discourage other children from verbalizing their own ideas.

Consequential Thinking

A third problem-solving skill involves *consequential* thinking—the ability to identify what might happen when one performs an interpersonal act. For example, the child whose toy was taken by another might think, "If I grab it back or tell her that I will hurt her then she will hit me. If I run to the teacher he will tell me to solve the problem myself. Crying won't help. Maybe if I ask, she will give it to me. If she won't return it then maybe I'll just take it back." Proper evaluation depends on being able to consider the consequences of various potential solutions.

A presentation might focus on consequential thinking by having the puppets try out some of the solutions suggested by the children. The children and the facilitator could then note the consequences. For example, Seymour is unable to convince the other puppets that he won't hurt them because they won't stay around to listen to him. And, though he might someday find potential friends, these puppets are the only possible friends he can have at this time. The children might observe that their efforts to convince the other puppets that Seymour will not really harm them actually results in a lessening of tensions. In this situation the children could learn that they can assume an active role in negotiating conflict.

Awareness of Emotional Consequences

Becoming aware of *emotional* consequences is another important aspect of this problem-solving skill. By observing the interaction and talking with both the facilitator and the puppets, the children could learn that Seymour feels sad when the others run away and that the others feel frightened because Seymour looks so different.

Developing Causal Thinking

Finally, puppet interactions can help children develop *causal thinking*, the ability to relate one event to another over time. Causal thinking reflects an awareness of events that influence our behavior. For example, the young child described earlier might conclude that the offender wants her toy because she does not have anything interesting to play with or because she wants revenge. Also, the child who has her toy taken might also realize that the violation will have some effect on her own behavior. Thus, if she decides to grab the toy back, and one of the teachers questions her motives, she might respond, "Well, she took it from me; I was playing with it first!"

In a puppet show involving Seymour, causal thinking could be encouraged by the following type of interaction:

| Facilitator: | "Seymour feels lonely. Why do you think he feels that way?" |
| Child(ren): | "No one wants to play with him. They are afraid." |

Young children are fascinated by puppets. Because they belong in the realm of fantasy, puppets encourage children to think imaginatively and creatively.

C. Smith

Facilitator:	"Well, why do you think they are afraid?"
Child(ren):	"'Cause they think he might hurt them . . . but he won't."
Seymour:	"No, I won't hurt them."

Understanding the relationship between interpersonal acts is an important step in avoiding and resolving interpersonal problems. Of course, children make many errors and have many misconceptions about causes. Accuracy is of secondary importance, though. What is important is that children begin to contemplate the possible motives and influences underlying the behavior of others.

Designing and Presenting Puppet Skits

Identifying the Problem

The examples of puppet interactions listed above only begin to convey the range of events that occur during a puppet show. Puppet skits should tell an interesting story which emphasizes interaction among the puppets. Puppets should not be used to lecture children. The brief problem-solving exchanges described earlier are important for giving direction to the story; they should never become so complex as to distract the children from following and enjoying the story.

In addition to Seymour's problem with his appearance, other presentations can be structured around the following types of problems:

- a puppet feels sad but refuses to cry;
- a puppet experiences the death of a pet;
- a puppet and her friend have a disagreement and become enemies;
- a puppet claims he is never afraid because he thinks fear is a sign of weakness;
- a puppet learns how to defend herself against aggression;
- a puppet learns how to express affection.

In our preschool class parents would often ask us to introduce a problem they were concerned about. Sometimes the problem was observed in the class itself. In each case, the goal was to help the children learn developmentally appropriate personal-social skills (Smith 1976).

Development of a Presentation Outline

Once the core problem is identified, the next step is to develop a presentation outline. This outline can be a *script* format that details everything the puppets say and do. The outline can then be taped to the back of the stage. The advantage of a script is that it provides security. The disadvantage is that it is sometimes difficult to follow and often appears rigid or "canned."

Greater freedom can be provided by a *scenario* outline that describes the action that is to take place (see scenario outline). The scenario outline does not have the rigidity of the script but may be more difficult for the puppeteers to follow because it is more open-ended. It might be easier for beginners to write out the entire play and switch to a scenario approach later when they become more certain of themselves.

All puppet presentations should be simple and clear stories of interest to young children. The puppets should not engage in complicated actions or tiresome lectures since adults who use puppets to make self-righteous sermons destroy the magic that gives puppetry its great power. Because of its theatrical traditions, classroom puppetry should be entertaining as well as educational.

Preparation and the Introduction

Just before the presentation of the puppet show, the puppeteer and/or facilitator should set up the puppet stage that can be commercially made, a table on its side, cut out of a cardboard box, a room divider, a clothesline stretched across a room, or a tension rod placed in a doorway with a blanket thrown over it. The stage should not be so high that children will have to strain their necks to see the action or so low that the puppeteer is forced into an uncomfortable position.

Performances should be scheduled at times when children are ready to relax and rest, e.g., when free play is over, just before or after snack or lunch, or just before children are ready to go home. The facilitator and the puppeteer could begin by sitting in front of the stage and briefly introducing the story. In the show "Seymour Finds a

---

Scenario Outline

Seymour Finds a Friend

Purpose   To help children understand that physical appearance is not an effective way to determine another person's worth; to help them understand feelings associated with rejection; to promote effective problem-solving responses to rejection based on appearances.

Puppets: **Seymour**   A puppet who looks scary but actually prefers friendly relationships. Voice is scratchy, unusual sounding.

Prissy   A softspoken lamb who is easily frightened.

Herbie   A mouse who is also easily frightened. (This show requires two puppeteers. If a helper cannot be found then the plot should be adjusted to exclude Herbie.)

Props: A blanket.

Plot: Scene One. Seymour enters (on left) and introduces himself to the children. He talks about his great interest in making friends with the other puppets. Prissy enters (far right), talks briefly with the children, and begins to move to the left. When Seymour gets her attention, Prissy becomes very frightened and runs away. Seymour reacts with sadness and briefly talks with the children and facilitator about how he feels. He then leaves.

Scene Two. Herbie appears (far left) and engages children in brief conversation. Seymour enters (on left) and moves toward Herbie. As soon as he sees him, Herbie quickly says something like, "Oh, look at him; he looks scary!" Herbie then runs away. Again, Seymour expresses disappointment and appeals to the children for help. (**Note:** At this point a probem-solving interaction should occur. Seymour could try out some of the children's suggestions. Some may not work. Someone, though, may offer an idea that would work. The remainder of this outline is based on one possible solution.) This solution could begin when Seymour comments that maybe if they didn't see him the other puppets would talk to him. Children comment on this possibility. Seymour then leaves.

Scene Three. Seymour returns (on left) with blanket and asks the facilitator to cover him. Following this both Prissy and Herbie appear (on right) and comment on that "weird looking thing" they saw earlier. They notice the blanket, move next to it, and begin to talk with Seymour. After a few moments of friendly conversation they both ask Seymour to take the blanket off. Seymour asks if they would run away. They respond by insisting that they would not run away from such a friendly person. When the facilitator removes the blanket, both Prissy and Herbie become afraid and begin to run away. Herbie escapes but the facilitator gently reaches up and stops Prissy from leaving. Prissy gradually loses her fear as the facilitator and children gently insist that Seymour is not harmful and encourage her to stay. As she overcomes her fear, she moves closer to Seymour to get a better look at him. She studies him closely and touches his face and hair. As she does this, she, Seymour, and the children comment about his appearance. Finally, Prissy expresses some relief about Seymour. She thanks the children for helping her understand her mistake. Seymour also expresses his appreciation for their help. The two then agree to go over to Seymour's house to play, and the presentation ends.

C. Smith

Friend," the discussion could focus on things that look scary but are not really harmful. The group could also discuss the wide variation of physical characteristics among people.

The Presentation

During the presentation the puppeteer and facilitator should keep several important points in mind. If they enjoy their involvement, the puppeteer and facilitator will transmit their enthusiasm to their children. They should also take advantage of the theatrical aspects of puppetry. The puppeteer can create special voices for the puppets and produce the types of movements the puppets need to make to convey the range of emotions and attitudes that are a part of the story. The puppeteer should talk more loudly than normal in order to project the sound adequately to the children. Furthermore, both the facilitator and puppeteer should be kind to themselves when they make mistakes. Children are very accepting of little failures, especially if the adults can see the humor in the situation. One of the common errors I still make is getting my voices mixed up with the puppets. The children think this incongruity is outrageously funny, so I simply chuckle at my own mistake and make adjustments in my voice. The ability to accept and learn from one's mistakes is an important contribution to professional development.

Follow Up

After a puppet show is completed, the puppeteer and facilitator can meet with the children to discuss the preceding events, clarify any difficulties, and reinforce the points introduced. If time permits, a group activity that strengthens the intended effects of the puppet show could immediately follow the presentation. "Seymour Finds a Friend" could be followed by a body-awareness activity like body drawing, where each child lies down on a large sheet of paper, has his or her outline drawn by a partner, and then completes his or her own features with crayons, chalk, and/or paint.

The enthusiasm of the preschool child for informal and brief puppet shows clearly demonstrates their effectiveness as a strategy for encouraging the development of problem-solving techniques.

The enthusiasm preschool children have demonstrated for informal and brief puppet shows clearly indicates that the use of puppets can be an effective strategy for motivating and teaching young children to develop effective problem-solving techniques. Puppets can be used to introduce a variety of issues important to children. Seymour represents any individual who has been touched by racism, sexism, and other forms of ridicule; Mr. Grump is the mean man down the street who seems to have special hostility for children; Mr. Chucklebelly is the type of happy individual who seems to find humor in most any situation; Queen Sarah represents the type of gentle kindness and nurturance which most of us find so healing, while Prissy the Lamb reflects a type of reasonable assertiveness necessary to overcome barriers created by sex-role stereotypes. Thoughtful teachers can create puppet characters based on their own experiences and those of their children.

One does not need to be a professional to begin. Young children do not expect our "homemade" presentations to be as sophisticated as a Sesame Street production.

Through diligent work, inexperienced but enthusiatic puppeteers can improve their technique and gradually become more skillful in creating that special magic which touches a child's imagination.

References

Andersen, B. E. *Let's Start a Puppet Theatre.* New York: Van Nostrand Reinhold, 1973.

Batchelder, M. *The Puppet Theatre Handbook.* New York: Harper, 1974.

Bates, E. *Potpourri of Puppetry.* Canyon, Tex.: West Texas State University, 1974.

Hanford, R. T. *The Complete Book of Puppets and Puppeteering.* New York: Drake, 1976.

Lee, M. *Puppet Theatre.* Fair Lawn, N.J.: Essential Books, 1958.

Richter, D. *Fell's Guide to Hand Puppets.* New York: Frederick Fell, 1970.

Smith, C. A. "Peopleteaching: An Approach to Identifying and Enhancing Personal-Social Competencies in Young Children." Presented at the National Association for the Education of Young Children annual conference, Anaheim, Calif., November 1976.

Spivack, J.; Platt, J. J.; and Shure, M. B. *The Problem-Solving Approach to Adjustment.* San Francisco: Jossey-Bass, 1976.

Karen L. Haswell, Ellen Hock, and Charles Wenar

Techniques for Dealing with Oppositional Behavior in Preschool Children

The teacher asks a group of children to put away their blocks and join her in a circle activity. From one boy comes a firm "No, I don't want to," and the more the teacher pleads, cajoles, or commands, the louder grow the child's refusals. Finally the teacher turns her back and proceeds to the next activity. Soon afterward, the boy replaces his blocks and cheerfully joins the activity, seeming to forget the conflict of wills that had consumed him only moments before.

In another situation, a freckled four-year-old dances menacingly around the wet paint she's been asked not to touch. "I'm going to touch it, here it goes!" she chants, smiling at the forbidding adult. She never breaks the adult's prohibition by touching the paint, but she has successfully engaged the adult in a struggle for control of the interchange, with herself in the driver's seat.

Any adult who has taught or cared for preschoolers has likely witnessed similar scenes of children's opposition to suggestions and directives of adults. Such oppositional behavior can be widely varied in style—it may range from silent ignoring of the adult to an assertive "No," to playful, coy refusals. Children may refuse certain activities which only the day before they had begged to do. Despite the varied nature of these behaviors, however, they frequently share a common function: to assert autonomy from adult control.

The development of oppositional behavior

The period of oppositional behavior begins between 18 months and two years of age (the infamous "terrible two's"), reaches its zenith at three-and-one-half to four years, and has usually declined by age five-and-one-half to six years (Levy and Tulchin 1925; Levy 1956; Caille 1933; Mayer 1935; Escalona 1973). Despite the frustration it causes for educators and parents, the noncompliant and seemingly stubborn behavior characteristic of this period represents an important milestone in children's cognitive and emotional development. Children's intellectual conquest of the concept of negation and the

Karen L. Haswell, Ph.D., is Assistant Professor of Psychology, Department of Psychiatry and Behavioral Science, University of Louisville School of Medicine, Louisville, Kentucky.

Ellen Hock, Ph.D., is Professor, Department of Family Relations and Human Development, and Clinical Professor, Department of Pediatrics, The Ohio State University, Columbus.

Charles Wenar, Ph.D., is Professor of Psychology, Department of Psychology, The Ohio State University, Columbus.

While the negativistic phase between the ages of 18 months and 4 years may be baffling and infuriating for adults, it is nevertheless a normal and crucial facet of the child's development.

Haswell, Hock, and Wenar

semantic *no,* along with their realization of self as a separate being with a separate will, make possible the refusal of others' wills. Thus, the preschool child may refuse to comply with an adult's request or suggestion, not because she or he does not like the suggestion, but because of the strong need to assert autonomy. The young child may refuse a well-meaning adult's offer of help because "I want to do it myself." The struggle for autonomy and independent mastery of the world is at the heart of much oppositional behavior. While this negativistic phase may be baffling and infuriating for adults, it is nevertheless a normal and crucial facet of the preschool child's development. Successful negotiation of the struggle for autonomy provides the child with a capacity for independent effort that is important for academic and social achievement in middle childhood (Erikson 1963).

Most of our understanding of this period of socioemotional development is based on research conducted sometime ago (Levy and Tulchin 1923; 1925; Reynolds 1928; Goodenough 1929; Rust 1931; Nelson 1931; Caille 1933; Mayer 1935; Frederickson 1942). We conducted a study (see Haswell, Hock, and Wenar 1981) to re-examine the parameters of normal negativistic behavior in 63 three-and-one-half- to four-year-old children. One set of observations was conducted during the presentation of age-appropriate items from a standardized intelligence test (Stanford-Binet, L-M). Other observations were made in a standardized play situation where the child was requested by the researcher to play in various ways with several toys. Records were made of the types of requests that elicited oppositional behavior, the various forms of oppositional behavior, and the subjects' responses to coaxing, prohibitions, and timing of requests. Subjects' mothers also participated in a standard interview where they were asked to describe their child's typical responses to common requests in the home (for example, to take

a bath, dress, go to bed, pick up toys). Mothers described their own responses to their child's oppositional behavior, and the relative success of various techniques for managing negativism and encouraging autonomy. Mothers' management styles were rated along descriptive dimensions such as flexibility and sensitivity.

Results showed that oppositional behavior to some requests and some situations was universal among the subjects. The frequency and style of negativism varied from direct verbal opposition ("No, I won't do it."), to indirect verbal opposition ("I'm gonna do *this* now."), to physically pushing toys away or leaving the room, to passive opposition (the silent stare).

Techniques for dealing with negativism

While it is important to recognize the positive implications of the child's development of autonomy, of which the negativistic period is a part, it is nevertheless helpful to have techniques for minimizing resistance in certain situations where compliance is of practical necessity. Furthermore, optimal development in this stage may be defined as the child's achievement of a healthy balance between independence and dependence through the provision of structure and opportunities for autonomous action.

Be flexible when making transitions

Flexibility is helpful in dealing with the resistance frequently encountered when a child is asked to change activities or to interrupt an ongoing activity (e.g., leave free play to come to circle activities). In our study it was found that children who demonstrated the least resistance to such changes had mothers who were rated as significantly more flexible. These mothers

Busy teachers may also unwittingly bypass many opportunities to praise cooperative behavior.

took into account their child's individual temperament and likes and dislikes when making requests. For the preschool teacher, this may translate into developing an awareness of the individual child's ease in changing activities or their speed in warming up to new tasks, so that new activities can be introduced at a comfortable pace and the arousal of unnecessary resistance can be avoided.

Schaffer and Crook (1980) had mothers issue commands for certain types of play activities to their two-year-old children. The greatest compliance occurred when mothers monitored the child's attention and either made requests when the child's attention was focused on them, or gently guided the child's attention to the object of the directive before starting it. Maternal directives that interfered with the child's activity had little chance of eliciting compliance. Thus, the teacher who aids children in gradually shifting their attention

away from an ongoing activity and toward the area of the adult's interest may meet more success when directives are given.

Give verbal alerts about the transitions

Many of the mothers interviewed in this study successfully managed some outbursts of oppositional behavior by giving one or more verbal alerts of upcoming changes in activities; for example, "In five minutes, it will be time for you to put your toys away and come to dinner." This technique allows the child to begin adjusting to the change and also to bring the activity to some closure. Likewise, teachers can alert the entire group that a change of activity will be occurring.

Offer choices

Another technique that can be used effectively to provide opportunities for autonomous action and to circumvent some

Haswell, Hock, and Wenar

oppositional behavior is giving the child some choices of activity, even when choices are limited (see Veach 1977). Since oppositional behavior is often an expression of the preschooler's need to assert autonomy, giving the child options from which to choose removes much of the motivation for noncompliance. Allowing children to exercise autonomy at some times in the day may serve to reduce their need to express it at other times. Activity choices have long been an integral part of the daily schedule of quality early childhood programs. For example, children might choose between an organized art activity and time for coloring, between a nap and quiet reading time.

Give children time to comply

If a child does not immediately comply with a request many adults repeat the directive, sometimes several times. Forehand and Scarboro (1975) found that this natural tendency may be counterproductive. When mothers of five-year-olds instructed their child to play with particular toys in a playroom, the greatest noncompliance occurred in the seconds immediately after a mother's command, but declined with time. Furthermore, as the number of commands increased, there was an increase in oppositional behavior immediately following the commands. Thus, achieving a child's compliance to a request seems most likely if the adult waits for a brief period to see if the child will comply, before repeating the request.

Rapid-fire repetition of requests will likely serve to increase oppositional behavior, rather than decrease it. Roberts et al. (1978) observed the interactions of three- to seven-year-old children with their mothers, noting the degree of the child's noncompliance to mothers' commands. The experimenters then trained mothers to wait at least five seconds after issuing commands without physically or verbally interfering to try to elicit compliance. Comparisons of pre- and post-training compliance rates showed that mothers were more successful in getting the requested response if they waited for a brief time. In the Haswell, Hock, and Wenar study, a ten-second interval between repetitions of a directive was used and was frequently effective in overcoming initial noncompliance. Thus, the research data confirm that patience and timing are key elements in working with young children.

Act positively

The type of verbal and nonverbal directives or suggestions used by adults may also have a significant influence on children's compliance. In a study observing the home interactions of two- and three-year-old boys with their mothers and fathers, children's actions were classified as compliance, noncompliance, or neither, and instances of parental verbal control were categorized as command-prohibition, suggestion, or control with reasoning; i.e., giving a justification for the command or prohibition (Lytton 1975; Lytton and Zwirner 1975). Parental actions preceding the verbal control were classified as physical control or restricting, negative action (expression of displeasure, threat), positive action (expression of love, hugging, smiling), and neutral action. Results showed that suggestions tended to facilitate compliance more than command-prohibition and control with reasoning statements. Furthermore, when positive action accompanied a verbal suggestion, compliance was further facilitated. When physical control or negative action (criticism) accompanied verbal statements by parents, noncompliance increased. Similarly, an observational study of 30 preschool boys and their mothers found that noncoercive disciplinary techniques were significantly more effective than coercive techniques for terminating episodes of negativism (Smolak, Bellar, and Vance 1977). Lytton (1975) also observed parents' reactions to children's compliance or non-compliance, and noted that in over 50 percent of the instances, children were given no reinforcement or reward for compliance. In only 15 percent of instances was a positive response given to the child following compliance.

The approaches found most effective in these studies of home interactions might also be useful in early childhood group programs. Teachers might attempt to use suggestions rather than commands, when possible, and should be aware that affection or praise may significantly increase the rate of compliance to suggestions. Teachers may want to monitor their own behavior in response to children's compliance. Just as parents in Lytton's study failed to reward compliance, busy teachers may also unwittingly bypass many opportunities to praise cooperative behavior.

Use time out

Despite the normalcy of oppositional behavior and its positive developmental implications, it is nevertheless necessary to sometimes regulate such episodes for practical reasons. What can be done in the face of persistent, unyielding negativism? One technique that has been shown to be effective is time out, wherein the adult's attention is removed from the child's behavior, or the child is removed from the situation. When mothers were instructed to stop playing with their five-year-olds or leave the room when oppositional behavior occurred in response to requests, and then the series of commands was given again (Scarboro and

Forehand 1975), the amount of oppositional behavior was significantly less. One subject in the Haswell, Hock, and Wenar study became markedly resistant to entering the laboratory. His resistance became more intense with each further attempt by the investigator and the child's mother to gain compliance. Once the adults ceased demanding compliance and removed their attention from this power struggle, however, the child's fervent *"no's"* ceased and he complied docilely.

Thus, in some instances, particularly when confronted with intense or persistent oppositional behavior, the preschool teacher may effectively choose to ignore the negativism and refuse to engage in a power struggle with the child. In many instances, removal of attention may bring an end to a negativistic episode.

Conclusion

Much negativistic behavior is an expression of the preschool child's growing need for autonomy, a basic psychosocial task in the early years. While the rise and decline of oppositional behavior is to be expected, there are children who fail to establish appropriate autonomy in the preschool years. Some children may develop a lasting pattern of rebelliousness, and others may remain excessively compliant and dependent. Our goal must be to aid children in developing a healthy balance between autonomy and cooperation, by providing both opportunities for independent action and experiences with compliance to reasonable social demands.

References

Caille, R. K. "Resistant Behavior of Preschool Children." In *Child Development Monographs, No. 11*. New York: Teachers College Press, 1933.

Erikson, E. H. *Childhood and Society*. New York: Norton, 1963.

Escalona, S. K. "Basic Modes of Social Interaction: Their Emergence and Patterning During the First Two Years of Life." *Merrill-Palmer Quarterly* 19 (1973): 205–232.

Forehand, R., and Scarboro, M. E. "An Analysis of Children's Oppositional Behavior." *Journal of Abnormal Child Psychology* 3 (1975): 27–31.

Frederickson, N. "The Effects of Frustration on Negativistic Behavior of Young Children." *Journal of Genetic Psychology* 61 (1942): 203−226.

Goodenough, F. "The Emotional Behavior of Children During Mental Tests." *Journal of Juvenile Research* 13 (1929): 204−219.

Haswell, K.; Hock, E.; and Wenar, C. "Oppositional Behavior of Preschool Children: Theory and Intervention." *Family Relations* 30 (1981): 440−446.

Levy, D. M. "Oppositional Syndromes and Oppositional Behavior." In *Psychopathology of Childhood*, ed. P. H. Hoch and J. Zubin. New York: Grune & Stratton, 1956.

Levy, D. M., and Tulchin, S. H. "The Resistance of Infants and Children During Mental Tests." *Journal of Experimental Psychology* 6 (1923): 304−322.

Levy, D. M., and Tulchin, S. H. "The Resistant Behavior of Infants and Children, II." *Journal of Experimental Psychology* 8 (1925): 209−224.

Lytton, H. "Disciplinary Encounters Between Young Boys and Their Mothers and Fathers: Is There a Contingency System?" *Developmental Psychology* 15 (1975): 256−268.

Lytton, H., and Zwirner, W. "Compliance and Its Controlling Stimuli Observed in a Natural Setting." *Developmental Psychology* 11 (1975): 769−779.

Mayer, B. A. "Negativistic Reactions of Preschool Children to the New Revision of the Stanford-Binet." *Journal of Genetic Psychology* 46 (1935): 311−334.

Nelson, J. F. "Personality and Intelligence." In *Child Development Monographs, No. 6.* New York: Teachers College Press, 1931.

Reynolds, M. M. "Negativism of Preschool Children." In *Teachers' College, Columbia University, Contributions to Education, No. 288.* New York: Teachers College Press, 1928.

Roberts, M. W.; McMahon, R. J.; Forehand, R.; and Humphreys, L. "The Effect of Parental Instruction-Giving on Child Compliance." *Behavior Modification* 9 (1978): 793−798.

Rust, M. M. "The Effect of Resistance on Intelligence Test Scores of Young Children." *Child Development Monographs, No. 6.* New York: Teachers College Press, 1931.

Scarboro, M. E., and Forehand, R. "Effects of Two Types of Response Contingent Time-Out on Compliance and Oppositional Behavior of Children." *Journal of Experimental Child Psychology* 19 (1975): 252−264.

Schaffer, H. R., and Crook, C. K. "Child Compliance and Maternal Control Techniques." *Developmental Psychology* 16 (1980): 54−61.

Smolak, L.; Bellar, E. K.; and Vance, S. "Relationships Between Parental Disciplinary Techniques and Negativism in Preschoolers." Paper presented at the annual meeting of the American Psychological Association, San Francisco, August 1977.

Veach, D. "Choice with Responsibility." *Young Children* 32, no. 4 (May 1977): 22−25.

Patsy Skeen and Patrick C. McKenry

The Teacher's Role in Facilitating a Child's Adjustment to Divorce

"At first it's so terrible you could really die, but then it gets better." (Andy—age 9)

"If I'd only kept my room clean [like Daddy asked], he wouldn't have left me." (Alice—age 4)

"Silence." (Becky—age 5)

These actual responses of children involved in divorce are typical of those observed by teachers. Such observations are increasing as the lives of an alarming number of children are being disrupted—at least temporarily—by divorce. The divorce rate has more than doubled in the past ten years. Currently almost four out of ten marriages end in divorce (United States Bureau of the Census 1976). More than 60 percent of these divorcing couples have children at home. Because almost 50 percent of all divorces occur in the first seven years of marriage, the children involved in divorce are usually quite young (Norton and Glick 1976). It is estimated that 20 percent of the children enrolled in elementary school have divorced parents. In some of the kindergarten and first grade classes, this figure is closer to the 40 to 50 percent level (Wilkinson and Beck 1977).

Revision of a paper presented at the 1978 National Association for the Education of Young Children Annual Conference.

The period of disorganization following divorce is usually extended. The family living standard is likely to change and a nonworking mother often goes to work. One parent generally leaves the home and siblings can be lost as well (Derdeyn 1977). Because divorce is a crisis involving disruption of the family structure, the role of the school and the teacher are of particular importance. A child's sense of continuity and stability is likely to be dependent upon the availability of extrafamilial supports such as the school, as well as upon what protection and concern can be mobilized in the parent-child relationship during this time (Kelly and Wallerstein 1977).

The purpose of this article is to provide information that will enable the teacher to be a positive support to children and families during divorce. Research and theory concerning the effects of divorce on children, parenting through divorce, and the role of the school is summarized. Practical suggestions for the classroom teacher are presented.

Children and Divorce

Without exception divorce is a significant event in the life of any child. For the child, divorce may represent a sense of loss, a sense of failure in interpersonal relationships, and the beginning of a difficult transition to new life patterns (Magrab 1978). It cannot be assumed, however, that children will all react to divorce in the same way. For the most part, they are healthy, normal children who are confronted with an extremely stressful situation (Wilkinson and Beck 1977). Research

Patsy Skeen, Ed.D., is Assistant Professor, Child and Family Development, University of Georgia, Athens, Georgia.

Patrick C. McKenry, Ph.D., is Associate Professor, Family Relations and Human Development, School of Home Economics, Ohio State University, Columbus, Ohio.

Some children of divorce exhibit more empathy for others, increased helping behavior, and greater independence than do children from intact families.

Hetherington et al. (1978) suggest that divorce is often the most positive solution to destructive family functioning. Divorce can have a positive influence. For example, some children of divorce exhibit more empathy for others, increased helping behavior, and greater independence than children from intact families. However, the ease and rapidity with which divorce may be obtained and the recent emphasis on "creative" and "positive" divorce may mask the pain, stress, and adjustment problems inherent in divorce.

Available research findings on children of divorce tend to agree that divorce is to an extent a developmental crisis for children (Jones 1977; Magrab 1978; Wilkinson and Beck 1977). Wallerstein and Kelly (1977) comment that they drew heavily from crisis intervention theory in their research, and Hetherington, Cox, and Cox (1976) use the term *critical event* to describe divorce as it affects families. Cantor's (1977) review of the literature revealed that in a period of parental divorce, children often show marked changes in behavior, particularly in school, and the changes are likely to be in the direction of acting-out behaviors.

Kelly and Wallerstein (1976) and Wallerstein and Kelly (1975, 1976) have researched the impact of the divorce process on children. In their preschool sample, they found that the children's self-concept was particularly affected. The children's views of the dependability and predictability of relationships were threatened, and their sense of order regarding the world was disrupted. Some suffered feelings of responsibility for driving the father away. Older preschoolers were better able to experience family turbulence and divorce without breaking developmental stride. The older preschoolers were also better able to find gratification outside the home and to place some psychological and social distance between themselves and their parents. However, heightened anxiety and aggression were noted in this group.

findings indicate that the experience of divorce itself is less harmful than the nature of the parents' personalities and relationships with their children (Despert 1962; McDermott 1968; Westman and Cline 1970). The child's reactions also depend upon such factors as the extent and nature of family disharmony prior to divorce, emotional availability of important people to the child during the divorce period, and the child's age, sex, and personality strengths (Anthony 1974; McDermott 1968).

Some evidence indicates that children of divorce may be better adjusted than children remaining in two-parent homes where there is ongoing tension, conflict, and stress (Nye 1957; Landis 1960; Hetherington, Cox, and Cox 1978).

Lois Duncan

Young children may respond to divorce with pervasive sadness, fear, feelings of deprivation, and anger.

Almost half of the children in this preschool group were found to be in a significantly deteriorated psychological condition at the followup study one year later.

Kelly and Wallerstein (1976) reported that young schoolage children respond to divorce with pervasive sadness, fear, feelings of deprivation, and some anger. At the end of one year, many still struggled with the task of integrating divorce-related changes in their lives. For older schoolage children, Wallerstein and Kelly (1976) found that divorce affected the freedom of children to keep major attention focused outside the family, particularly on school-related tasks. These children displayed conscious and intense anger, fears and phobias, and a shaken sense of identity and loneliness. At the end of one year,

the anger and hostility lingered, and half the children evidenced troubled, conflictual, and depressed behavior patterns.

Hetherington et al. (1976) characterized behaviors of children of divorce as more dependent, aggressive, whiny, demanding, unaffectionate, and disobedient than behavior of children from intact families. Hetherington et al. (1976) noted three areas of anxiety: fear of abandonment, loss of love, and bodily harm. Anthony (1974) noted other behaviors of low vitality, restlessness, guilt, shame, anxiety, depression, low self-esteem, failure to develop as a separate person, a preoccupation with death and disease, inability to be alone, regression to immature behavior, separation and phobia anxiety, and an intense attachment to one parent. With certain

Skeen and McKenry

groups of children—i.e., handicapped, adopted, and chronic illness cases such as asthmatics, epileptics, and diabetics—the divorce process might precipitate a psychosomatic crisis requiring hospitalization. Jacobson (1978) found the more the amount of time spent with the father was reduced during a 12-month period following divorce, the more a child was likely to show signs of maladjustment. Anthony (1974) concluded that the major reaction *during* divorce is grief associated with guilt, while the major reaction *after* divorce is shame coupled with strong resentment.

Hozman and Froiland (1977) suggested that the experience of losing a parent through divorce is similar to that of losing a parent through death. They adopted the Kubler-Ross model for dealing with loss. In this model, children go through five stages as they learn to accept loss of a parent. Initially, children deny the reality of the divorce. Denial is followed by anger and then bargaining in which children try to get parents back together. When they realize that their efforts cannot persuade parents to live together again, they become depressed. The final stage is acceptance of the divorce situation.

Anthony (1974) and Hetherington et al. (1978) cautioned against expecting all children and parents to react the same way in divorce. Each individual's behavior depends upon his or her unique personality, experiences, and the support system available.

Parenting During Divorce

For parents, divorce is a time of marked stress in everyday living and emotional as well as interpersonal adjustment. Feelings of loneliness, lowered self-esteem, depression, and helplessness interfere with parenting abilities (Hetherington et al. 1978). Several studies have noted a serious deterioration in the quality of the mother-child relationship in divorced families be-

cause of the mother's emotional neediness and her ambivalence about her new role as single parent (McDermott 1968; Hetherington et al. 1976; Wallerstein and Kelly 1976). After divorce, some fathers may become freer and less authoritarian. However, other fathers who are absent from the household may become less nurturant and more detached from their children with time (Hetherington et al. 1976; Weiss 1975).

During divorce, specific developmental needs of children are often unmet because of parental preoccupation with their own needs and parental role conflicts. When compared to parents in intact families, Hetherington et al. (1976) found that divorced parents of preschoolers were less consistent and effective in discipline, less nurturant, and generally less appropriately behaved with their children because of the preoccupation with the divorce process. When compared to parents in intact families, divorced parents communicated less well and made fewer demands for mature behavior of their children (Hetherington et al. 1976).

In summary, parent-child relationships are altered as a result of divorce. Parenting becomes difficult as the structure of the family breaks down and parents must make interpersonal adjustments such as dealing with stress, loneliness, and lowered self-esteem. However, there are many unanswered questions concerning parenting capabilities and behaviors during divorce. A great deal more research needs to be done before we can draw definitive conclusions in this area.

Schools and Divorce

The important role that schools can play in facilitating children's adjustment has not been clearly addressed in the divorce literature. Because children spend a great number of hours in school, as compared to time with parents, it is reasonable to assume that schools may be providing emotional support and continuity to a large number of children from divorcing parents. In other words, schools as a major socializing institution for children may play a more vital role in offsetting some of the negative impact of family disruption that accompanies divorce than previously thought (Jones 1977).

Key relationships in the family are often disrupted in part because of the geographic inaccessibility of the noncustodial parent. In addition, the custodial parent may be emotionally unavailable in the usual role to the child. Therefore, it has been argued that the school has an obligation to intervene with children of divorce to prevent reactions from being repressed and thus to prevent future disorders. Because parents are often involved in conflicts over financial support, visitation rights, and a battle for the children's loyalties, the teacher may be forcibly thrust into the role of an interim parent substitute (McDermott 1968).

Many children find some support within the school setting because their attitudes and performance in school provide gratification which is sustaining to them in the face of divorce stress. Kelly and Wallerstein (1977) found that the attention, sympathy, and tolerance demonstrated by teachers who had been informed about the divorce were supportive to a number of children who were feeling emotionally undernourished at home. In their study, teachers became a central stable figure in the lives of several children in the months following the separation, in some cases the only stable figure in these children's lives.

School personnel should be interested and involved in providing developmental assistance to individuals faced with critical life situations such as divorce. To date, few strategies have been published concerning ways that teachers can provide specific assistance to the child involved in divorce (Wilkinson and Beck 1977). Existing strategies that have been developed have been directed primarily to the school psychologist and guidance counselor. The following specific techniques are suggested for the classroom teacher who perhaps first notices behavioral changes and is in a position to help the child on a long-term basis. The teacher's role is discussed in three sections: working in the classroom, working with parents, and working with counselors.

What Can the Teacher Do?

In the Classroom

Team teachers, Harriet Sykes and George Brown, have just discovered that over one-half of the families of their kindergarten children have been involved in divorce. They decide that they want to help the children in their classroom grow through the divorce experience. What can they do?

Be a Careful Observer

1. Look for behavioral cues that help you understand how a child is feeling and what problems and strengths the child might have. Free play, art activities, puppet shows, and individual talks with the child are particularly good opportunities for observation.

2. Observe the child frequently, over a period of time, and in several types of situations such as at quiet time, in group work, alone, in active play, in free play, and at home. Such varied observations allow the teacher to construct a more complete picture of the total child and reduce the likelihood that judgments will be made on the basis of a "bad day."

3. Be a good listener to both verbalization and body language.

Make a Plan

1. When teachers are attempting to understand, predict, and intervene with behavior, it is important to first determine the child's physical, social, emotional, and cognitive developmental levels. A plan can then be developed to meet the child's individual needs. Direct observation, parents, counselors, and relevant literature

Sken and McKenry

are good sources of information to use when planning.

Provide Opportunities for Working Through Feelings

1. Help the child recognize and acceptably express feelings and resolve conflict through the use of curriculum activities such as painting, flannel board, clay, drawing pictures, writing experience stories about the child's family, dramatic play, doll play, books about alternate family styles, free play, woodworking, music, and movement.

2. If the child appears to be going through the Kubler-Ross stages, prepare to help the child deal with the feelings in each stage. Give the child time for a resolution in each stage.

3. Allow children the solitude and privacy they sometimes need.

4. Support the establishment of divorce discussion and/or therapy groups for children led by trained leaders or counselors.

Help the Child Understand Cognitively

1. Help the child understand cognitively what his or her situation is, how and why he or she feels, how feelings can be expressed, and the consequences of such expression. Many discussions over an extended period of time will be necessary before such cognitive understanding is established.

2. Provide opportunities for the child to be successful in controlling his or her life. For example, make sure equipment and learning materials are matched to the child's abilities. Tell the child about the sequence of the day's events and notify the child about changes in schedule well ahead of time. Give the child opportunities to make as many choices as he or she can handle.

3. Books and discussions can be used to give information about divorce in general and promote peer acceptance and support for a child from a divorced family. (See Relevant Books, p. 236.)

Florence Sharp

Teachers are especially significant to the family because they probably spend as much or more time with the child than any other adult outside the family.

Maintain a Stable Environment

1. Remain consistent in expectations for the child. This may be the only area of consistency in a rapidly changing and difficult period of the child's life.

2. Although children must be dealt with patiently and might regress to immature forms of behavior at times, avoid overprotecting the child.

3. Even though the child might have problems, he or she should not be allowed to "run wild." Because parents may be having difficulty setting limits for the child, it is extremely important for the classroom teacher to lovingly, but firmly, set reasonable limits for the child's behavior.

4. Make a special effort to love the child. Let the child know that he or she is

important and worthwhile through smiles, hugs, praise, and attention to appropriate behaviors. However, avoid "being a mother or father" or allowing the child to become overly dependent upon you since you and the child will separate at the end of the year.

5. Prepare the child for separation from you at the end of the year (or an extended absence from you during the year) by telling the child ahead of time about the separation, why it will occur, and what will happen to the child. A visit to the new teacher and room can be very helpful. The child must be reassured that you are not leaving because he or she is "bad" or because you have stopped loving the child.

6. Encourage the child to work through stressful situations (e.g., a move to a new house) by talking about and role playing the situation in advance.

Examine Your Attitude

1. Avoid expecting a child to manifest certain kinds of problems simply because parents are divorcing. Children are skillful in "reading" adult expectations and often will behave accordingly. Adults might also assume that divorce is the reason for a behavior problem when in actuality other factors are the causes. Children have different reactions to divorce just as they do to all other aspects of life.

2. Examine personal feelings and values about divorce. Feelings and values consciously and unconsciously affect the way teachers interact with children and parents.

3. Try to help each child grow through divorce. Remember that divorce can have the positive effects of ending a highly dysfunctional family and providing growth opportunities for family members.

Working with Parents

Andy Robinson's mother has just told Andy's teacher, Mr. Wang, that she and her husband are going to get a divorce. She is worried about how this will affect Andy and wants to do whatever she can to assist her son. How can Mr. Wang help?

1. Realize that since divorce is a stressful time, teacher-parent communication should be especially supportive and positive.

2. Understand that parents are in a crisis situation and may not be able to attend to parenting as well as you or they would like.

3. Support the parent as an important person about whom you are concerned.

4. Provide books written for both children and adults for the parent to read concerning divorce. (See Relevant Books, p. 236.)

5. Encourage parents to be as open and honest as possible with the child about the divorce and their related feelings.

6. Urge parents to assure their children that divorce occurs because of problems the parents have. The children did not cause the divorce and cannot bring the parents back together.

7. Encourage parents to elicit their children's feelings.

8. Assure parents that children will need time to adjust to divorce and that difficulties in the child's behavior do not mean that the child has become permanently psychologically disturbed.

9. Encourage parents to work together as much as possible in their parenting roles even though they are dissolving their couple role. The attitudes that parents display toward each other and their divorce are vital factors in the child's adjustment. The use of the child as a messenger or a "pawn" in the couple relationship is particularly harmful to the child.

10. Help alleviate parental guilt by telling parents that their child is not alone. Indicate to parents that there is also evidence that children from stable one-parent families are better off emotionally than children in unstable, conflictual two-parent families.

11. Encourage parents to take time to establish a meaningful personal life both as a parent and as an important person

Skeen and McKenry

apart from the child. This can be their best gift to their children.

12. Provide an informal atmosphere in which parents can share their problems and solutions.

13. Correctly address notes to parents. "Dear Parent" can be used when you are not sure if the child's parents are divorced or if the mother might have remarried and have a different name from the child.

Working with Counselors

Becky's teacher, Ms. Jones, has been patiently listening for two hours to Becky's father talk about the pain he feels and how hard it is to cope with life as a single man after 15 years of marriage. Ms. Jones wants to help but is at her wits end. What can she do?

1. Refer children and parents to competent counselors in the community instead of trying to assume the role of counselor. A great deal of harm can be done by well-meaning listeners who "get in over their heads" and do not know how to handle a situation.

2. The American Association for Marriage and Family Therapy (1717 K St., N.W., Washington, DC 20006) and the American Psychological Association (1200 17th St., N.W., Washington, DC 20036) maintain lists of qualified counselors. Counselors belonging to these organizations also generally indicate such membership in yellow page phonebook listings. However, the teacher should find out firsthand about the effectiveness of a counselor before referrals are made. Former clients, other teachers, and a personal visit to the counselor are good sources of information.

3. Work with the counselor when appropriate. The teacher can provide a great deal of information as a result of daily observation and interaction with the child. The teacher might also help carry out treatment strategies in the classroom.

In summary, divorce is a time of crisis for parents and children. The role of the school becomes particularly important during divorce since the family support system is under stress. Teachers are especially significant to the family since they probably spend as much or more time with the child than any other adult outside the family. When teachers are skilled and concerned, they can help parents and children grow through divorce.

References

Anthony, E. J. "Children at Risk from Divorce: A Review." In *The Child in His Family*, ed. E. T. Anthony and C. Koupernils. New York: Wiley, 1974.

Cantor, D. W. "School-Based Groups for Children of Divorce." *Journal of Divorce* 1 (1977): 183-187.

Derdeyn, A. P. "Children in Divorce: Intervention in the Phase of Separation." *Pediatrics* 60 (1977): 20-27.

Despert, L. *Children of Divorce*. Garden City, N.J.: Dolphin Books, 1962.

Hetherington, E. M.; Cox, M.; and Cox, R. "The Aftermath of Divorce." In *Mother/Child, Father/Child Relationships*, ed. J. H. Stevens and M. Mathews. Washington, D.C.: National Association for the Education of Young Children, 1978.

Hetherington, E. M.; Cox, M.; and Cox, R. "Divorced Fathers." *The Family Coordinator* (1976): 417-429.

Hozman, T. L., and Froiland, D. J. "Children: Forgotten in Divorce." *Personnel and Guidance Journal* 5 (1977): 530-533.

Jacobson, D. S. "The Impact of Marital Separation/Divorce on Children: Parent-Child Separation and Child Adjustment." *Journal of Divorce* 1 (1978): 341-360.

Jones, F. N. "The Impact of Divorce on Children." *Conciliation Courts Review* 15 (1977): 25-29.

Kelly, J. B., and Wallerstein, J. S. "Brief Interventions with Children in Divorcing Families." *American Journal of Orthopsychiatry* 47 (1977): 23-39.

Kelly, J. B., and Wallerstein, J. S. "The Effects of Parental Divorce: Experiences of the Child in Early Latency." *American Journal of Orthopsychiatry* 46 (1976): 20-32.

Landis, J. "The Trauma of Children when Parents Divorce." *Marriage and Family Living* 22 (1960): 7-13.

Magrab, P. R. "For the Sake of the Children: A Review of the Psychological Effects of Divorce." *Journal of Divorce* 1 (1978): 233-245.

McDermott, J. F. "Parental Divorce in Early Childhood." *American Journal of Psychiatry* 124 (1968): 1424-1432.

Norton, A. J., and Glick, P. C. "Marital Instability: Past, Present and Future." *Journal of Social Issues* 32 (1976): 5-20.

Nye, F. I. "Child Adjustment in Broken and in Unhappy Unbroken Homes." *Marriage and Family Living* 19 (1957): 356-361.

United States Bureau of the Census. *Current Population Reports,* Series P-20, No. 297. Washington, D. C.: U.S. Government Printing Office, 1976.

Wallerstein, J. S., and Kelly, J. B. "Divorce Counseling: A Community Service for Families in the Midst of Divorce." *American Journal of Orthopsychiatry* 47 (1977): 4-22.

Wallerstein, J. S., and Kelly, J. B. "The Effects of Parental Divorce: Experience of the Child in Later Latency." *American Journal of Orthopsychiatry* 46 (1976): 256-269.

Wallerstein, J. S., and Kelly, J. B. "The Effects of Parental Divorce: Experience of the Preschool Child." *Journal of Child Psychiatry* 14 (1975): 600-616.

Weiss, R. *Marital Separation.* New York: Basic Books, 1975.

Westman, J. C., and Cline, D. W. "Role of Child Psychiatry in Divorce." *Archives of General Psychiatry,* 23 (1970): 416-420.

Wilkinson, G. S., and Beck, R. T. "Children's Divorce Groups." *Elementary School Guidance and Counseling* 26 (1977): 204-213.

Relevant Books

Books for Children

Picture Books

Adams, F. *Mushy Eggs.* New York: C. P. Putnam's Sons, 1973.

Caines, J. *Daddy.* New York: Harper & Row, 1977.

Kindred, W. *Lucky Wilma.* New York: Dial Press, 1973.

Lexau, J. *Emily and the Klunky Baby and the Next-Door Dog.* New York: Dial Press, 1972.

Lexau, J. *Me Day.* New York: Dial Press, 1971.

Perry, P., and Lynch, M. *Mommy and Daddy Are Divorced.* New York: Dial Press, 1978.

Stein, S. B. *On Divorce.* New York: Walker & Co., 1979.

Elementary and Middle School

Alexander, A. *To Live a Lie.* West Hanover, Mass.: McClelland & Stewart, 1975.

Bach, A. *A Father Every Few Years.* New York: Harper & Row, 1977.

Blue, R. *A Month of Sundays.* New York: Franklin Watts, 1972.

Blume, J. *It's Not the End of the World.* New York: Bradbury Press, 1972.

Corcoran, B. *Hey, That's My Soul You're Stomping On.* New York: Atheneum, 1978.

Donovan, J. *I'll Get There. It Better Be Worth the Trip.* New York: Harper & Row, 1969.

Duncan, L. *A Gift of Magic.* Boston: Little, Brown & Co., 1971.

Fox, P. *Blowfish Live in the Sea.* Scarsdale, N.Y.: Bradbury Press, 1970.

Gardner, R. *The Boys and Girls Book about Divorce.* New York: Bantam Books, 1977.

Goff, B. *Where Is Daddy?* Boston: Beacon Press, 1969.

Greene, C. *A Girl Called Al.* New York: Viking Press, 1969.

Hoban, L. *I Met a Traveller.* New York: Harper & Row, 1977.

Johnson, A., and Johnson, E. *The Grizzly.* New York: Harper & Row, 1964.

Klein, N. *Taking Sides.* New York: Pantheon Books, 1974.

LeShan, E. *What's Going to Happen to Me? When Parents Separate or Divorce.* New York: Four Winds Press, 1978.

Nahn, P. *My Dad Lives in a Downtown Motel.* Garden City, N.J.: Doubleday, 1973.

Mazer, H. *Guy Lenny.* New York: Delacorte Press, 1971.

Mazer, N. *I, Trissy.* New York: Dell Publishing Co., 1971.

Newfield, M. *A Book for Jodan.* New York: Atheneum, 1975.

Rogers, H. *Morris and His Brave Lion.* New York: McGraw-Hill, 1975.

Simon, N. *All Kinds of Families.* Chicago: Whitman, 1976.

Steptoe, J. *My Special Best Words.* New York: Viking Press, 1974.

Stolz, M. *Leap Before You Look.* New York: Harper & Row, 1972.

Talbot, C. *The Great Rat Island Adventure.* New York: Atheneum, 1977.

Walker, M. *A Piece of the World.* New York: Atheneum, 1972.

Books for Teachers and Parents

Gardner, R. *The Parents Book about Divorce.* Garden City, N.J.: Doubleday, 1977.

Grollman, E. *Explaining Divorce to Children.* Boston: Beacon Press, 1969.

Hunt, M., and Hunt, B. *The Divorce Experience*. New York: McGraw-Hill, 1977.

Kessler, S. *The American Way of Divorce: Prescriptions for Change*. Chicago: Nelson-Hall, 1975.

Krantzler, M. *Creative Divorce*. New York: M. Evans & Co., 1974.

Salk, L. *What Every Child Would Like Parents to Know about Divorce*. New York: Harper & Row, 1978.

Sinberg, J. *Divorce Is a Grown Up Problem: A Book about Divorce for Young Children and Their Parents*. New York: Avon, 1978.

Stein, S. B. *On Divorce*. New York: Walker & Co., 1979.

Stevens, J., and Mathews, M., eds. *Mother/Child, Father/Child Relationships*. Washington, D.C.: National Association for the Education of Young Children, 1978.

Turow, R. *Daddy Doesn't Live Here Anymore*. Garden City, N.J.: Anchor Books, 1978.

Weiss, R. *Marital Separation*. New York: Basic Books, 1975.

Journals

Journal of Divorce. Editor: Esther O. Fisher. Haworth Press, 174 Fifth Ave., New York, NY 10010.

The Single Parent: The Journal of Parents Without Partners, Inc. Editor: Barbara Chase. Parents Without Partners, Inc., International Headquarters, 7910 Woodmont Ave., Bethesda, MD 20014.

Erna Furman

Helping Children Cope with Death

Perhaps there are some among you who find the topic of death particularly trying because you have recently lost a loved one or because you suffer from old bereavement wounds that are still sore and painful. To those who are hurting and struggling to cope, I extend my sympathies and also my apologies lest this article contain thoughts that might inadvertently make things harder for you.

Many of us go through life for long periods without thinking about death. When it suddenly strikes very close to us, it comes as a shock, not only because it always represents a loss but also because we get the horrible feeling that "this could be me; this could happen to me, to my family, to my children and friends." We have a tendency to deal with this fear by adopting one of two extreme attitudes. We may feel the impact as though the tragedy had really happened to us. We put ourselves in the shoes of the bereaved or of the dying and feel so overwhelmed and anxious that we are unable to extend ourselves appropriately to those who need our help. At the other extreme, we shield ourselves and behave as if "this is not real; this did not happen to me; I don't want to hear, read, or talk about it." This reaction too prevents us from extending a helping hand because it keeps us from coming to terms with our own feelings. Often we waver from one extreme to the other until, hopefully, we reach a kind of middle ground where we are able to feel, "There but for the grace of God go I; it is not me but it could be." When we arrive at this hard-to-reach point we begin to be able to think and feel with others and to help them as well as ourselves.

Many years ago at the Hanna Perkins (therapeutic) Nursery School, we were working without thinking about death. Then within one year, two mothers of young children died, leaving their families as well as therapists, teachers, peers, and friends stunned. We had to cope with the immediate reality and struggle to come to terms with what had happened. But this was only the beginning. In the course of the next few years, we found that, without having sought cases of bereavement, we had in intensive treatment 23 children of all ages who had lost a parent through death. Each analyst who treated a bereaved child and worked with the family found it so difficult and painful that we turned to each other to share and learn together. We hoped that in this way we would be better able to understand and help our patients and, perhaps, formulate some thoughts that might be of general interest and serve to assist others (Furman 1974). I would like to share with you some of the things we learned, trying to pick out what might be particularly helpful to teachers of young children.

Erna Furman, B.A., is a faculty member of the Cleveland Center for Research in Child Development and Assistant Clinical Professor, Department of Psychiatry, Case Western Reserve University Medical School, Cleveland, Ohio.

As you know, it does not take the death of a parent to bring children to an encounter with death. Many grandparents, siblings, relatives, and pets die. There are also many daily events which bring children face to face with death, be it a passing funeral procession or a dead worm in the backyard. The worst bereavement is the death of a parent. It is a unique experience distinct from all other losses, such as divorce or separation, and distinct from other experiences with death. Many nursery school teachers may be fortunate enough never to have a pupil whose parent dies, but they are surely called upon to help with some less tragic bereavements and the many daily encounters with death—the ants a child steps on or the dead mouse someone brings for show-and-tell (Hoffman 1974).

The danger of parental bereavement does not lie in the formation of isolated symptoms or difficulties. The main danger is that it may arrest or distort a child's development toward becoming a fully functioning adult.

Our bereaved children came to treatment with many different symptoms. Parental death is unique; it happens to unique people who respond in unique ways. Our patients most often responded in a disturbed, unhealthy fashion, sometimes at the time of the bereavements, sometimes not until many years later. But we were deeply impressed that some children only about two years of age, because of very optimal circumstances, could master their tragic loss. By contrast, we had much older patients who could not master it at all. I do not mean to imply that the two-year-olds master this stress more easily; on the contrary, it is harder. Nor is it short-lived for them; it lasts longer. I am not speaking of the degree of pain and anguish, but the ability to master ultimately. To me that means that these children were upset, struggled and suffered, but were able to mourn their par-

ents and to progress in their development. The danger of parental bereavement does not lie in the formation of isolated symptoms or difficulties. The main danger is that it may arrest or distort a child's development toward becoming a fully functioning adult. Many of the factors involved touch upon the role of the teacher and offer an opportunity to develop in children those qualities which will enable them to master a future bereavement or to help them and their peers to cope with a current loss or minor encounter with death.

Helping Children Understand Death

The first crucial factor is children's ability to understand death in its concrete manifestations, *i.e.*, to understand that death means no life, no eating, no sleeping, no pain, no movement. Those children who at the time of bereavement already had a rather good grasp of the concrete facts of death had a much easier time. We found that children from toddler age on show interest in dead things. They find dead insects or birds. When they can tell that a sibling is different from a teddy bear, that one is animate and the other not, they can also begin to understand what *dead* means. For example, when the toddler plays with a dead fly and notes that it does not move, it helps to confirm the child's observation by using the word *dead* and explaining that the fly will never move again because it is dead. Most young children have not yet been helped to acquire this kind of basic concrete understanding of what *dead* means, how things die, and what we do with the corpse. It is much easier to acquire concrete understanding of death from insects or small animals, since they do not have great emotional significance for the child; this knowledge paves the way for later understanding of death in people.

McDonald (1963) studied the responses of the peers of our two bereaved Hanna Perkins Nursery School pupils. She found that children's first interest focused on what death is. They could not direct themselves to the aspects of loss, empathy, or sympathy for a peer's loss until they could understand concretely what death means. McDonald also noted that each of the children's questions required a special effort of thoughtful awareness and listening by the teachers. Initially, and without knowing it, teachers closed their eyes and ears and implied, without words, that death was not a welcome topic. Once their attitude changed, the children's questions just poured out. It is very difficult for all of us to talk about death, even dead insects. Most of us were not helped in this respect when we were children so we tend not to help children or do not know how to help. With special effort and by struggling to come to terms with questions about death ourselves, it is possible to overcome our difficulty to some extent.

Support for Parents

Parents usually do not mind when teachers talk at school about death as it relates to insects, worms, or even animals. Some teachers have found it helpful to meet with parents to discuss how such incidents are handled. Parents, perhaps even more than teachers, find it very difficult to talk with children about death, fearing that sooner or later the child will say, "Will I die?" "Will you die?" We are frightened of the answers that we would rather not give. However, the eventual next step in children's understanding death is that of relating it to themselves and to those they love and need. A meeting with parents on this subject does sometimes help to bring such questions into the open and offers the teacher an opportunity to help the parents. Whether a teacher wishes to arrange such meetings depends on the teacher's relationship with the parent group and the extent to which both sides are ready to grapple with the subject of death.

When a child asks, "Can this happen to me or to my mommy?" the answer should take into account the child's sense of time.

A parent is hesitant to say, "No, I won't die," because he or she eventually will die. Yet should the parent say, "Yes, I will die," the child understands this to mean tomorrow or next week. We find that a young child can best understand when the parent says, "No, I do not expect to die for a long, long time," stressing the *no*, and adding that he or she expects to enjoy the child as a grown-up and have many years of being a grandparent.

Children before age five or six are incapable of abstract thinking and therefore unable to grasp religious or philosophical explanations. They usually distort them into concrete and often frightening concepts that have little to do with religion.

Parents usually also raise the question of spiritual answers to the question of death. Children before age five or six are incapable of abstract thinking and therefore unable to grasp religious or philosophical explanations. They usually distort them into concrete and often frightening concepts that have little to do with religion. I know some very religious parents who chose not to introduce religious explanations to their

James Baritot

children under the age of five precisely because they knew these concepts would be distorted and might later interfere with the children's attitudes about religion. By contrast, doubting or unbelieving parents quite often use explanations that involve *heaven* and *God*. This happens because they have not thought matters through themselves and want to shield the child from something frightening. In shielding the child they only shield themselves and create confusion in the child. Something that is not really believed by the adult cannot come across as true or reassuring to the child.

In our experience the most understanding parents have given concrete explanations of death and burial. When, in response to what they had heard from others, the children asked, "What about heaven?" or "Does God take people away?" the parents replied, "Many people believe that. Many people believe other things too and as you get older you will learn about them and will understand them better. Right now it is important that you understand how we all know when someone is dead."

The concrete facts of death are usually much less frightening to children than to adults. An anecdote about one of Barnes' (1964) patients illustrates this point. A father had struggled very hard to help his young children understand what *dead* meant and what being in a coffin meant because their mother had died. Some months later their grandfather died. As the father tried to tell his little girl that they would choose a nice box with a soft blanket inside so that grandfather would be very comfortable, the little girl interrupted him and said, "But daddy, if he is really dead then it doesn't matter about his being comfortable in the coffin." For that moment the child certainly had a better grasp than the father.

Bearing Unpleasant Feelings

Another factor which facilitates a child's mastery of bereavement is the ability to bear unpleasant feelings, particularly sadness and anger. Obviously, there is no way to anticipate the kind of feelings that come with a bereavement. Separations are very different from a loss through death, but there are some similarities. Separations, to a small extent, involve the same feelings of longing, sadness, and anger that we find in much greater intensity at a time of bereavement. Young children are able to bear these feelings to an incredible extent if they have been given appropriate help in developing this strength.

How does one help a child achieve such mastery? Basically there are two ways. One is to expose children only to bearable separations. When separations are too long they become unbearable and therefore not conducive to experiencing feelings. A very few hours of separation are bearable for a baby, perhaps half a day for a toddler, and at most a couple of days for a nursery school child. But it takes more than adjusting the lengths of separation. The second important step is the adults' willingness to help children recognize their feelings, express them appropriately, and cope with them. Before and after the separation this is the parents' task; during the separation the caregiving person can help.

The goal of assisting bereaved persons is not to foreshorten their or our own pain and anguish but to strive toward inner mastery.

It is often thought that children who do not react, do not make a fuss, or even enjoy the parents' absence, are well-adjusted, good children. To me, these children have not built appropriate mental muscles to bear unpleasant feelings. They shut themselves off from such feelings and therefore have no control of them. For nursery school teachers an excellent time to practice with children in building up the mental muscles for knowing and bearing unpleasant feelings is, of course, during entry to nursery school. At that time one can help parents understand that children who have no feelings, who react as though nothing has happened, or who immediately "love" the school, are children who are shut off from their feelings and in danger of stunting their emotional growth. Many mothers who do not welcome the child's unhappy or angry response to separation at the start of school would be very concerned if the child did not react feelingly to the loss of a loved person or readily preferred someone else in that person's stead. Yet how could a child acknowledge very intense feelings without previous help to cope with them in less threatening situations?

Coping with Bereavement

So far we have considered how difficult it is to talk about death even in terms of animals and insects, and how hard to bear loneliness, sadness, and anger in terms of brief separations. We know, of course, how much greater the hardship is when we have to think about and feel fully the total loss of a loved person. There is no easy way to cope with bereavement. There is no shortcut, either for the bereaved or for those who help them. The goal of assisting bereaved persons is not to foreshorten their or our own pain and anguish but to strive toward inner mastery. Even if we achieve it, it does not mean that we have come to terms with death once and for all. In order to be able to help we too have to empathize anew with each bereavement and struggle through it again.

I would like to turn now to what teachers can do, and often have done, when a child in the nursery school suffers the death of a parent, sibling, or close relative. I do not have any easy remedies to offer, and my suggestions are much more easily said than done because pain and anxiety are an essential part of the task.

The teacher's first question often is, "Should I mention the loss to the child?" I have heard time and again about the fear of causing a child hardship by referring to his or her loss. Some years ago I met a boy whose father had died. His teacher had reported that the boy had no feelings about, or reaction to, the death of the father. When I saw this boy, said "Hello" and expressed my natural sympathy, he broke into tears at once. He cried for an hour and I had to see him a second time before he could begin to talk. I asked him later why he had never shown his feelings at school. The boy replied, "You know, that teacher was so mean! He never even bothered to come to me and say 'I am sorry your father died.' I would never show my feelings to that kind of guy." I suspect that this was not a mean teacher but that his reaction of silence built a barrier between the child and himself.

This and similar experiences have convinced me that the teacher has to take the first step by mentioning the loss and expressing sympathy in a way that implies, "This will be with us a long time. I hope you will feel free to come to me, talk with me, or feel with me about it." In practice, some children will come to the teacher much more than others. However often they do or do not come, the teacher needs to empathize with each and every feeling that may arise and help children tolerate them. This means not to falsify feelings, not to hold them back, not even to pour them out in order to be rid of them, but to recognize and contain them.

It is most important that the children understand not only that the parent or sibling is dead, but also what the cause of death was.

At opportune times the teacher can also help by talking with the child about the factual aspects of the bereavement—how the loved one died, where he or she is buried, and changes in the family setting and routine. I think it is equally important for the teacher to report to the parent what the child shows, thinks, or feels about this experience so that the parent can further

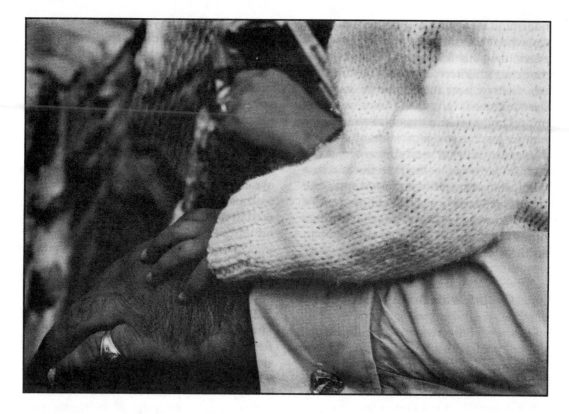

help the child and perhaps be alerted to some aspect which has not yet been expressed at home.

In addition to work with the child, a second area in which the teacher can be helpful is with the parents or surviving parent. Hopefully, before a loss occurs, the teacher will have built the kind of relationship with the parent which will make it possible for him or her to inform the teacher as a friend, a special professional friend who has the parent's and child's welfare at heart. The parent will welcome talking with this teacher and perhaps accept some suggestions—how to tell the child about the death, how to talk it over with the child, whether to take the child to the funeral, what plans to make for the immediate future.

Assisting Parents

Let me now share with you some of the things we have found helpful to parents at such a time. Adults with young children do not die uncomplicated deaths; the deaths are always untimely. This is also true about the death of siblings. It is most important that the child understand not only that the parent or sibling is dead, but also what the cause of death was. When these two things are not understood, when they are distorted or denied, it is impossible for the child even to begin mourning. I do not mean overwhelming the child with frightening details. Hopefully a teacher can help a parent to tell the child enough and in such a manner that the child can achieve a considerable amount of understanding.

Parents always want to know whether they should take the child to the funeral, and what they should say about it. We can only give an answer after we learn more about the specific situation. The child's attendance at the funeral will depend on the type of service, how the parent feels about it, how comfortable the parent is with the rites the family observes, and how able the parent is to extend himself or herself emotionally to the child during the funeral.

Many families are willing to adapt the services to the needs of all the family. Children often find an open casket difficult. They find long services difficult. If the funeral rites are not suitable for a young child or if the parent is unable to care effectively for the child during the services, it is better that the child remain at home with a familiar person and with the full verbal knowledge of what is happening during that time. I had a patient who was sent to the zoo on the day of her father's funeral in the hope that she would not have to be sad. This hope was not fulfilled, and the arrangement produced an almost insurmountable barrier within the child and between child and surviving parent. Mourning has to happen together. Pain and anguish have to be shared. It is not fair to shut out the child.

When it comes to immediate plans for the future, the teacher can sometimes impress upon parents how very important it is for the child to keep the home and remaining family together. Adults often find it much easier to leave the place of distress, to throw away the things that remind them of the deceased. For children the opposite holds true. They need the concrete continuation and help of their surroundings in order to come to terms with what is missing. Sometimes people have asked how parents and children can ever be of support to one another when they have such different needs. When parents understand that their children's greatest need is continued physical and emotional care by the surviving parent, they usually compromise for the sake of the child and find that they benefit as well. Being a good parent brings a measure of self-esteem that cannot be gained in any other way and is especially helpful at a time of bereavement when so many other things seem not worthwhile.

Helping Others in the Group

Along with assisting the bereaved child and parent, the teacher has to extend help to the other children in the nursery school.

This usually starts by discussing with the bereaved parent what to tell the other children and their families. Hopefully the bereaved parent is able to share the truth in simple realistic terms with his or her own child and is willing to have this information passed on. Then the teacher needs to take a few painful hours to call every parent in the nursery group. Each call is long and difficult and should, if possible, include several items: a brief account of what happened to their child's peer, which terms or phrases will be used in the nursery school to discuss the sad event, how the parents can tell their own child and how helpful it would be if the child learned the news first from them, and how to cope with some of the child's questions.

If a bereaved parent is initially unable to allow discussion of the cause of death, the teacher may have to say, for example, "Chris's father died. It is still too hard for Chris's mommy to talk about it, but she will tell us what happened later and I will share it with you." Hopefully, the teacher's relationship with the parent will help to make this delay brief.

Mourning . . . is a process that is not always visible from the outside. . . . Sometimes there are no overt signs of upset and yet the feelings may be there.

The next morning all children will have been told of the death, even if not its cause, by their parents, and the teacher can sit down with them and initiate the first discussion of facts and feelings. The most important point to cover is, "This talk is only a beginning. We will talk about it and feel about it often and for a long time. It will be with us because it is a sad and scary thing."

There are usually three main questions that arise sooner or later: "What is dead?" "Can it happen to me?" and "Can it happen to you?" Until these questions are accepted and coped with, it is generally not possible for the peers or for their parents to

Furman

extend genuine sympathy to the bereaved. When we are able to assist children in gaining gradual mastery, many months of painful struggle seem indeed worthwhile.

The Mourning Process

If the death is understood, if its cause is understood and the disposal of the body is understood, and if the bereaved child is reasonably sure of his or her own survival and of having bodily and emotional needs met to a sufficient extent, mourning will start of itself. It is a process that is not always visible from the outside because, contrary to what many people think, mourning does not consist of wailing, rages, crying, or complaining. Sometimes there are no overt signs of upset and yet the feelings may be there.

I worked with a mother and child. The little boy lost his father two years previously and experienced some difficulty in the aftermath. The mother told me that she had never cried in front of the child, since she only cries when she is alone in bed. The boy, who supposedly had not reacted at all to his father's death and had certainly never cried or raged, told me in his separate interview that he was not a person who ever cried in front of people. He only cried when he was alone in bed and nobody knew that he cried. He cried night after night but his mother never cried. Although mother and child expressed feelings in the same form, they did not know that the other even had feelings. It was sad to see how hard they had made it for themselves and for each other. However, even if they had not cried at all they might have been able to mourn because mourning is a mental process that consists primarily of two parts: on one hand, a very gradual and painful detachment from the memories of the deceased, and on the other hand almost the opposite, a taking into oneself some traits or qualities of the deceased. How much there is of each part and whether the proportion leads to a healthy adaptive outcome depend on many factors, including the age of the bereaved person, the nature of the bereavement, the preceding relationship, the personality of the deceased. With young children it is particularly important that they take into themselves the healthy rather than the sick attributes of the dead parent and that they detach themselves sufficiently, so that, in time, they will be free to form a parental bond with a new person.

Sometimes parents intuitively understand the ways in which their child's long inner mourning proceeds and sense when the child encounters difficulties. Sometimes it is much harder. It certainly is not a mark of failure to seek professional assistance at such a time. That is yet another area where the teacher can support the surviving parent. The sooner help is given, the better the chances of preventing possible damage to the child's growing personality.

This article is adapted from a talk given in May 1975 at the Seventh Annual Workshop of the Cleveland Center for Research in Child Development for Preschool Educators of North Eastern Ohio.

References

Barnes, M. J. "Reactions to the Death of a Mother." *The Psychoanalytic Study of the Child* 19 (1964): 334-357.

Furman, E. *A Child's Parent Dies*. New Haven, Conn.: Yale University Press, 1974.

Hoffman, Y. "Learning about Death in Preschool." *Review, Spring 1974*. Cleveland: Cleveland Association for the Education of Young Children, 1974, pp. 15-17.

McDonald, M. "Helping Children to Understand Death: An Experience with Death in a Nursery School." *Journal of Nursery Education* 19, no. 1 (1963): 19-25.

Judith E. Stalmack

S.W.A.P.—Strategies Which Affect Programs: A Framework for Staff Development

Although S.W.A.P. resurrects traditional early learning equipment—blocks, sand tables, etc.—it aligns this equipment with contemporary goals: helping aggressive and passive children, devising non-paper-and-pencil assessments, challenging the gifted, and raising the self-concept of the low achiever.

"Hey Gary, want to weight stuff?"
"OK," meeting at the balance scale.
"Hey. Let's weigh these blocks."
"Mine are in."
"Mine are in, too."
"Mine is getting filled up."
(dumping bucket) "Now mine is empty."
"Mine is *not empty*, because having some *in* means *not empty*. Right, teacher?"

"It takes three scoops to make the small sand castle."
"Yep—and six to make the big one," figured two kindergarteners.

Four-year-old Laura, collecting red, white, and blue objects from the sorting kit, insisted that the pink rings belong in the grouping " 'cause pink is made from red and white."

"Remember children, a triangle has only three sides."
"No, it doesn't! That line on the bottom is not a side. It's a *bottom*.
Stunned, the teacher wondered, "What would you say about a rectangle and a square? How many sides do those shapes have?"
The four-year-old thought. "D'pends

which way it's turned. One top, one bottom, and two sides."
"What do you say about a circle? Does it have a top and bottom?!"
"Sure! It has a top, bottom, and sides, but they're all smoothly connected."
The class stopped to look at the various shapes of objects in the room and labeled them according to top, bottom, and sides.

These are lessons in concepts—lessons for the teacher. In the class where the children had so logically theorized about the spatial orientation of shapes, the teacher gave her traditional directions for "Farmer in the Dell." "Get in the middle of the circle, Tommy." Then she thought—I have been using those words for ten years, never really thinking. "We sat right down and talked about *in the middle of*," she reported.

Judith E. Stalmack, M.A., is a former preschool coordinator, Waterford School District, Waterford, Michigan. Areas of her experience include organizational change, staff development, and program implementation and evaluation.

For four years, the S.W.A.P. (Strategies Which Affect Programs) plan, our plan for professional growth—an exchange of ideas, observations, and equipment between programs and teachers—involved more than 20 schools and over 35 early childhood, kindergarten, and special education teachers in the Waterford School District, Waterford, Michigan. It included studies of block play, sand and water discovery centers, concept learning, and logico-mathematical thinking. Enriching the classroom environment for thousands of children, at the same time, it made a difference in the teachers' attitudes and effectiveness.

How S.W.A.P. originated

Waterford was probably not much different from most school districts in the 1970s—trying its best to meet the challenge to teach more earlier. In the kindergarten rooms, desks and dittos had replaced walking boards and balance scales; colorful and creatively conceived workbooks for reading and math cut into time for socializing, pretending, and problem solving. There were no sets of blocks—just bins of mismatched leftovers; sand tables were stored. Curriculum statements such as "we teach reading" or "we do not teach reading" varied from school to school, but one common line was obvious: we don't have time for play. Enrichment sessions for four-year-olds, although not caught in the same curricular squeeze as kindergarten, suffered the same lack of discovery-oriented materials.

A nucleus of early childhood teachers enrolled in graduate courses at Oakland University faced two problems. First, their coursework tended toward the theoretical rather than the practical, and second, the lack of play materials and the absence of an administrative sanction of a play curriculum were not conducive to experimenting with a play philosophy. Teachers need assistance to bridge the gap between theory and practice (Argyris and Schon 1974). According to Spodek (1974, p. 90), teachers teach the way they do more as a result of the pressures of the current setting in which they are teaching rather than because of any pre-service or in-service training. Harris (1964) refers to this pressure as "the reality structure."

There was a need to restructure, as much as possible, a "conducive reality" for these teachers. Classroom materials were needed so that they might plan for guided play periods. At the same time, the district needed to be prodded into a review of its preprimary curriculum. Curriculum incentive funds were available, so the first S.W.A.P. proposal, an exchange and study of wooden unit blocks, was written. The proposal was funded and the success of that pilot project ignited the interest of other district teachers and administrators. Subsequent proposals, varying the theme but following the basic model, were submitted and funded annually.

S.W.A.P. is an on-the-job staff development model that makes the teaching day an effective in-service day with a minimum outlay of training dollars. Simultaneously, it stimulates practical, meaningful exchanges between programs and personnel.

Our experience has shown that S.W.A.P. can update teachers and administrators on current research; it can retrain teachers shifted into early childhood placements; and it can give teachers a backbone of experience and information to support their stand against a dependency on programmed math and reading lessons before first grade.

The S.W.A.P. model allows two levels of participation. For teachers who choose to conscientiously complete the project's annual workplan, it becomes an effective, intensive professional growth experience. For the broad spectrum of early childhood administrators and teachers in the district, S.W.A.P. can be a stimulating and unifying catalyst.

Our S.W.A.P. model can be used to meet the staff development needs of any

Elaine Wickens

By joining S.W.A.P., teachers can study and experience the teaching/learning potential of specific classroom materials and begin to understand, through their own observations, how these materials meet the developmental needs of young children.

program based on the teaching/learning potential of play. It could be adapted to train day care staff at a single center, develop Head Start personnel, serve as a support network for a group of family day care providers, or be used as a parent education project in a cooperative nursery school. Although our project was supported by district incentive funds awarded to innovative curriculum proposals, the budget for new equipment could adequately cover project costs, in any program, as long as someone in the program takes responsibility for leadership.

How does S.W.A.P. work?

S.W.A.P. is an exchange system that is an *in-service* program; thus it differs from the standard *service* flow of films and kits from an instructional materials center. Equipment is shared, studied, and tested by a group of teachers through a cooperative workshop/workplan. Workshops traditionally have been used for in-service training; S.W.A.P. includes a workplan for long-term staff development. Swapping materials between classrooms is cost effective and increases the time that equipment is in use. To implement the project in a single center, staff might simply agree to swap time with the curriculum materials being studied.

As part of their workplan, teachers study a research paper or text giving the viewpoint or teaching methods of an early childhood expert. Because even experts do not agree as to what constitutes the best curriculum for children (Katz 1977; Simon and Boyer 1974), each S.W.A.P. teacher *individually*, and then collectively, verifies or disputes the text by recording classroom observations pertaining to the study topic. This skill-building experience of recording classroom observations and the subsequent realization of the value of such records is a significant staff development goal.

By joining S.W.A.P., teachers can study and experience the teaching/learning potential of specific classroom materials and begin to understand, through their own observations, how these materials meet the developmental needs of four-, five-, and six-year-old children. Few classrooms could afford to purchase all the block accessories, all the sand play tools, or all of the numerous math games in a catalog; neither would one teacher display all at one time. Swapping equipment is a budget consideration—and a good selling point for the proposal.

The framework for each S.W.A.P. follows a similar pattern.

1. A study theme evolves from needs expressed by the teachers, and a project text dealing with the topic is selected.

2. All preprimary teachers in the district are invited to participate. They are encouraged to form preschool/kindergarten S.W.A.P. teams.

3. Equipment is purchased. Large equipment is shared by preprimary teachers in the same building; e.g., sand tables or block carts on wheels. Small accessories or games are packaged in kits and circulated between schools on a two- or three-week schedule.

4. Teachers, in their own classrooms, encourage and observe the children's interaction with the S.W.A.P. materials for a period of three to five months.

5. Teachers observe in other preprimary classrooms to strengthen peer contact and professional exchange; visits between preschool and kindergarten are especially encouraged so that teachers will see the different ways older and younger children manipulate the same equipment.

6. Project information and experiences are shared with *all* preprimary personnel in a monthly newsletter.

7. Parent education materials relative to each S.W.A.P. topic are developed. For example, a handout was published to explain the reintroduction of blocks in kindergarten.

8. Formal workshops and informal teacher-team conferences are held throughout the year. Whenever possible, arrangements are made to meet and discuss both theory and application with the author of the project text. During a final wrap-up session, participating teachers collectively evaluate the impact of the materials on their classes and formulate a curriculum position statement.

Why S.W.A.P.?

Several factors contribute to the effectiveness of the project as a staff development strategy. Because S.W.A.P. makes equipment available to the teacher, the physical structure of the classroom is changed. S.W.A.P. helps teachers adjust to new behavior patterns that will enhance the use of the materials by involving teachers in an assessment of a new teaching model and allowing them time to internalize a commitment to the model. In essence, teachers are given the same hands-on, discovery-learning situation that is purported to be good for children. S.W.A.P. also generates support from peers, supervisors, and parents for the curriculum.

S.W.A.P. is characterized by a high degree of teacher-selected activity and a strong emphasis on process. McNeil and Popham (1973) stress that teaching techniques should never, in pre-service or in-service education of teachers, be presented as "scientifically confirmed answers about how a teacher should proceed to effect desirable consequences in learners. Instead, such skills should be presented as hypotheses to be tested" (p. 24). This challenge to experiment is crucial to S.W.A.P.

Programs stressing guided play periods demand teaching techniques involving complex cognitive and emotional interactions. Teacher-as-facilitator methods are not as easily taught or as quickly learned as those established for programmed curricula. Staff members may hold different views of their teaching role based on their experience and their pre-service training in different institutions during eras of different educational emphasis (Hunter 1976). If the effectiveness of a program depends on the degree to which a specific curriculum orientation is reflected in the teaching behavior of the staff (Berk 1976; Evans 1975; Hunter 1976; Parker and Day 1972), then it would seem that time spent together on defining goals and roles and examining teaching tools and techniques

The prospect of new equipment and fresh ideas for classroom activities continually attracts new teachers to S.W.A.P., while professional contact with grade-level peers remains another incentive.

is a necessity.

The open framework of S.W.A.P. is also consistent with supervisory strategies proposed by Neagley and Evans (1964) who suggest that teachers change instructional habits only after they have actually *used* an educational procedure or techniques successfully. Experimenting with S.W.A.P. materials over an extended period of time provides an opportunity to feel successful with a new procedure or technique.

Hilliard (1974) states: "Two basic things help teachers to grow. One is relevant professional information, and the other is continuing feedback . . ." (p. 19). The S.W.A.P. project provides teachers with information, but it also requires them to keep observation checklists and running records or to take snapshots of the effects of specific materials and methods on the children. Although the value of recording observations is unquestioned (Almy 1959; Cohen and Stern 1975; Lindberg and

Swedlow 1976), it is seldom practiced by teachers.

The S.W.A.P. framework meshes well with Spodek's (1974) "onion construct" which describes layered levels of resistance to planned in-service programs. Resistance is stronger as core beliefs are approached.

Any practice influencing reading, according to Spodek, is close to the core of attitudes most crucial to teachers of young children, and a play-oriented S.W.A.P. could affect an early reading program by taking time from it. Also, to imply that the role of the teacher need not be front and center of an activity tampers with a core belief of some. S.W.A.P. initiates contact with teachers and tempts them to join, however, on the most comfortable, least threatening level—classroom materials. The teacher is free, when workshops and workplans are over, to respond on a deeper level.

Katz (1977) points out that teachers ex-

Stalmack

perience stages of development in much the same way that children do. S.W.A.P.'s open framework appears to meet the needs of teachers at any stage of professional development.

S.W.A.P. in action

The Block S.W.A.P.

Teachers were especially curious to discover whether children would follow the stages of development in block play outlined by Hirsch (1974). Teachers were also interested in observing the problem-solving potential of block play, its influence on math and language, and its impact on socialization and imagination. They wanted to experiment with suggested classroom techniques for guiding block play and managing cleanup.

Observation checklists for the block S.W.A.P. were developed with the assistance of the teachers (table 1). Although the checklists were not intended to be used daily, they were to be used often enough to collect significant feedback so that the teachers could verify what they were being told about the value of blocks.

One checklist reminded teachers of the many ways to facilitate block play. Another checklist helped teachers to gain a better understanding of child development. After using the checklist on stages of block play (table 2), one kindergarten teacher said, "I can actually gauge the maturity of my kindergartners by observing their level of block play. The stage of their block building is a good predictor of their overall capability." Another wrote, "The recorded observations and what they reveal have helped me in my conferences with parents." During the postassessment of the block S.W.A.P., one teacher commented, "I thought that much of what I read in *The Block Book* by Hirsch was pure jargon; I almost dared the book to defend itself. One day I couldn't seem to talk the children into playing with

the blocks, so I tried a teaching trick right out of the text. I arranged two blocks at right angles to each other, said nothing to the children (who were nowhere around anyway), and left the area. Was I surprised when that 'gestalt theory' did attract children to finish the structure."

After their intensive study of block play, the block S.W.A.P. teachers increased their appreciation for the effectiveness of block play on children's learning.

The Concept Training S.W.A.P.

Another S.W.A.P. centered on a study of Palmer's concept training curriculum (1978) using balance scales, walking boards, and magnifiers to teach concepts such as long/short and front/back. At the close of the project, teachers in the concept training S.W.A.P. indicated the following: "I feel the S.W.A.P. made me more aware of how I word things to children. Why do we say the fire alarm goes *off* when we mean *on*?" "Anytime you can get involved with the kids and objects to explain a concept—the quicker they catch on." "S.W.A.P. helped me understand a child's cognitive development better. I would definitely like to continue and expand my awareness of concept development."

Evaluation of the Program

S.W.A.P. has been an effective, intensive professional growth program; it has unified and stimulated administrators and teachers. The prospect of new equipment and fresh ideas for classroom activities attracts teachers to S.W.A.P., while professional contact with grade-level peers remains another incentive. At the same time, the exchange of materials offers hundreds of children a continuing and wide variety of novel stimuli during play periods.

Evaluations of each S.W.A.P. reveal, however, that teachers who conscientiously complete their workplan exhibit a far greater understanding and acceptance of the project information than those who

Table 1.
Block S.W.A.P.—Play checklist

Teacher _____

_____ **Kindergarten**

_____ **Preschool**

Play Period	Number of Children	Type of Play				Play Theme accessories, comments, etc.	Observer	Teacher's Role									
									Facilitator, by								
		solitary	parallel	associative	cooperative			Motivating	Participating	Verbalizing	Questioning	Challenging	Informing	Enriching	Modeling	Reinforcing	
Date: Time:																	
Date: Time:																	

Table 2.
Block S.W.A.P.—Stages in block building

Teacher _____

_____ **Kindergarten**

_____ **Preschool**

Fill in spaces with children's names as you observe their work/play. See if you can detect transitions or growth over a period of time. (Is the information helpful in analyzing the maturity of the child?)

Date	Stage 1 Carrying	Stage 2 Rows— Vertical and horizontal	Stage 3 Bridges	Stage 4 Enclosures	Stage 5 Decorative patterns	Stage 6 Naming for play	Stage 7 Naming and use for play

are less involved. These teachers discover what works, or does not work, for them as individuals. Teachers who maintain the observation schedule for several months see themselves—and their supervisors view them—as greatly improved facilitators in the topic area. The change in their teaching pattern is longer lived and often transferred to other areas in the curriculum. These teachers continue to implement their new ideas by ordering the equipment for their own classrooms or by continuing to borrow it from the S.W.A.P. center.

S.W.A.P., as a staff development strategy, helps teachers become skilled at teaching children younger than that for which they were originally trained. In some cases, teachers experience an insight different from that expected; for instance, during the block S.W.A.P. one teacher complained that the children did not seem interested in block play. On the postassessment she wrote, "I think I've discovered why the children ignore the blocks. *I* do. I'm so busy and wrapped up in the art activities I've planned, I don't award attention to children in any other activity."

The S.W.A.P. in-service model reinforces several theories regarding change for teachers (Amidon and Flanders 1971; MacDonald 1966; Sarason 1971; Zaherick 1977):

1. Change is natural and should be viewed not as a threat but as an opportunity.
2. Fundamental change is slow and gradual and requires time and effort. Any quick change is illusory.
3. New experiences can lead to a change in value positions, but the thought that this might happen can be unsettling. Teachers need to make changes at their own pace.
4. Understanding and accepting new or different teaching behaviors requires more than factual knowledge. It is also imperative to *want* to do something different—and ultimately to believe one *can*.
5. The environment must encourage and facilitate the change process.

Organizing an effective staff development program requires a process of designing strategies to help teachers bring about changes in themselves. Such strategies should not be static how-to's, but rather dynamic, hands-on, discovery-oriented experiences.

Bibliography

Almy, M. *Ways of Studying Children.* New York: Teachers College Press, 1959.

Amidon, E. J., and Flanders, N. A. *The Role of the Teacher in the Classroom.* Rev. ed. Minneapolis: Association for Productive Teaching, 1971.

Argyris, C., and Schon, D. *Theory in Practice: Increasing Professional Effectiveness.* San Francisco: Jossey-Bass, 1974.

Beller, E. K. "Research on Organized Programs of Early Education." In *Second Handbook of Research on Teaching,* ed. R. M. W. Travers. Chicago: Rand McNally, 1973.

Berk, L. E. "How Well Do Classroom Practices Reflect Teacher Goals?" *Young Children* 32, no. 1 (November 1976): 64-81.

Cohen, D. H., and Stern, U. *Observing and Recording the Behavior of Young Children.* New York: Teachers College Press, 1975.

Evans, E. D. *Contemporary Influences in Early Childhood Education.* 2nd ed. New York: Holt, Rinehart & Winston, 1975.

Harris, B. M. *Supervision for Affecting Instructional Changes–Problems and Strategy.* Report of the Conference, Department of Supervisors and Directors of Instruction. Montgomery, Ala.: State Department of Education, 1964.

Hilliard, A. G. "Moving from Abstract to Functional Teacher Education: Pruning and Planting." In *Teacher Education,* ed. B. Spodek. Washington, D.C: National Association for the Education of Young Children, 1974.

Hirsch, E. S., ed. *The Block Book.* Washington, D.C.: National Association for the Education of Young Children, 1974.

Hunter, M. *Prescription for Improved Instruction*. El Segundo, Calif.: TIP Publications, 1976.

Katz, L. *Talks with Teachers*. Washington, D.C.: National Association for the Education of Young Children, 1977.

Lindberg, L., and Swedlow, R. *Early Childhood Education: A Guide for Observation and Participation*. Boston: Allyn & Bacon, 1976.

MacDonald, J. B. "Helping Teachers Change." In *The Supervisor: Agent for Change in Teaching*. Washington, D.C.: Association for Supervision and Curriculum Development, 1966.

McNeil, J. D., and Popham, J. W. "The Assessment of Teacher Competence." In *Second Handbook of Research on Teaching*, ed. R. M. W. Travers. Chicago: Rand McNally, 1973.

Neagley, R., and Evans, N. D. *Handbook for Effective Supervision of Instruction*. Englewood Cliffs, N.J.: Prentice-Hall, 1964.

Palmer, F. H. *One to One: A Concept Training Curriculum for Children Ages Three to Five Years*. Stony Brook, N.Y.: Early Intellective Development, 1978.

Parker, R., and Day, M. *Comparisons of Preschool Curricula: The Preschool in Action*. Boston: Allyn & Bacon, 1972.

Sarason, S. B. *The Culture of the School and the Problem of Change*. Boston: Allyn & Bacon, 1971.

Simon, A., and Boyer, E. G. *Mirrors for Behavior III: An Anthology of Observation Instruments*. Philadelphia: Research for Better Schools, 1974.

Spodek, B. *Teacher Education—of the Teacher, by the Teacher, for the Child*. Washington, D.C.: National Association for the Education of Young Children, 1974.

Wolfgang, C. H. *Helping Aggressive and Passive Preschoolers Through Play*. Columbus, Ohio: Merrill, 1977.

Zaherick, J. A. "How to Decide How to Teach." *The Elementary School Journal* 78 (1977): 22-30.

List of articles

Bradbard, M., and Endsley, R. "How Can Teachers Develop Young Children's Curiosity? What Current Research Says to Teachers." 35, no. 5 (July 1980): 21–32.

Davidson, J. "Wasted Time: The Ignored Dilemma." 35, no. 4 (May 1980): 13–21.

Elkind, D. "Child Development and Early Childhood Education: Where Do We Stand Today?" 36, no. 5 (July 1981): 2–9.

Fein, G. "Pretend Play: New Perspectives." 34, no. 5 (July 1979): 61–66.

Francks, O. "Scribbles? Yes, They *Are* Art!" 34, no. 5 (July 1979): 14–22.

Frost, J., and Henniger, M. "Making Playgrounds Safe for Children and Children Safe for Playgrounds." 34, no. 5 (July 1979): 23–30.

Furman, E. "Helping Children Cope with Death." 33, no. 4 (May 1978): 25–32.

Garcia, E. "Bilingualism in Early Childhood." 35, no. 4 (May 1980): 52–66.

Goetz, E. "Early Reading: A Developmental Approach." 34, no. 5 (July 1979): 4–11.

Griffing, P. "Encouraging Dramatic Play in Early Childhood." 38, no. 2 (January 1983): 13–22.

Haswell, K.; Hock, E.; and Wenar, C. "Techniques for Dealing with Oppositional Behavior in Preschool Children." 37, no. 3 (March 1982): 12–18.

Herr, J., and Morse, W. "Food for Thought: Nutrition Education for Young Children." 38, no. 1 (November 1982): 3–11.

Honig, A. S. "The Young Child and You—Learning Together." 35, no. 4 (May 1980): 2–10.

Jensen, M., and Hanson, B. "Helping Children Learn to Read: What Research Says to Teachers." 36, no. 1 (November 1980): 61–71.

Kamii, C., and Lee-Katz, L. "Physics in Preschool Education: A Piagetian Approach." 34, no. 4 (May 1979): 4–9.

Kinsman, C., and Berk, L. "Joining the Block and Housekeeping Areas: Changes in Play and Social Behavior." 35, no. 1 (November 1979): 66–75.

Koblinsky, S.; Atkinson, J.; and Davis, S. "Sex Education with Young Children." 36, no. 1 (November 1980): 21–31.

Lamme, L. "Handwriting In an Early Childhood Curriculum." 35, no. 1 (November 1979): 20–27.

McDonald, D., and Ramsey, J. "Awakening the Artist: Music for Young Children." 33, no. 2 (January 1978): 26–34.

Ramsey, P. "Multicultural Education in Early Childhood." 37, no. 2 (January 1982): 13–24.

Schickedanz, J. "'Hey! This Book's Not Working Right.'" 37, no. 1 (November 1981): 18–27.

Skeen, P., and McKenry, P. "The Teacher's Role in Facilitating a Child's Adjustment to Divorce." 35, no. 5 (July 1980): 3–12.

Smith, C. "Puppetry and Problem-Solving Skills." 34, no. 3 (March 1979): 4–11.

Smith, R. "Early Childhood Science Education: A Piagetian Perspective." 36, no. 2 (January 1981): 3–10.

Stalmack, J. "S.W.A.P.—Strategies Which Affect Programs: A Framework for Staff Development." 36, no. 6 (September 1981): 16–24.

Stipek, D. "Work Habits Begin in Preschool." 38, no. 4 (May 1983): 25–32.

Williamson, P. "Literature Goals and Activities for Young Children." 36, no. 4 (May 1981): 24–30.

Index

Information about NAEYC

NAEYC is . . .

. . . a membership organization of people committed to fostering the growth and development of children from birth through age eight. Membership is open to all who share a desire to serve and act on behalf of the needs and rights of young children.

NAEYC provides . . .

. . . educational services and resources to adults who work with and for children, including

■ *Young Children, the* Journal for early childhood educators

■ **Books, posters, brochures, and videos** to expand your knowledge and commitment to young children, with topics including infants, curriculum, research, discipline, teacher education, and parent involvement

■ An **Annual Conference** that brings people from all over the country to share their expertise and advocate on behalf of children and families

■ **Week of the Young Child** celebrations sponsored by NAEYC Affiliate Groups across the country to call public attention to the needs and rights of children and families

■ **Insurance plans** for individuals and programs

■ **Public policy information** for informed advocacy efforts at all levels of government

■ The **National Academy of Early Childhood Programs,** a voluntary accreditation system for high-quality programs for young children

■ The **Information Service,** a computerized central source of information sharing, distribution, and collaboration

For free information about membership, publications, or other NAEYC services . . .

. . . Call NAEYC at
202-232-8777 or 800-424-2460 or write to
NAEYC
1834 Connecticut Avenue, N.W.
Washington, DC 20009-5786